Praise for *T*

—WINNER—

2008 Silver Freedom Fighter Award
Independent Publisher Book Awards

2008 Silver Book Award for Social Change/
Activism/Peaceful Solutions
Nautilus Book Awards

"Most Valuable Political Book [of 2007]. Her detailing of the
parallels between steps taken by the current administration
and moves made by the 20th century's most notorious
dictators to transform democracies into authoritarian states
is as convincing as it is chilling."

—John Nichols, "The Beat" blog, *The Nation*

"One of the most important books that's been written,
certainly in the last decade or two, and perhaps in my
lifetime."

—Thom Hartmann, bestselling author and host of
The Thom Hartmann Program

"Naomi Wolf's *The End of America* is a vivid, urgent,
mandatory wake-up call that addresses momentous issues of
tyranny, democracy, survival: Who are we now? How did it
come to this? For enlightenment and hope, we would all do
well to carry about and give to all our allies Naomi Wolf's
profound and urgent essay. It is the book we need to carry
with us as we regroup and rally for the return of justice and
political sanity."

—Blanche Wiesen Cook, author of the three-volume
Eleanor Roosevelt and distinguished professor at John Jay College

ALSO BY NAOMI WOLF

The End of America

The Treehouse

Misconceptions

Promiscuities

Fire with Fire

The Beauty Myth

GIVE ME LIBERTY

A HANDBOOK FOR AMERICAN REVOLUTIONARIES

NAOMI WOLF

SIMON & SCHUSTER PAPERBACKS
NEW YORK LONDON TORONTO SYDNEY

SIMON & SCHUSTER PAPERBACKS
A Division of Simon & Schuster, Inc.
1230 Avenue of the Americas
New York, NY 10020

First Simon & Schuster trade paperback edition September 2008

SIMON & SCHUSTER PAPERBACKS and colophon are registered
trademarks of Simon & Schuster, Inc.

For information about special discounts for bulk purchases,
please contact Simon & Schuster Special Sales at
1-800-456-6798 or business@simonandschuster.com.

Designed by Davina Mock

Manufactured in the United States of America

1   3   5   7   9   10   8   6   4   2

Library of Congress Cataloging-in-Publication Data

Wolf, Naomi.
Give me liberty / Naomi Wolf.
p. cm.
Includes bibliographical references and index.
1. Civil rights—United States.   2. Civil rights movements—
United States.   3. Rule of law—United States.   I. Title.
JC599.U5W63 2008
323.60973—dc22   2008024264

ISBN-13: 978-1-4165-9056-9
ISBN-10:   1-4165-9056-0

For the citizens I've met on this journey,
who are holding the line

CONTENTS

Contents

PART III:
America: The User's Guide

Contents

Contents

Even the smallest spark of freedom could set
[an] entire world ablaze. That's why dissidents were
held in isolation, dissident books were confiscated, and
every typewriter had to be registered with the authorities.
The regime knew the volatile potential of free thought
and speech, so they spared no effort at extinguishing
the spark. . . . Dissidents understood the
power of freedom because it had already
transformed our lives.
—NATAN SHARANSKY, *The Case for Democracy*

It has been said that each generation
must win its own struggle to be free.
—ROBERT F. KENNEDY

It is their mores, then, that make the Americans
of the United States . . . capable of maintaining
the rule of democracy. . . . Too much importance
is attached to laws and too little to mores. . . . I am
convinced that the luckiest of geographical circumstances
and the best of laws cannot maintain a constitution in
spite of mores, whereas the latter can turn even the most
unfavorable circumstances . . . to advantage. . . . If,
in the course of this book, I have not succeeded
in making the reader feel the importance I attach
to the practical experience of the Americans,
to their habits, laws, and, in a word, their mores,
I have failed in the main object of my work.
—ALEXIS DE TOCQUEVILLE, *Democracy in America*

GIVE ME
LIBERTY

PART I: WHAT IS "AMERICA"?
NOT A COUNTRY, A STATE OF MIND

The summer before last, I traveled across the country talking about threats to our liberty. I spoke and listened to groups of Americans from all walks of life. They told me new and always harsher stories of state coercion.

What I had called a "fascist shift" in the United States, projections I had warned about as worst-case scenarios, was now surpassing my imagination: in 2008, thousands of terrified, shackled illegal immigrants were rounded up in the mass arrests which always characterize a closing society;[1] news emerged that the 9/11 report had been based on evidence derived from the testimonies of prisoners who had been tortured—and the tapes that documented their torture were missing—leading the commissioners of the report publicly to disavow their own findings;[2] the Associated Press reported that the torture of prisoners in U.S.-held facilities had not been the work of "a few bad apples" but had been directed out of the White House;[3] the TSA "watch list," which had contained 45,000 names when I wrote my last book, ballooned to 755,000 names and 20,000 were being added every month;[4] Scott McClellan confirmed that the drive to war in Iraq had been based on administration lies;[5] HR 1955, legislation that would criminalize certain kinds of political thought and speech, passed the House and made it to the Senate;[6] Blackwater, a violent paramilitary force not answerable to the people, established presences in Illinois and North Carolina and sought to get into border patrol activity in San Diego.[7]

The White House has established, no matter who leads the nation in the future, U.S. government spying on the e-mails and phone calls of Americans—a permanent violation of the Constitution's Fourth Amendment.[8] The last step of the ten steps to a closed society is the subversion of the rule of law. That is happening now. What critics have called a "paper coup" has already taken place.

Yes, the situation is dire. But history shows that when an army of citizens, supported by even a vestige of civil society, believes in liberty—in the psychological space that is "America"—no power on earth can ultimately suppress them.

Dissident Natan Sharansky writes that there are two kinds of states—"fear societies" and "free societies."[9] Understood in this light, "America"—the state of freedom that is under attack—is first of all a place in the mind. That is what we must regain now to fight back.

The two societies make up two kinds of consciousness. The consciousness derived of oppression is despairing, fatalistic, and fearful of inquiry. It is mistrustful of the self and forced to trust external authority. It is premised on a dearth of self-respect. It is cramped. People around the world understand that this kind of inner experience is as toxic an environment as is a polluted waterway they are forced to drink from; it is as insufficient a space as being compelled to sleep in a one-room hut with seven other bodies on the floor.

In contrast, the consciousness of freedom—the psychology of freedom that is "America"—is one of expansiveness, trust of the self, and hope. It is a consciousness of limitless inquiry. "Everything," wrote Denis Diderot, who influenced, via Thomas Jefferson, the Revolutionary generation, "must be examined, everything must be shaken up, without exception and without circumspection."[10] Jefferson wrote that American universities are "based on the illimitable freedom of the human mind. For here we are not afraid to follow truth wherever it may lead, nor to tolerate any error so long as reason is left free to combat it."[11] Since this state of mind is self-trusting, it builds up in a citizen a wealth of self-respect. "Your own reason," wrote Jefferson to his nephew, "is the only oracle given you by heaven, and you are answerable not for the rightness but the uprightness of the decision."[12]

After my cross-country journey, I realized that I needed to go back and read about the original Revolutionaries of our nation. I realized in a new way from them that liberty is not a set of laws or a system of government; it is not a nation or a species of patriotism. Liberty is a state of mind before it is anything else. You can have a nation of wealth and power, but without this state of mind—this psychological "America"—you are living in a deadening consciousness; with this state of mind, you can be in a darkened cell waiting for your torturer to arrive and yet inhabit a chainless space as wide as the sky.

"America," too, is a state of mind. "Being an American" is a set of attitudes and actions, not a nationality or a posture of reflexive loyalty. This tribe of true "Americans" consists of people who have crossed a personal Rubicon of a specific kind and can no longer be satisfied with anything less than absolute liberty.

This state of mind, I learned, has no national boundaries. The Tibetans, who, as I write this, are marching in the face of Chinese soldiers, are acting like members of this tribe; so did the Pakistani lawyers who recently faced down house arrest and tear gas in their suits and judicial robes. Nathan Hale, Patrick Henry, and Ida B. Wells, who risked their lives for liberty, acted like "Americans." When the crusading journalist Anna Politkovskaya insisted on reporting on war crimes in Chechnya, even though her informing her fellow citizens led—as she knew it well could—to her being gunned down on her doorstep as she went home to her fourteen-year-old daughter, she was acting like an American.[13] When three JAG lawyers refused to sell out their detainee clients, they were being "Americans." When Vietnam vet David Antoon risked his career to speak out in favor of the Constitution's separation of church and state, he was being an "American." When journalist Josh Wolf went to jail rather than reveal a source, he was being an "American" too. Always, everywhere, the members of this tribe are fundamentally the same, in spite of the great deal that may divide them in terms of clothing and religion, language and culture. But when we quietly go about our business as our rights are plundered, when we yield to passivity and switch on the Wii and hand over our power to a leadership class that has no interest in our voice, we are not acting like true Americans. Indeed, at those moments we are essentially giving up our citizenship.

The notion that "American-ness" is a state of mind—a rigorous psychodynamic process or a continued personal challenge, rather than a static point on a map or an impressive display in a Fourth of July parade—is not new. But we are so used to being raised on a rhetoric of cheap patriotism—the kind that you get to tune in to in a feel-good way just because you were lucky enough to have been born here and can then pretty much forget about—that this definition seems positively exotic. The founders understood "American-ness" in this way, though, not at all in our way.

And today, I learned as I traveled, we are very far from experiencing this connection to our source. Many of us feel ourselves clouded within, cramped, baffled obscurely from without, not in alignment with the electric source that is liberty. So it is easy for us to rationalize always further and more aggressive cramping and clouding; is the government spying on us? Well . . . Okay . . . So now the telecommunications companies are asking for retroactive immunity for their spying on us? Well . . . Okay . . . Once a certain threshold of passivity has been crossed, it becomes easier and easier, as Benjamin Franklin warned, to trade liberty for a false security—and deserve neither.

What struck me on my journey was how powerless so many Americans felt to make change. Many citizens I heard from felt more hopeless than did citizens of some of the poorest and youngest democracies on the planet. Others were angrier than ever and were speaking up and acting up with fervor. I felt that all of us—the hopeless and the hopeful—needed to reconnect to our mentors, the founders, and to remind ourselves of the blueprint for freedom they meant us to inherit. I wrote this handbook with the faith that if Americans take personal ownership of the Constitution and the Bill of Rights, they can push back any darkness. The first two sections of this refresher guide to our liberties recall what America is supposed to be; the last third is a practical how-to for citizen leadership for a new American Revolution.

There are concrete laws we must pass to restore liberty and actions we must take to safeguard it. You will find them in the last third of this handbook. But more crucial

than any list of laws or actions is our own need to redis-
cover our role as American revolutionaries and to reclaim
the "America" in ourselves—in our consciousness as free
men and women.

Do we have the right to see ourselves this way? Absolutely. Many histories of our nation's founding focus on a
small group, "a band of brothers" or "the Founding
Fathers"—the handful of illustrious men whose names we
all know. This tight focus tends to reinforce the idea that
we are the lucky recipients of the American gift of liberty
and of the republic, not ourselves its stewards, crafters,
and defenders. It prepares us to think of ourselves as the
led, not as the leaders.

But historians are also now documenting the stories of
how in the pre-Revolutionary years, ordinary people—
farmers, free and enslaved Africans, washer-women, butch-
ers, printers, apprentices, carpenters, penniless soldiers,
artisans, wheelwrights, teachers, indentured servants—
were rising up against the king's representatives, debating
the nature of liberty, fighting the war and following the
warriors to support them, insisting on expanding the franchise, demanding the right to vote, compelling the more
aristocratic leaders of the community to include them in
deliberations about the nature of the state constitutions,
and requiring transparency and accountability in the legislative process.[14] Even enslaved Africans, those Americans
most silenced by history, were not only debating in their
own communities the implications or the ideas of God-
given liberty that the white colonists were debating;[15] they
were also taking up arms against George III's men in
hopes that the new republic would emancipate them.
Some were petitioning state legislatures for their freedom;
and others were even successfully bringing lawsuits against

their owners, arguing in court for their inalienable rights as human beings.[16] This is the revolutionary spirit that we must claim again for ourselves—fast—if we are to save the country.

When Abraham Lincoln said that our nation was "conceived in Liberty"[17] he was not simply phrasemaking; our nation was literally "conceived" by Enlightenment ideas that were becoming more and more current, waking up greater and greater numbers of ordinary people, and finally bearing on our own founders, known and unknown, with ever-stronger pressure.

Key Enlightenment beliefs of the colonial era are these: human beings are perfectible; the right structures of society, at the heart of which is a representational government whose power derives from the consent of the governed, facilitate this continual evolution; reason is the means by which ordinary people can successfully rule themselves and attain liberty; the right to liberty is *universal,* God given, and part of a natural cosmic order, or "natural law"; as more and more people around the world claim their God-given right to liberty, tyranny and oppression will be pushed aside. It is worth reminding ourselves of these founding ideas at a time when they are under sustained attack.

The core ideals, the essence, of what the founders imperfectly glimpsed, are perfect. I am often asked how I can so champion the writing and accomplishments of the better-known founders. Most of them were, of course, propertied, white, and male. Critics on the left often point out their flaws in relation to the very ideals they put forward. John Adams was never comfortable with true citizen democracy.[18] "Jefferson's writings about race reveal that he saw Africans as innately deficient in humanity and culture." [19] When a male slave escaped from Benjamin Franklin in England, Franklin sold him back into slavery.[20]

But the essence of the idea of liberty and equality that they codified—an idea that was being debated and developed by men and women, black and white, of all classes in the pre-Revolutionary generation—went further than such an idea had ever gone before. It is humanity's most radical blueprint for transformation.

More important, the idea itself carries within it the moral power to correct the contradictions in its execution that were obvious from the very birth of the new nation. An enslaved woman, Mum Bett, who became a housekeeper for the Sedgwick family of Massachussetts, successfully sued for her own emancipation using the language of the Declaration of Independence;[21] decades later a slave, Dred Scott, argued that he was "entitled to his freedom" as a citizen and a resident of a free state.[22] The first suffragists at the Seneca Falls Convention, intent on securing equal rights for women, used the framework of the Declaration of Independence to advance their cause.[23] New democracies in developing nations around the world draw on our founding documents and government structure to ground their own hopes for freedom. The human beings at the helm of the new nation, whatever their limitations, were truly revolutionary. The theory of liberty born in that era, the seed of the idea, was, as I say, perfect. We should not look to other revolutions to inspire us; nothing is more transformative than our own revolution. We must neither oversentimentalize it, as the right tends to do, nor disdain it, as the left tends to do; rather we must reclaim it.

The stories I read and reread of the "spirit of 1776" led me with new faith to these conclusions: We are not to wait for others to lead. You and I are meant to take back the founders' mandate, and you and I are meant to lead. You and I must protest, you and I must confront our representatives, you and I must run for office, you and I must write the op-eds, you and I must take over the battle. The founders—the unknown as well as the well-known Americans who "conceived" the nation in liberty—did not intend for us to delegate worrying about the Constitution to a cadre of constitutional scholars, or to leave debate to a class of professional pundits, or to leave the job of fighting for liberty to a caste of politicians. They meant for *us* to defend the Constitution, for *us* to debate the issues of the day, and for *us* to rise up against tyranny: the American who delivers the mail; the American who teaches our children; ordinary people.

In my reading, I went back as if to contact our mentors. I looked for practical advice and moral support from those who had stood up for the ideal. We need a strategy for a new American uprising against those who would suppress our rights; we need what Lincoln would have called "a new birth of freedom."[24] As readers of Tom Paine's *Common Sense* had to realize, we are not declaring war on an oppressor—rather, we have to realize that the war has already, quietly, systemically, been declared against us.[25]

Today we have most of our rights still codified on paper—but these documents are indeed "only paper" if we no longer experience them viscerally, if their violation no longer infuriates us. We can be citizens of a republic; we can have a Constitution and a Congress; but if we, the people, have fallen asleep to the meaning of the Constitution and to the radical implications of representative and direct democracy, then we aren't really Americans anymore.

• • •

So we must listen to the original revolutionaries and to current ones as well, and explain their ideas clearly to new generations. To hear the voices of the original vision and the voices of those modern heroes, here in the U.S. and around the world, who are true heirs to the American Revolution is to feel your wishes change. "[Freedom] liberated us the day we stopped living in a world where 'truth' and 'falsehood' were, like everything else, the property of the State. And for the most part, this liberation did not stop when we were sentenced to prison," wrote Sharansky.[26] "I was not born to be forced," wrote Henry David Thoreau. "I will breathe after my own fashion. Let us see who is the strongest . . . they only can force me to obey a higher law than I."[27] You want to stay in that room where these revolutionaries are conversing in this electrifying way among themselves. It feels painful but ultimately cleansing and energizing. You want to be more like them; then you realize that maybe you can be—then finally you realize that you already are.

Our "America," our Constitution, our dream, when properly felt within us, does more than "defend freedom." It clears space to build the society that allows for the highest possible development of who we ourselves personally were meant to be.

We have to rise up in self-defense and legitimate rebellion. We need more drastic action than e-mails to Congress.

We need the next revolution.

FREEDOM IS INTENDED
AS A CHALLENGE

Oh, Freedom . . . Oh, Freedom over me.
— African-American spiritual

We have to change our understanding of what our legacy is if we are to renew the revolution that is America.

Is the American promise a greeting card? Hardly. We are meant to sign our contract with American liberty in a kind of existential blood.

We tend to assume that our American legacy promises us liberty and the pursuit of happiness—no questions asked. But I learned from my reading of the founders' work that just as you aren't promised freedom in the American contract without the reciprocal expectation that you will risk yourself to defend freedom, so you aren't promised happiness or even the purely self-regarding right to pursue happiness. That's a myth.

THE DECLARATION OF INDEPENDENCE:
YOUR CONTRACT AS LIBERTY'S WARRIOR

The American contract is codified in Thomas Jefferson's short but stunning Declaration of Independence. Jefferson wrote it as a distillation of sentiments that were common among his fellow colonists:

We hold these Truths to be self-evident, that all Men are created equal, that they are endowed by their Creator with certain unalienable Rights, that among these are Life, Liberty, and the Pursuit of Happiness.—That to secure these Rights, Governments are instituted among Men, deriving their just Powers from the Consent of the governed, that whenever any Form of Government becomes destructive of these Ends, it is the Right of the People to alter or to abolish it, and to institute new Government, laying its Foundation on such Principles, and organizing its Powers in such Form, as to them shall seem most likely to effect their Safety and Happiness. Prudence, indeed, will dictate that Governments long established should not be changed for light and transient Causes; and accordingly all Experience hath shewn, that Mankind are more disposed to suffer, while Evils are sufferable than to right themselves by abolishing the Forms to which they are accustomed. But when a long Train of Abuses and Usurpations, pursuing invariably the same Object, evinces a Design to reduce them under absolute Despotism, it is their Right, it is their Duty, to throw off such Government, and to provide new Guards for their future Security.

This language, while beautiful, is quite difficult; it is the formal language of a very formal century far removed from our own. Most of the "fake patriotism" bullet points we get from the Declaration focus on its first sentence and an early clause in it, the famous "Life, Liberty, and the Pursuit of Happiness." (Or as a Svedka vodka ad has it, "Life,

Liberty, and the Pursuit of Happy Hour." Or as a Cadillac ad puts it, "Life, Liberty and the Pursuit.")

Since our attention is usually called to that opening shot, most of us think of the Declaration as being no more disturbing or personally demanding than a nicely lit HBO special about 1776. We tend to think that the Declaration intends something pleasant and benign: people like to pursue their individual pleasures, God wants it to work out this way, and everyone's interests are best served by our having the right to do so. Out of context, this phrase evokes a smiley-faced, noncombative, self-absorbed version of the American task.

But it turns out that the Declaration of Independence is about our continual duty as Americans to rebel—not so much about our continual enjoyment as Americans of the pleasures of shopping and team sports. Indeed, historian Pauline Maier points out in *American Scripture: Making the Declaration of Independence* that the Declaration of Independence's first long sentence asserts above all the "right of revolution." [1]

What Is "the Pursuit of Happiness"?

The founders saw two ideas, individuality and happiness— as in "the Pursuit of Happiness" above—as being closely related.

But again, our contemporary understanding of both these terms is far distorted from how the founders intended us to interpret them: we tend to think of both as lifestyle opportunities—scope for personal preferences to play out upon. A whole marketing wavelength around us is all about this predicate of "individuality" and "happiness": MySpace, MyTunes, MyFavorites, my personal checking, my monogram, my pet, my cubicle, my retirement goals. In contemporary America, "happiness" is what you get when you activate your "liberty" to express your "individuality." "Happiness" today is often defined as personal satisfaction that stops with the individual, and even personal pleasure and joy.

But to Jefferson and his Enlightenment contemporaries, the "individual" and "happiness" had different meanings than what we assume they do today. To Jefferson, "happiness" would not have been the opposite of the eighteenth-century term "melancholy," which today we would call sadness or depression. Rather, to many of the founders, "happiness" was a fortunate state of enfranchisement in the context of an open, just society. This sense of the word descended to the revolutionary generation from Greek literature: to the founders, "happiness" meant the development of one's full power as an individual, and one's respecting of the "sacred rights" and consciences of others in a condition of freedom.[2] (Robert Kennedy picked up this definition when he wrote, "Long ago the Greeks defined happiness as 'the exercise of vital powers along lines of excellence in a life affording them scope.'")[3]

For instance, Jefferson wrote in 1787: "Happy for us, that when we find our constitutions defective & insufficient to secure the *happiness* of our people, we can assemble with all the coolness of philosophers & set it to rights, while every other nation on earth must have recourse to arms to amend or restore their constitutions."[4] In 1803 he defined the nation's well-being in terms of people's "liberty" and "security," which in turn make them feel *"at . . . ease"* and lead them to act on behalf of a whole. In 1814, he wrote to a friend, Miles King, using "happiness" in the context of

honesty, kindness, and respect for others' personal and religious freedoms: "He [God] formed us moral agents. . . .
he is far above our power; but that we may promote the
happiness of those with whom he has placed us in society, by
acting honestly toward all, benevolently to those who fall
within our way, respecting sacredly their rights, bodily and
mental, and cherishing especially their freedom of conscience, as we value our own."[5,6]

So the right to "the Pursuit of Happiness" we inherit is
not a pleasure pursuit such as catalog shopping or an in-
dulgence in a personal lifestyle choice, whether a doll col-
lectors' convention or an S&M gala.

To most of us, nonetheless, the first clause alone *is* the
Declaration of Independence. We remember it because
our civics textbooks and politicians stick to this section; but
we also remember it because the modern ear can more
easily understand the words of the opening clause than
those of the second half.

But then—the rest of the text! If you read to the end
and translate into contemporary English—which I bet your
middle school civics textbooks never did for you—you will
find that Jefferson put together a most radical document
with most challenging implications for every one of us. And
Pauline Maier points out that what Jefferson was doing by
constructing his paragraph as he did—using an eighteenth-
century way of building a set of ideas so the most important one comes last—makes it all the more indefensible to
take the first famous clause out of context.

So the rest of Jefferson's passage is just as crucial for us
to understand—Maier would say even more crucial. And it
illuminates a completely different role for us.

With translation for a modern reader, it means something like this:

That to guarantee these rights for themselves, men create governments that derive their rightful [or "proper"] power from the consent of those who are governed; that whenever any form of government starts to be destructive to the goals of life, liberty, and the pursuit of happiness, the people have a *right* to change *or even destroy* that form of government; and the people have a right then to create a new form of government—one that is founded upon the kind of principles, and that takes the kind of shape, that seems to them to be most likely to guarantee their safety and good fortune.

It is obviously not prudent to change or to destroy long-established governments for superficial reasons, or in response to [difficult] circumstances that are transient; and experience shows that it is human nature for people to put up with suffering if the suffering is bearable. But when a long series of abuses and violations of their rights appears to be directed at one primary goal—that of reducing a given people to having to live under conditions of absolute despotism—*then it is the people's right—indeed, it is their duty*—to throw off this kind of government, so as to establish new forms of protection for their security in the future.

This part of the declaration is not saying: "Hurrah, you are born free, enjoy your bingo or your yoga as you see fit." Nor is it simply justifying in ringing terms the domestic political decision to separate the fate of the young North American colonies from the oppressive "protection" of mother England. Rather, it is saying something darker and more personally demanding: you have a sacred obligation to take the most serious possible steps and undergo the most serious kinds of personal risks in defense of this freedom that is your natural right; and you *must* rise up against those who seek to subdue you—wherever and whenever they appear.

Did Mrs. Jones in eighth grade put that on your test? I didn't think so. My own civics class had no such focus on personal resistance. Was that mandate in the shaded box in your textbook? Or was there, much more likely, a photo of the actual unexplicated and illegible parchment document? Maier makes the point that the document itself, starting at the fifty-year anniversary after the Revolution, became and remains today a kind of sacred relic for a secular nation—but that the relic has itself been promoted and publicized often at the expense of anyone explaining the more rebellious message it intended to convey to us, the heirs of Jefferson's revolutionary manifesto.[7]

The pretty but illegible scroll that had become so iconic was in my textbook in middle school. That translated mandate to protest and confront abusive power? Didn't make it in. The Fourth of July gives us fireworks and speeches—not, usually, a reminder that we inherit a sworn duty to rebel at injustice.

If we actually learned this entire passage as the nation's and our own personal manifesto, would we tolerate today the state spying on us illegally? Would we tolerate the passage of laws today that allow the executive to bypass the people's representatives entirely—giving Americans effectively a condition of being subject to taxation and other commitments without representation? Would we be okay with our rights and liberties being chipped away? Would we change the channel?

The more I read the Declaration, the more unsettled I

became. Did this mean that I was not free to sit by, check out, scan the catalogs, go on a long vacation, tend my own garden when I was sick of the mess on the homefront? Did this mean that I personally had to step up to confront abusive power?

How altogether different and more difficult an experience of oneself and one's country it would be if a "declaration of independence" for Americans means accepting a personal commitment to defend liberty. Jefferson left us not a guarantee of a life basking in a lawn chair, but rather a guarantee of a life of personal upheaval and sacrifice when necessary.

I kept going over and over Jefferson's language. I was looking, I realized, for a loophole. Did the philosopher of Monticello make any allowance for my personal complacency? Didn't the language somewhere let me off the hook? Didn't he know I was *busy*?

No, I was forced to conclude, not anywhere. Thomas Jefferson implicated *me*.

And you too.

"Liberation" is not only about a historical moment in the past. It is, as African-American slaves knew for centuries, a destination of the mind. Jews who were not alive during the historical liberation from Egypt understood this too, as have many others. So the Declaration's specific call to liberation from George III's tyranny is also a timeless contract that implicates each one of us forever, bestowing upon us certain rights but charging us too with certain responsibilities, and not at one moment of time but continually. This meant I was going to have to feel more outrage and less detachment, do more fighting and less settling. And there wasn't a time when my commitment could expire; it wasn't "one revolution" or "in your college days" that we were asked to fight. It is whenever our country—meaning, liberty—needed us. Even when we are old. Even when we are sick of it. Even if we have done it before.

Jefferson and Adams both lived long, productive lives. Both men fought for and won the first revolution and served their country as leaders; in old age, both longed to be left in peace, the former at his farm in Monticello and the latter at his estate in Massachusetts.[8]

But both stepped up again and again to aid the nation when called to, very much against their personal inclinations, because they understood the status of "being an American" existentially, that it means that one has signed on to fight the permanent revolution.

So real patriotism means understanding that the Declaration of Independence charges us *categorically* and *always* as Americans to rise up in person against threats to liberty. A friend remarked that the words in the Declaration seemed to force one to ask of oneself, "Am I a revolutionary on behalf of freedom?"

I realized that he was right. That *is* the question that the Declaration demands that each of us ask ourself.

Well, am I willing to be?

Are you?

FAKE PATRIOTISM

What are we supposed to do to reclaim freedom? We need to understand that we are bombarded with both fake patriotism and fake democracy. Only then can we get to the real American mandate.

The key ways, the phrases and metaphors, in which we are often asked to think about America tend to make us stupid, complacent, and inert. They are also, if you go back to what the great Americans wished us to identify as love of country, just plain wrong. Today, politicians often ask us to think of ourselves as a kind of "chosen people" by birthright: "Our nation is chosen by God and commissioned by history to be a model to the world," as George W. Bush asserted during the 2000 election campaign.[1]

Over the past four decades, patriotism was often defined as uncritical support for U.S. policies—such as the Vietnam War–era bumper sticker MY COUNTRY, RIGHT OR WRONG. Patriotism was also branded as support for U.S. militarism, whatever the context or conflict or cost. Sometimes patriotism was identified with "Christian America" and sometimes even as direct evangelism in the context of statecraft. Finally patriotism was rebranded as the active silencing of dissent. John McCain, for instance, whose campaign messaging in 2008 was grounded in a theme of patriotism, recently called in public for members of MoveOn.org to be kicked out of the country.[2] But all these rebrandings of patriotism would have dismayed the great

Americans who had all at various times criticized U.S. military actions, U.S. policies, the establishment of any state religion, and most of all, criticized those who would silence disagreeing voices and dissent.

How did "patriotism" become so dumbed down? There are many reasons. During the Vietnam War, the left often abandoned a claim on the notion of "patriotism." Young antiwar leaders challenged the mythology of the stars and stripes—fair enough—but spent less energy re-investigating and reanimating the ideals the flag was intended to represent. By disdaining America's own most radical heritage, the left let the right "brand" patriotism. Today's leaders on the left rarely assert that the most radical revolution in human history has already taken place—in 1776—and that it is spreading in fits and starts around the globe. Their message rarely calls on citizens to reclaim the American Revolution above any other.

And unfortunately for everyone across the political spectrum, the religious right, especially during the 1970s and 1980s, redefined patriotism in ways that would have appalled Paine, Jefferson, Washington, and Adams—not to mention the Republican president Abraham Lincoln. "Patriotism" became identified with blind loyalty and a sense that America is innately better than the rest of the world.

So today, we often believe that we as Americans are "the Elect"—a special, almost a chosen, people, who are uniquely entitled to a place in the sun. Where did that idea originally come from? For it is actually a direct heresy against the founders' intent.

The founders did not create liberty for America, but America for liberty, which they understood as part of universal law. The notion of an America that was above other nations because we were somehow better, already "saved"—rather than an America that was continually *called* to become better, continually charged with saving itself—is an idea that only came into vogue about fifty years after the revolution of 1776. This idea emerged out of the religious revival movement called the Second Great Awakening.[3] The founders and the greatest Americans of the previous generation would have been apoplectic at the conception that the U.S. is simply saved, simply special, whether or not it does good works.

Rather, our calling America to face itself is central to the task the founders and great Americans explicitly left us.

In 2008, presidential contender Barack Obama was pilloried in the mainstream press because he associated with a minister, the Reverend Jeremiah Wright, who gave speeches blisteringly critical of U.S. policies.[4] In a sermon, "The Day of Jerusalem's Fall," delivered soon after the September 11 attacks in 2001, Wright said, "We bombed Hiroshima, we bombed Nagasaki, and we nuked far more than the thousands in New York and the Pentagon, and we never batted an eye . . . and now we are indignant because the stuff we have done overseas is now brought back into our own front yards. America's chickens are coming home to roost." Wright called on his parishioners to respond to this by rededicating themselves to God. Yet Reverend Wright's call for the U.S. to look in the mirror has been deemed unpatriotic—so unpatriotic, in fact, that the Republican opposition is turning these quotes into an ad campaign in the South.

But such challenging language would have been right at home alongside the sermons of the Puritans whom we celebrate at Thanksgiving, as well as alongside many of the speeches of Abraham Lincoln,[5] Frederick Douglass,[6] Martin Luther King,[7] and Robert Kennedy.[8]

The great Americans defined America as a chance for us not to flatter but rather to confront ourselves. They did not define patriotism as a smug legacy of entitlement, but as a universal challenge that always included the demand for self-correction. But we are so used to being raised on a rhetoric of artificial patriotism—the kind that you get to tune in to in a feel-good way just because you were lucky enough to have been born here and then can pretty much forget about—that this definition seems positively foreign today.

The phony patriotism we are fed starts with the misuse of sources that go back to the very beginning of the republic. John Winthrop was a minister who sailed with a small band of Puritans from England, where they were violently persecuted, to Massachussetts in 1630. When the emigrants arrived in harbor after the harrowing journey, he gave a sermon, "A Model of Christian Charity."[9]

Since Reagan, modern politicians cite this sermon, saying that we *are* or that "we will be" a "city on a hill"—implying that we are innately good and that God has set us permanently up above other nations to be an effortless role model to them.[10]

But this is the opposite of the message of the author of the "city on a hill" sermon. The original phrase Winthrop used is from Jesus's Sermon on the Mount in the Gospel of Matthew: "Ye are the light of the world. A city that is set on [a] hill cannot be hid. Neither do men light a candle, and put it under a bushel, but on a candlestick, and it giveth light unto all that are in the house. Let your light so shine before men, that they may see your good works, and glorify your Father which is in heaven."[11] Winthrop knew perfectly well that the "city on a hill" metaphor he was invoking was about doing good deeds, about behaving righteously and justly. The whole point of the metaphor in the Gospel that it is good works, and not ethnic or racial identity, let alone national identity, that gives "light."

But Reagan often misquoted Winthrop. Reagan declared, "Standing on the tiny deck of the *Arabella* in 1630 off the Massachusetts coast, John Winthrop said, 'We *will* be as a city upon a hill.' "[12] Reagan not only got the verb wrong, he also regularly omitted the rest of the paragraph.

John Winthrop did not write that we *are* like a "city on a hill," nor did he declare that "we *will* be" like one. Rather he said that we *shall be* like a city on a hill. "Shall" is a seventeenth-century conjugation of the verb "should"; it is not a declarative term, it is an imperative one. "Thou shalt not commit adultery" doesn't mean "You won't." It means "You should not," or "You must not." That is, Winthrop's is an active demand *for* goodness, not by any means a claim *of* goodness. Winthrop was saying clearly that we have to earn the blessing that is "America" and that the way we deserve it is by engaging continually in acts of righteousness. Furthermore, Winthrop wrote that if we were to fail to act justly, *we* would *deserve* the curses that would come our way—a point Abraham Lincoln would make just as confrontationally and unflinchingly more than 200 years later.

Both Winthrop and later Lincoln and Rev. Martin Luther King would say to Americans that if we failed to be just, we would deserve the hostility that would come our way from others, both from friends and enemies; *deserve* the darkness that God would have in store for us; and even *deserve* the famine or violence that we might have to endure. "If we act unrighteously," warned Winthrop in the often-elided paragraph, ". . . we shall open the mouths of enemies to speak evil of the ways of God and all professors for God's sake; we shall shame the faces of many of God's worthy servants, and cause their prayers to be turned into curses upon us till we be consumed out of the good land whither we are going."[13]

Abraham Lincoln's second inaugural address, which he gave to the nation on March 4, 1865, confronts this as well. A terrible war had been ravaging the nation for years when Lincoln gave this speech. Almost one million Americans were dead or wounded, cities had been destroyed, and vast stretches of the nation had been reduced to wasteland. Surely this was a moment for a politician to assuage a nation or at the very least give the war some ("Mission Accomplished") spin.

Yet this speech is so radically different from any presidential speech in the midst of or at the end of a war that I had ever heard in my lifetime that I had to read it through several times to believe my eyes:

> Fellow-Countrymen: . . . . On the occasion corresponding to this four years ago all thoughts were anxiously directed to an impending civil war. All dreaded it, all sought to avert it. While the inaugural address was being delivered from this place, devoted altogether to *saving* the Union without war, urgent agents were in the city seeking to *destroy* it without war—seeking to dissolve the Union and divide effects by negotiation. Both parties deprecated war, but one of them would *make* war rather than let the nation survive, and the other would *accept* war rather than let it perish, and the war came. . . .

Both read the same Bible and pray to the same God, and each invokes His aid against the other. . . . "Woe unto the world because of offenses; for it must needs be that offenses come, but woe to that man by whom the offense cometh." If we shall suppose that American slavery is one of those offenses which, in the providence of God, must needs come, but which, having continued through His appointed time, He now wills to remove, and that He gives to both North and South this terrible war as the woe due to those by whom the offense came, shall we discern therein any departure from those divine attributes which the believers in a living God always ascribe to Him? Fondly do we hope, fervently do we pray, that this mighty scourge of war may speedily pass away. Yet, *if God wills that it continue until all the wealth piled by the bondsman's two hundred and fifty years of unrequited toil shall be sunk, and until every drop of blood drawn with the lash shall be paid by another drawn with the sword, as was said three thousand years ago, so still it must be said "the judgments of the Lord are true and righteous altogether."* [14] [Emphasis mine; translation: "If God wills that the war shall continue until all the profit generated by enslaved Americans' 250 years of forced and unpaid labor shall be paid out by both sides waging the war, and until every drop of blood drawn from those Americans with the (overseer's) whip shall be paid by another drop of blood drawn by combat (blood from soldiers drawn by the violence of the war)—then, as was said three thousand years ago, 'the judgments of the Lord are true and righteous altogether.' "] [15]

Was that message in our civics books or in our SAT history books? That Lincoln believed on a spiritual level that America would have to pay with blood and money for the crime of slavery?

Fake patriotism stressed that Dr. King said he had a dream. That is a very benign sentiment. We aren't taught that he gave a 1967 sermon at Riverside Church in New York in which, speaking about the fact that the war was sending the poor disproportionately to fight and die in Vietnam, he said, "I know I could never again raise my voice against the violence of the oppressed in the ghettos without having first spoken clearly to the greatest purveyor of violence in the world, my own govenment. . . . If America's soul becomes totally poisoned, part of the autopsy must read, Vietnam. It can never be saved so long as it destroys the deepest hopes of men the world over."

Imagine if a president told us Americans today, as Winthrop, Lincoln, and King did, that we are engaged in committing great wrongs in which blowback is inevitable and even spiritually just: the crime, say, of subverting democratically elected governments overseas and then subsidizing and training death squads to murder citizens, or waging illegal wars against nations not at war with us. What if an American president told us to our faces that some of the hostility directed toward us now from the Middle East derives from our own policies, such as torturing prisoners, and that some of the hostility is justified? What if an American president held a mirror up to our own faces as Lincoln so outrageously did in his second inaugural address?

Would we assassinate him? Or would we look in the mirror?

Lincoln clearly suffered personally when he fell short

of what he knew he was supposed to be. The great patriots all believed that true Americans *should* suffer if they looked in the mirror and saw that they fell short. Lincoln once wrote a friend, Joshua Speed, who had advocated his right to own slaves and had argued, as many did at the time, that that right was enshrined in the Constitution. Lincoln noted that one reason he opposed slavery was that it made him feel personally miserable:

"You know I dislike slavery. . . . I also acknowledge your rights and my obligations under the Constitution in regard to your slaves." But Lincoln went on with a seemingly casual aside: "I confess I hate to see the poor creatures hunted down and caught and carried back to their stripes [lashes] and unrequited toil; but I bite my lip and keep quiet."[16]

He then evoked an image that would be emotionally unanswerable:

> In 1841, you and I had together a tedious low-water trip on a steamboat from Louisville to St. Louis. You may remember, as I well do, that from Louisville to the mouth of the Ohio there were on board ten or a dozen slaves shackled together with irons. That sight was a continual torment to me, and I see something like it every time I touch the Ohio or any other slave border. It is not fair for you to assume that I have no interest in a thing which has, and continually exercises, the power to make me miserable. You ought rather to appreciate how much the great body of the Northern people do crucify their feelings, in order to maintain their loyalty to the Constitution and the Union. I do oppose the extension of slavery because my

judgment and feelings so prompt me, and I am under no obligations to the contrary. If for this you and I must differ, differ we must. . . .

As a nation we began by declaring that "all men are created equal." We now practically read it, "all men are created equal, except negroes." When the Know Nothings [a racist group] get control, it will read, "all men are created equal, except negroes and foreigners and Catholics." When it comes to this, I shall prefer emigrating to some country where they make no pretense of loving liberty—to Russia, for instance, where despotism can be taken pure, and without the base alloy of hypocrisy.[17]

Lincoln pointed out that the Northerners who opposed slavery had to "crucify" their feelings about it to carry on with business as usual. From a shift in consciousness, action—a bloody war and the Emancipation Proclamation—followed; but the war that was waged and the laws that were passed were outcomes first of a change in consciousness.

Is the way Winthrop, Lincoln, and King asked their audiences to be patriotic—that is, to face themselves—the way commentators and political leaders ask us to be patriotic today?

Would we experience our own gift of freedom more intensely if our leaders demanded this of us in calling us to patriotism, and if we demanded such moral clarity of ourselves?

FAKE DEMOCRACY

I realized that my own feelings about American citizenship were changing as I read, or reread, the founders. At first I thought I would focus on helping citizens *affect* the political process and speak up to their leaders. But I felt my expectations shifting—drastically rising. The founders had made it clear that we were *not* supposed to see ourselves only as constituents, voters, or recipients of the leadership of our representatives. We, ordinary people, were also supposed to run things ourselves.

Having heard so many people's feelings of powerlessness in relationship to really engaging our liberties, I sat down to find the practical knowledge, to research the information a citizen would need to take command of the nation again.

As I did so, to my dismay, I hit a series of walls.

I had assumed that 2000–2008 was the period when liberty was under special assault. But on my travels, citizens warned me that the erosion went back three decades. Indeed, I found that a subtle set of tactics had, since the citizen uprisings of the 1960s and 1970s, been replacing some elements of real liberty and democracy with fake stand-ins. These sleights of hand are so elusive each alone that we do not feel as we should the monstrous impact of them taken altogether. I tried the doorknobs to citizen leadership and found so many jammed—or encountered maddening arrows to nowhere that sent me down blind alleys marked "empowerment" and "citizen action."

The systemic assault amounted to a war. It is war by other means, and not very sexy ones. It is being waged through, unglamorously enough, bureaucracy. It is civic death by a thousand cuts.

THE WAR ON LIBERTY

"Every government degenerates when trusted to the rulers of the people alone," wrote Jefferson. "The people themselves therefore are its only safe depositories."[1] So I set out to try to use some of my basic rights: my right to assemble and to speak aloud in a public forum; to try to run for local office or to help another ordinary citizen run; and to vote or help register people to vote. But the process turned out to be like a reality show in which the goal is to make the contestants go home, one by one. Again and again I would find my efforts stymied or cut off at the knees by a thousand suffocating regulations. If the regulations didn't kill the actual event or activity, they were sure to kill the spirit.

Eventually I wondered, is this barrier of petty regulations and restrictions what citizens intuit is out there when they express such depressed, hopeless feelings about the real prospect of using their rights?

We have not just had our rights undermined—we have also had our expectations lowered. I realized that over three decades we've been taught to have less hope that *we* should run, *we* should lead, *we* should be able to win, and to have just about no real hope left anymore that if we do not like what our representatives are doing, we have the right and the realistic ability to throw our own hat in the ring and defeat them ourselves.

I found vanishing civic education; vanishing or falsified entry points for citizen leaders; vanishing votes; and vanishing space in which to march, protest, or speak out.

These vanishing access points to liberty led us to a situation in which we are continually told we live in a nation far freer than the one our founders left us—but it is actually a nation in which key aspects of our liberty have transmuted themselves into a dimension of make-believe.

Vanishing Civic Education

The founders knew that you had to continually educate people about liberty in order to continue to possess liberty.

According to historian George Grant, by the beginning of the nineteenth century U.S. educators realized that "if their great experiment in liberty . . . was to be maintained over the course of succeeding generations, then an informed patriotism would have to be instilled in the hearts and minds of the young." So, from the middle of the nineteenth century to the middle of the twentieth, we had an educational tradition: "rising citizens were presented with small handbooks—brief guides to the essential elements of the American creed."[2]

What happened in the middle of the twentieth century and into the 1960s? Dispossessed citizens, such as those in the civil rights movement, began to register voters and to learn to claim their constitutional rights. We know that regulations restricting voting rights proliferated in the South as a consequence. Is it a coincidence that at the same time the tradition of making sure such American rights handbooks were widely available came to an end, that civics education began to disappear, and that permits restricting assembly started to proliferate?

But in the 1960s and early 1970s, the nation also saw effective consumer boycotts led by poor migrant workers; effective antiwar demonstrations led by very young students; and effective lawsuits against corporations that polluted or discriminated brought by ordinary citizens. Those who profited from leading the political process and the corporate sector realized that decision-making could no longer continue without regard to the voices of ordinary Americans clamoring for a seat at the table.

No one today gives American kids handbooks about American rights and freedoms when they get a learner's permit to drive. Adults don't get such handbooks when they register to vote. Today, it is only naturalized immigrants who are still consistently required to pass a test giving them an orientation in "informed patriotism."[3] So today it is not uncommon for newly naturalized citizens to know more about the American system and its ideals than do the rest of their neighbors. The result? Native-born citizens are often baffled by democracy's workings and unsure what American ideals really are.

This confusion and lack of awareness well suits corporate and special interests who want us to give up our leadership role in the nation. And it's not just the power elite that are happy to reap the benefits of a gathering blackout of information about liberty. Many theorists are comfortable with it as well.

Many younger Americans have inherited intellectual baggage that undermines their awareness of democracy. When New Left activists of the 1960s started the antiwar and free speech student movements, they didn't usually take their framework from Montesquieu or Thomas Paine; rather, as I noted, Marx and Lenin set the tone. So some gifted young people in that era who wanted to be activists tended to think not about "reform" but "revolt"; not about "citizen engagement" but "the people's uprising"; not about the truly revolutionary implications of American open debate but about the need for "ideological correctness"; not about the incredibly revolutionary potential of the engaged universal U.S. vote, but about the post-Marxist idea that voting at all puts off "the revolution" and the collapse of a corrupt system.

The result of all this? In the Reagan era, when the Iran-Contra scandal showed U.S. officials operated in disregard of the rule of law, many college students were preoccupied with theories of post-structuralism and deconstructionism. These theories were often presented to students as an argument that the state—even in the United States—is only a network of power structures, rather than a radical catalyst for liberty. This trend also helped consign to the attic of unfashionable ideas the notion that the state could be built up by ordinary people to be a true platform for freedom. Finally, theories that globalization is the ultimate evil found their ascendancy on college campuses. Many idealistic young people, involved in movements against sweatshops and against the World Trade Organization, came to see democracy as merely a cosmetic gloss on the monolith of global capitalism rather than as the only true corrective to the growing excesses and abuses of global capitalism.[4]

But our nation needs young people's engagement now more than ever. Young people are always in the vanguard of any movement to sustain or advance liberty. Students led the charge for freedom in Prague and Mexico City in

1968, in Chile in 1973, in Beijing and throughout Eastern Europe in 1989. Young people helped lead the way in the U.S. civil rights movement, the women's movement, the free speech, gay rights, and antiwar movements.[5] Many are leading the charge for social justice and freedom today, and they deserve their revolutionary inheritance to help them. If more of the remarkable young people I met had been taught those core principles, they would feel much angrier—but not nearly as often so hopeless.

But the blacking out of information about liberty doesn't require a fancy theory. You can disempower future citizens by simply wiping out civics altogether.

As the founders knew, if citizens are ignorant of or complacent about the proper workings of a republic "of laws, and not of men," then any leaders of any party—or any tyrannical Congress, or even a tyrannical majority—can abuse the power they hold.

But studies show that today a third of young Americans don't really understand what our system is, and even if they do understand it, they don't necessarily agree that it is a good idea. According to the National Center for Education Statistics, only 47 percent of high school seniors have mastered a minimum level of U.S. history, 66 percent of civics. Only 14 percent perform at or above the "proficient" level for history, 27 percent for civics.

The Intercollegiate Studies Institute found in 2007 that U.S. college students missed almost half the questions on a civics literacy test. Only 45.9 percent of those surveyed knew that the clause "We hold these truths to be self-evident, that all men are created equal" is in the Declaration of Independence.[6] The study also found what many other studies confirm: that civics illiteracy equals disengagement. Conversely, the more students know about the system, the more likely they are to vote and engage in other ways.

Few young Americans today understand, for instance, how the Constitution and the Bill of Rights protect them *personally*. Few get it on a gut level that the Fourth Amendment keeps armed agents of the state from bursting into their dorm rooms or their apartments, ripping through their papers, and hauling off their computers, often as a prelude to framing them on false charges, or simply to terrorize them and make them feel that they are never really safe or experiencing truly private life—a kind of vulnerability that other citizens suffer around the world. Few young people realize that the "due process" and "habeas corpus" that the Constitution guarantees for them means that they can't personally be locked up in a dungeon by agents of the state and left to languish indefinitely.

The Knight Foundation has found an alarming decline in U.S. student support for the First Amendment: in a 2004 survey, more than a third of the young respondents believed that the First Amendment *went too far* in guaranteeing freedom of speech and of the press.[7] By 2006, the number who held that view had swelled to almost *half.* In the absence of a powerful education about what America really is, and in the face of a hyped "war on terror" that portrays our liberty, as well as our checks and balances, as threats to security, the Constitution and the Bill of Rights that the founders left us have become controversial.

Not long ago, I gave a talk at a major university in the Midwest. "They're going to raze our meadows and put in a shopping mall!" a young woman in the audience wailed. "And there's nothing we can do!" she said, to the nods of young and old alike.

I asked how old she was. When she said twenty-six, I

suggested that she run for city council. She stared at me with complete incomprehension. It took me a long time to convince her and her peers in the audience that what I'd suggested was possible, even if she didn't have money, a major media outlet of her own, or a political "machine" behind her.

Here are some actual quotes from smart, idealistic young Americans: "I show my true convictions by refusing to vote." "The two parties are exactly the same." "Congress is bought and paid for." "Elections are just a front for corporations." "My teacher says you shouldn't believe anything you read in the newspapers at all." While there is plenty of truth to all of these remarks, there is plenty of power we still have to push back. And the same young people are not being taught about that power. Many of the young people I met had an overwhelmingly intense critique of what's wrong with the republic but little information about using the power they have to fight back.

Even those young people who are politically engaged don't have much faith in our system's potential. "I was taught that it's set up for the elites and for old white men and that there's not much you can do about it," said Christopher Le, twenty-eight, who works on suicide prevention programs in Austin, Texas. Le's mother was a "boat person" who fled Vietnam with her four-month-old son so that he could be raised in freedom. But few Americans I met under thirty had been given the gist of this kind of faith in the ideals of the United States. As Le put it, "No one taught us that democracy was this shining, inspiring thing."[8]

Vanishing Entry Points for Citizen Leaders

I had told the young woman in Wisconsin to run for city council. Now I needed to see if I knew how to run myself and if I could help other people run. But I found that not only was usable information about democracy disappearing, so were the entry points to citizen leadership. I accumulated a stack of research materials from all the main resources a citizen would plausibly turn to if he or she wanted to run for office: state and city government, governors' offices, Congress, county sources, and so on.

I kept having a bizarre intellectual experience. I would be reading material that purported to be about how a given city or town council worked, or about how you put an initiative on a ballot, or about how a state senate works. But again and again, after reading the PR-heavy overview and admiring the many informative sites to click on in a given website menu, I would search and search for the key piece for citizens, the action step: how do *you,* the reader, the ordinary citizen, run for city council? How would I? How do *you or I,* the ordinary citizens, put the initiative on the ballot? How do you or I help draft a bill for our representative?

That button or banner was almost never there—and if it was, it was often inoperable in practice.

For example, when you go to the website for Atlanta, Georgia, and click "City Council," it shows everyone on the council—including a nice full-color photo of the council members—but *does not tell you how to run.*[9] Keep clicking "City Council"—nothing will connect you to any description of or information about how *you* can start the process of running to become a city council member. When you enter in the search box the words "run for office" the site brings up all the city departments and nice descriptions of what they do—but *does not tell you how to run for them.* If you enter the word "ballots" you get ninety documents, none of them about how *you* get on the ballot for your city, Atlanta. If you click on "Boards and Commissions," you get a frankly *fake* process. You will be offered descriptions of the boards and commissions in Atlanta, but if you want to apply to be on a board or commission you get a tiny window that offers you all of two thousand characters—not words, characters—to describe why you want to serve; in another miniature window, you get five thousand *characters* for your CV. But you can find no information about who is assessing your application, what determines a successful applicant, what the deadline is, when you will hear back, what the availability is for seats on the various boards or commissions, which are open, what the terms of service and meeting requirements are, and so on. In a sidebar, a happy little questionnaire lets you check various areas of interest—e.g., arts, education—as if for a vague online dating service, but not the actual board or commission on which you wish to serve, as if for a democracy. It is a *fake* application process. There is no way to know how to get one of those seats for yourself if you are a citizen—no way to compete fairly with the donors, cronies, members of special interests, lovers, business colleagues, or other people filling the seats that an American citizen should have free and fair and equal access to.

A document that the U.S. Senate produces by the thousands, ostensibly for citizens, with a robust "here you are, guys!" title, "How Our Laws Are Made," [10] purports to explain to regular people how a bill becomes a law. It is forty-nine pages long. It was first put together in 1953, and it still sounds that way. Buried on page 3 in the midst of a mass of impenetrable language is a *single paragraph* acknowledging that a voter can play a direct role in the process, that an individual has the right to (not the obligation or duty to) petition the "member" to get a law passed, changed, or repealed. But there is no practical explanation whatsoever of how an ordinary person can find out in his or her state how to drive an issue for his or her congressman, let alone how to help the representative draft a bill himself or herself.

A website for the Illinois state legislature sends you to find out about every single bill that is coming up to become a law—and identifies them all by number so you have absolutely no idea what issues your representatives are talking about, let alone any effective way to step in and put pressure on when something is coming up that you may care about.[11]

A Shasta County, California, document purports to show citizens there how to put an initiative on the ballot.[12] Now, this—starting an initiative—is, as we will see, one of the main ways that ordinary people can reclaim the country and fight back. I have been to Shasta County; it is a mellow, plainspoken place. But the guidelines for the people's actions were written as if translated from Urdu. My own education was useless; my head swam: no terms *at all* were defined for ordinary use. What exactly is a "proponent"? What is the difference between "governing" and "governance"?

Feeling smaller and smaller, I began to turn to nongovernment sources to try to get help to follow the map that would let me have power—just a little power!—as a U.S. citizen.

Luckily, I ran into a friend, Curtis Ellis, who ran the press office for a congressman and who now as a political consultant trains ordinary people to run for office with an unusually grassroots-oriented firm. I told him about the difficulty I was having with government sources as I tried to identify information for ordinary people about driving their representatives' agenda or running for office themselves. Was I just stupid? What, I asked, could I tell people about how to more effectively pressure their representatives and how to engage directly in the process?

He laughed out loud at my consternation. He was not surprised. He confirmed that gatekeepers—the parties, lobbyists, and even issue groups—benefit from preventing citizens from getting involved. Those who are now in power don't really want a transparent system for citizen engagement, let alone a level playing field.

One morning, I stared at these mountains of printouts, really angry at myself. Even with a research assistant, a graduate education, and with the privilege of this project being my only full-time job, I still couldn't piece together the map of America—the map of how I and other ordinary citizens could work it, the map the founders had meant to bequeath to us. The last time I'd felt my brain fry like that was when I'd had to try decoding Elizabethan manuscript writing as a grad student.

Indeed, the materials seemed *designed* to make you conclude that democracy was just too complicated for ordinary people to take charge of. I felt as if I were in a scene in a thriller in which a character has to search under great pressure for a missing clue: I rifled page after page of printouts looking for what was not there. Finally, staring at my stack of yellow file folders— containing source after U.S. *government* source that left out the key action step that would let citizens actually enter the process and throw their weight around and make a difference—I faced a bitter conclusion. They don't want us weighing in, let alone driving the process.

I had set out hopefully to find out how we all could run for city council, state assembly, state legislature, governor, the House of Representatives or Senate, and the Presidency, as Benjamin Franklin, himself a working-class printer by origin, had intended us to do.

That innocent confidence was a long way from the Saturday, months later, when I found myself sitting, crumpled, on the floor between a TGI Friday's and a World's Best Yogurt at Newark Airport, literally crying on the phone to a friend. I am not ashamed of this abasement because I was actually heartsick. What I had grown up believing was real, true, and meaningful was in many ways a stage set with rats scurrying behind the scrim.

A maze had been constructed that had a nicely designed logo and attractive lettering that read DEMOCRACY over the entrance; once inside, the maze pointed citizens down various paths with various pretty arrows. But in reality it had few real pathways, and none to the true power center.

On most government sites we, the people, were positioned as docile voters or at most as volunteers—the lowly, grateful people who might put up the signs, humbly pass the petitions for the *real* candidates, and clean up the trash after leafleting. The prose cast us as the forelock tuggers; but Thomas Jefferson said that no one was born booted and spurred to ride on the backs of others.[13] Weren't we Americans supposed to tug our forelocks to no one? But it was hell on earth trying to find material that addressed us as the rightful leaders of the nation ourselves. Even Congress's own websites don't explain upcoming bills in clear English, don't offer you enough advance notice of the agenda to affect the outcome, and don't show how many citizens (who would be willing to have the information reported) contacted Congresspeople for or against various legislation.[14] So you are left to be alerted, if you're lucky, by some random organization, and you send your e-mail blindly, alone, as if dropping a penny into the ocean. It is an engineered experience of powerlessness.

The few exceptions to this rule were individual states such as Massachusetts, Vermont, California, and Iowa, which enjoyed unique histories of citizen leadership: the colonial activism of Massachusetts, the town meeting of Vermont, the referenda of California, and the caucuses of Iowa—that had left its citizens some protections.

Many people across the nation feel so frustrated and hopeless because they intuit the construction of this maze around them and do not want to spend their lives walking around with fake shiny keys fumbling with doors that will never open.

This dampening of aspiration is critical when it comes to our running for office—that is, when we try to touch the real third rail of power.

I did not start this journey with the feeling that learning to run for office was so important; no one I respected thought about that as a serious or even attractive possibility. But finally I realized, therein lies one main piece of evidence of this pernicious thirty-year reeducation of Americans to accept Democracy Lite. Given that no one I respect *does* feel strongly that he or she needs to know how to, or even wants to, run for office at any level at all, they—the parties, the lobbyists, and the issue groups that just do not want ordinary citizens involved, let alone causing a ruckus or finding themselves in charge—have already won.

Was it unfair for me to yearn for the relative simplicity of citizen leadership in the infant republic? Is the modern era simply too complex to let ordinary people lead?

Not at all. One of the myths of American patriotism is that we lead the world in using our liberties. Sadly, this is not true: we actually lag behind Western democracies in our rates of voting and our general knowledge of political issues when it comes to citizen leadership in a modern democracy.[15]

Nations and regions around the world have instituted "direct democracy," in which citizens make the laws themselves as well as enjoy representation. In Switzerland, if you as an ordinary Swiss national can get enough fellow Swiss citizens to sign your petition, you can get your issue voted upon in a nationwide referendum.[16] In British Columbia, randomly chosen citizens actually help draft the laws. In the United Kingdom, the Labour administration is spearheading a raft of new procedures to open up democracy to ordinary people: proposing easier ways for British citizens from all backgrounds to stand for Parliament; establishing easier ways for citizens to put initiatives upon ballots to be voted on by their neighbors; confirming new guarantees for civil liberties—even while the nation suffered severe terror attacks and is fighting the same "bad guys" that we are fighting. Britain is even making it easier for citizens to march, rally, protest, and make noise in public spaces closer to the entrances of the houses of Parliament, so that parliamentarians actually have to hear the voices of their constituents outside.[17] In Australia you *have* to vote—it's a law—and you get the day off work, so as to make it easier on you.[18] And so on, in democracies around the world, including the most sophisticated. It's not rocket science for ordinary people to run a modern complex state.

Is there a good reason for the tools of citizen governing to be so impenetrable? Should running things be reserved for "experts" and lifers? We should ask ourselves the same question the founders asked: are ordinary people smart enough to run America? The data is in. The answer is yes. Studies show, for instance, that voters exposed to "direct democracy" in the form of ballot initiatives, understand political information better, have a greater desire to follow public affairs, and are more likely to contribute money to interest groups in midterm elections. "Thus, the data suggest that ballot initiatives stimulate political participation beyond mere voting. . . . If ballot initiatives enhance a citizen's political participation and knowledge, it bolsters the case for participatory models of government, including recent proposals for national direct democracy mechanisms in the United States." [19]

I traveled to or looked at fragile, emerging democracies from Sierra Leone to Pakistan. Citizen engagement there often seemed more energizing and even joyful than it did here at home. I believe Americans deserve to feel as positive and in control of the process as do the new voters of Freetown: I did not want to give up.

So, taking the founders' mandate seriously, I set out to make use of some of my liberty in America.

I knew just where I wanted to go, and headed for midtown Manhattan.

I'd been following the transit of the Olympic torch around the world. The torch had started its journey in Beijing. China, which is hosting this year's Olympics, has been cracking down violently on human rights as well as going after supporters of Tibetan self-determination.[20] Ordinary people in Paris, Athens, and San Francisco who love liberty have thronged the torch and compelled it to change course—or to ride in a van.

That was as it should be. It was right, I felt, that thousands of lovers of liberty around the world had protested and engaged in physical action to thwart China's PR push. Responding to the crowds worldwide, heads of state such as Nicolas Sarkozy of France were starting to waver about showing up in Beijing for the opening ceremonies. The people, by using their rights to free speech and assembly, were standing up effectively for liberty.

I too wanted to serve my country and practice democracy. I located the New York City version of the global protest against China's oppression.

I found the protest at Forty-second Street and the West Side Highway, where the Chinese consulate is located.

I mean—the protest was *sort of* located *somewhere* in the vicinity of the Chinese consulate. For what was this? Something was off in this picture. This American crowd didn't look anything like the swarming, energized crowds thronging, even confronting face-to-face, China's officials in other cities around the world—in Athens, Paris, even Seoul—crowds that had been able to and dared to seize the torch itself.

It looked like—well, like a bunch of extras dressed like protesters, in a movie about protests, who were standing far away from the action, in some backstage area, waiting haplessly for their cue.

There was the entrance to the Chinese consulate. Four lanes of city traffic and a median away from it stood about seventy-five people, waving DON'T MISTREAT THE KOREAN REF-

UGEES signs. They had one plaintive megaphone. A dozen bored police officers cordoned the space around them. The group couldn't move. "Free Korean refugees! China violates freedom!" they shouted plaintively.

But what about Tibet? I scanned the immense intersection. Oh—there they were! I finally spotted them, by shading my eyes and squinting. Backed away from the consulate by six lanes of whizzing city traffic, I saw about a hundred people who were holding up FREE TIBET and NO OLYMPIC FREEDOM IN CHINA signs at a distant point on the horizon, right up against the Hudson River, and they were just as immobilized as the first group. They were positioned kitty-corner to, not even across from—not even really in any physical relationship to—the entrance to the Chinese consulate.

These lovers of liberty were entirely penned in behind a set of metal barriers of the kind that you see at state fairs managing the livestock. Thirty police officers marked the perimeter of the group. The whole assembly had been cordoned off so that the group was largely obscured by a big tourist concession selling Statue of Liberty snowies, and by the ticket office for a motorized ferry ride called the Beast, which had giant cartoon shark teeth painted on its prow.

When I cupped my ears, I could just hear their protest chants—distant, helpless—barely reaching me across the clanging river of traffic. That group had no megaphone at all.

I asked the leader of the Korea group closer to me why the other group was so far away from the consulate. "Permits," she explained, and added that the two groups of protesters had had to share a single permit.

Share a permit? I wondered. Was free speech, like the ozone layer, in short supply?

I asked the officers about the permit sharing. Officer MacEwan, a tall, pleasant, talkative man, and Officer Rogers, who was shorter, quieter, and more intense, answered all of my questions with courtesy.

"Why are they so far away from the consulate?" I asked.

Officer MacEwan pointed out some red paint on the embassy wall and two broken glass tiles. "They marched yesterday and look what happened," he said. "Violence is unacceptable. So now that group has to march over there." He pointed half a football field away to the citizens penned in by barriers behind the concession stand, obscured by the sign for the shark ride, and backed right up against the edge of the Hudson River.

Violence is, of course, unacceptable. Did two broken tiles and some paint constitute violence? It certainly constituted misbehavior. I had just been reading about the misbehavior of our forebears, who had dragged a luxurious carriage "and two sleighs" of the hated royalist stamp distributors into the "monstrous bonfire" they had made on Bowling Green. [21] I thought of Jefferson: "We are not to expect to be translated from despotism to liberty in a feather bed." [22]

But even if you should arrest the guy who broke the tiles or spilled the paint, what about everyone else? A group is penalized for something an individual does? Did I miss that in the First Amendment? "But"—I smiled sweetly—"wouldn't the First Amendment mean that you arrest the ones who throw paint or break tiles, but you don't penalize other people who are just protesting?"

"They had their chance," Officer Rogers said darkly.

They had their *chance*? I thought. That premise—taking away assembly rights of a whole group because of the actions of individuals—would have closed down the entire antiwar movement during the Vietnam era. And the civil rights movement before that. And the anti-child-labor movement before that.

"But . . . what about the rights of the people who didn't commit any crimes?" I asked. You can ask anything in New York if you are polite and female.

"We are supposed to be proactive," explained Officer MacEwan. I recognized that term: lawyers for the protesters who had been arrested, having committed no crimes, in warrantless sweeps in New York during the 2004 Republican National Convention and jailed en masse, had said that the city had switched to a "preemptive detention" model.[23] That was what "proactive" meant. Different terms, depending on which group you were part of, but the same outcome.

I thanked the officers and made my way with difficulty across the traffic whizzing down the busy West Side Highway to the forlorn pro-Tibet group. There I met Lieutenant Triuzzi, a well-groomed man in a trim, perfectly tailored navy-blue uniform.[24] He looked like an Italian film star.

Lieutenant Triuzzi leaned casually against the railing as the protesters tried to raise their voices above the traffic din. Yes, I could clearly now see that the protesters were actually held within a closed pen made of steel barriers. They could not move. You almost wanted to pet them.

Lieutenant Triuzzi and his colleagues stood outside the pen. As politely as his colleagues had, he explained that, yes, he was the permit guy, and sure, he would be happy to answer my questions about permits.

What's a "shared permit"? I asked. He answered that there had been an advance negotiation between the groups and the mayor's office. The groups couldn't *both* have permits, he said. They had to share one.

The two groups had asked, he explained, for eight hours of time for free speech; the mayor's office had countered with two; and a compromise had been reached at four hours. But since it was a shared permit, the Korea group could only use the bullhorn for an hour and a half.

"Then," said Lieutenant Triuzzi patiently, as if explaining a math problem to a fourth-grader, "the Tibet group gets the bullhorn for half an hour. That's two hours." He used his fingers to show me: two. "Then an hour for the Korea group again. Then an hour for the Tibet supporters. Four hours."

"Oh," I said.

"Our ideal, of course," he said, "would be zero."

The protest ended shortly thereafter, and I didn't get any of the time available with the bullhorn. But I still wanted to serve my country by speaking up, as I knew now that the Declaration of Independence insisted that I must do so.

I had tried to hold a rally: A community of Americans had been following a discussion about my call to take up the fight on behalf of liberty, on the website Firedoglake .com. The site has about a million citizens in its cybercommunity. The ones who had communicated with me online were hopeless about the chance to fight back against the war on liberty.

I had met free speech hero Daniel Ellsberg that week—the man who had risked a jail sentence of 115 years to leak to the nation the information about the Vietnam War contained in the Pentagon Papers. I had asked him what I should know about how to "rise up" effectively.[25] He told me that a three-day moratorium—with giant marches across the country—had brought business as usual to a halt and helped end the Vietnam War.

A moratorium! I got right online and whipped up my fellow Americans on Firedoglake.com. Let's have a moratorium of our own for the Constitution! I urged them to do mass sit-ins in front of town halls across the country, wear red, white, and blue, carry flags, hold vigils, stop traffic, bring everything to a halt to showcase a mass democracy movement. A wave of excitement followed in the online community. People started to plan, strategize, and volunteer. Maybe we could actually do something!

"But," wrote one well-informed citizen, "you need permits. And every city has different rules."

I could feel the thousands of people watching this discussion switch from energized "on" to the now default position of "off." I felt it myself. There was no way any longer to put together in America the kind of mass nationwide moratorium that Ellsberg knew could sway the path of a nation. The permits had outflanked us.

Nonetheless, a volunteer named Barbara Martinez and I showed up in Union Square on the designated day. We brought our petition and our flags. She brought a bullhorn. We began to read the Constitution and alert our fellow citizens to the dangers our liberty faced. I felt a little silly but kind of happy: people were drawing near and listening. A crowd started to gather. People started to sign.

"Um, that's illegal," explained one well-intentioned activist who passed by.

"What?" I asked.

"You can't use a bullhorn in New York City without a permit."

We *can't*?

We unplugged our bullhorn. We shouted our voices raw. "The Constitution is under threat! Save the Constitution! Save free speech!" No one could really hear us without a bullhorn.

Across the street a head-splitting, throbbing, but legal beat of pop music emerged onto the street from retailer American Eagle. Another stream of skull-banging legal noise poured out from retailer Forever 21.

We kept trying to speak to our neighbors, but no one could make out what we were saying. People drifted away. Yes, eventually we felt like random crazy people—but now voiceless random crazy people. We sheepishly folded our American flags, thanked one another, and drifted away ourselves.

Union Square, the site of over a century of robust citizen marches and protest speech, was left to the insistent music of the chain stores.

I went onto the city website, NYC.gov, to find out about applying for a permit so I could use a bullhorn to tell people about the threat to free speech.[26] Though by now I was no longer really in the mood, and neither were the thousands of people on Firedoglake.com who had gotten so excited with me.

I was discovering that activism is a lot like sex: if you can never act on the impulse of the moment, the moment is much more likely to pass and never present itself again.

To my amazement, I read the following: "Please fill out and submit the application below to request a special event permit." "Special event"? My free speech is a "special event"? Hopefully, not that special. The permit would be processed in up to thirty days. If it was a protest or rally I was applying for, it would be processed in five to seven days. But . . . was I reading this correctly? Was this possible? "If the application is approved, a permit will be mailed to the applicant. *If the application is not approved* [italics mine], the applicant will receive notification by mail. There is a $25.00 non-refundable, administrative processing fee for this form. This form is not a permit."

That was . . . it. No recourse if the permit was denied, no information about how to challenge a denial.

Could this be right? Was I hallucinating? "If the application is not approved . . . " But—but—isn't that *unconstitutional*? William O. Douglas, then Associate Justice of the Supreme Court, wrote in 1970, "[Our] First Amendment traditions have been watered down or discarded altogether. The First Amendment was designed so as to permit a flowering of man and his idiosyncrasies, but we have greatly diluted it. Although the Amendment says that Congress shall make 'no law' abridging freedom of speech and press, this has been construed to mean that Congress shall make 'some laws' to abridge that freedom."[27] Not to mention, I thought, the activity of Mr. Bloomberg's office in my own hometown.

Here it was right before me: the death blow to the heart of democracy not via a bloody coup but via neutral black-and-white bureaucratspeak. "If the application is not approved . . ."? By whom? Tito? Wasn't this America? Isn't this New York, site of the conscription protests in the nineteenth century and of Emma Goldman's speeches, of massive protests after the Triangle Shirtwaist Factory fire wiped out dozens of young women, burned to death because of greedy factory owners who had locked the doors?

I soon learned that restrictions like these and many others for 'free speech' permits are common throughout the country. The National Lawyers' Guild reports that there has been a definite upsurge of the severity of these restrictions over the past thirty years. (In some places in America you have to pay for 'free speech' even if you are penniless: The Maine Civil Liberties Union took on a case about whether the fees must be paid even if protesters are indigent and they have asked the U.S. Supreme Court to hear their appeal.)

How did this come to pass?

I called Michael Bloomberg in the mayor's office, to express how I felt about not being able to be sure about securing my bullhorn so I could warn my fellow New Yorkers about the threats to their liberty.

I started to call him on April 28, 2008, at 12:20 p.m. I got a direct earsplitting nonfax shriek. Tried again at 12:23. His line was busy. At 12:25—busy. Okay, it's a big city. At 12:30, I got a ringing tone! I was excited and readied my comments in my head; but the ringing tone turned, oddly, into yet another, differently pitched, ear-piercing nonfax shriek. At 12:33—busy; 12:35—busy; 12:40—busy.

I tried that for four more days, then gave up. I called 311, the city information hotline, and was told I couldn't actually phone his office. But I was undeterred: I would find a way to use my liberty, raise my voice somehow, somehow serve my country.

It was getting harder and harder for me to figure out how, though. I was feeling dejected. Feeling so powerless, I decided to go shopping. I headed onto Sixth Avenue, thinking of the nicely stocked aisles at Bed Bath & Beyond.

I was facing so many obstacles trying to serve my country and use my liberties: attempting to speak up, rally my neighbors, join a commission, find out how to help my congressperson draft a bill, figure out how to run for office or how to help my neighbors run. Perhaps there was another way I could serve my country.

I stopped in my tracks. Maybe Providence was helping me after all. There was a sign: US ARMY RECRUITING STATION, right there on Sixth Avenue. Not only was there a sign with words—the sign actually showed an arrow, in case I missed it or the words. The arrow pointed around to the entrance on Nineteenth Street.

I turned to Nineteenth Street—and how easy it was: yet another sign said US ARMY RECRUITING STATION and had another arrow, this one pointing vertically right to the door. Things were definitely getting easier. There was even a phone symbol next to the intercom. I pushed it and was let right in.

I had felt at an impasse. I couldn't really understand from the website what the bills meant that were before Congress. I knew the Chinese consulate couldn't hear me if I stood in a pen behind the Beast. Mayor Bloomberg did not, evidently, want my phone call, and it was hard for me to speak directly to my fellow citizens in Union Square. My kids would worry if I was arrested for using a renegade bullhorn, and I was a bit scared of preventive detention because I'd read that Sergeant Triuzzi's colleagues now carried Tasers. I knew Tasers could kill. But here at last my strong desire to serve my country was received with warmth, attentiveness, and practical help.

I didn't need to wait. I found myself in a spacious car-peted office with a broad bank of windows, the corners decorated with luxuriant potted plants. A courtly and charming young army recruiter, Staff Sergeant Keven W. Shockley, welcomed me and gestured for me to sit right down.

I said that I was interested in finding out about what it took to join the army and possibly serve in Iraq.

"How old are you?" he asked delicately.

I said that I was forty-five.

Sergeant Shockley assured me gallantly that I did not look forty-five.

Unfortunately, though, he said, given my age, he could only take me if I had legal, medical, or nursing experience. But had I been only three years younger, I could indeed have enlisted to serve and started the process right then and there. They take citizens between ages eighteen and forty-two.

I asked, out of curiosity, to see the initial paperwork that starts the application process to join the army. It was a simple one-page document. It asked me about my tattoos. It also asked if I had ever been convicted of a felony.

Had I been younger, Sergeant Shockley said, I would have taken a test online in his presence. I would have had my height and weight taken on a scale in the next room. The "prequel" sheet would show what I might be qualified for. If I failed the test the first time, I was not to worry. The U.S. Army had put in place a new nationwide program— "designed by Princeton Review, the people who do the SAT training"—that would tutor me one-on-one by phone using the latest methods.

When I passed that test, I would get a physical. Those medical tests would all be completed on the same day and in the presence of a recruiter who would be right there to walk me through the process.

At the end of that day, or a few days later, I would be given a range of jobs that I qualified for. Then and there I would get to choose one.

How soon could the whole process be over with? I asked.

If I passed my physical? Well, said Sergeant Shockley, I could be in basic training within a week to a week and a half. Had I been only three years younger, I could possibly have shipped out to Iraq soon thereafter.[28]

I thanked him for his time, impressed with at least one element of our system that was really connecting with citizens. Sergeant Shockley himself was available to me if I had any other questions at all: the card he gave me had his e-mail (Keven.Shockley@USAREC.Army.mil), landline (212-255-8229), and cell phone number (1-877-241-7747). He also said he would be willing to travel anywhere in Manhattan or the five boroughs to talk about the military—indeed, he would willingly come to the young women's group, which I ran, to make his presentation.

In parting, I received several gifts. I received a number of illustrated brochures: clearly written, beautifully photographed, accessible, and informative. In one, determined-looking women soldiers were decorating cakes and directing video cameras in one brochure. In another, a male soldier dressed in full battle fatigues, in an Afghanistan-like setting, was surrounded by children. I received a free DVD, titled *One on One*, which comprehensively explained the process of enlisting. The "Army Skill Training" brochure showed me how, had I been merely three years younger, I could have learned "everything from engineering to electronics, communications to medical." Its list of army military occupational specialties gave me possible career options ranging from counterintelligence agent to diver, from electric bass guitar player to bassoon player, from mental health specialist to mortuary affairs specialist. A final brochure promised a slightly younger me an attractive deal: forty days of paid vacation each year, medical and dental care, "professional quality sports and recreational facilities," low-cost life-insurance for coverage of $400,000, the chance of a $20,000 enlistment bonus, room and board, and the chance to serve my country.[29] It walked me through my nine weeks of basic training. I also got a coffee mug.

When I had knocked on the door to this avenue of my possible public service, I found that the entry point could not have been clearer, better guided, or better designed to help me through the process.

After Sergeant Shockley had walked me through the entire process, I thanked him and got up to go. On my way out the door, he added, speaking about military service, "You travel a lot. I have been to twenty countries."

He shook my hand as I got ready to leave.

"It's a fun life," he said.

I left wishing every other door I had knocked on was as supportive of citizen engagement as was the military.

FAKE VOTING RIGHTS

So I realized that there weren't many ways for me to use the rights—or perform the responsibilities—the founders had intended American citizens to have. But surely one right was left to me: the unimpeded right to vote and have my vote be counted. I knew how many people had risked or devoted their lives to giving every American the right to vote. Well, no, I discovered. New York University professor and voting-fraud activist Mark Crispin Miller recently told me that there is now a systematic drive to install everproliferating voting regulations aimed at penalizing ordinary people—not to punish organizations or parties, but to punish ordinary citizens. Miller, in his books *Fooled Again: The Real Case for Electoral Reform*, and *Loser Take All: Election Fraud and the Subversion of Democracy, 2000–2008*, has documented dozens of new regulations aimed at blocking registration, punishing voters' groups, even threatening them with arrest, purging voters from rolls, or preventing oversight of problems with electronic voting machines. Republican groups are training volunteers to "challenge" voters in November at the polling places themselves—sure to be an intimidating situation for many new or nervous voters. Some of these new barriers are fines. These fines are designed to hit Americans to the tune of $1,000 to $5,000 per person for each inadvertent bureaucratic mistake he or she might commit while trying to go to neighbors and friends to get out the vote in their communities. Ordinary people, of course, are now balking at volunteering in this way—reluctant to use the rights the founders left to them. Understandably: anyone except the very rich would be scared of being fined the price of a used but serviceable Honda Civic for the crime of practicing democracy.[30]

Other barriers are new laws that raise the bar set for voting. In 2008, the Supreme Court upheld an Indiana voter ID requirement that forbids people from voting unless they can present government ID. This will put up barriers to hundreds of thousands of voters who can't take a day off from low-paying jobs to travel and pay the fees to get a driver's license.

One aspect of "Fake Democracy" is the myth that our votes are wanted and our elections are sound in a way that shames other nations. But, in fact, former president Jimmy Carter, now head of the Carter Center, an organization that promotes transparent elections worldwide, says that the U.S. system is so flawed that it would not even qualify on the level of international norms to be monitored by international bodies. In an interview with NPR, Carter explained:

[The United States] would not qualify at all for instance for participation by the Carter Center in observing. We require for instance that there be uniform voting procedures throughout an entire nation. In the United States you've got not only fragmented from one state to another but also from one county to another. There is no central election commission in the United States that can make final judgment. It's a cacophony of voices that come in after the election is over with, thousands or hundreds of lawyers contending with each other. There's no uniformity in the nation at all. There's no doubt that there's severe discrimination against poor people because of the quality of voting procedures presented to them. Another thing in the United States that we wouldn't permit in a country other than the United States is that we require that every candidate in a country in which we monitor the elections have equal access to the major news media, regardless of how much money they have. In the United States, as you know, it's how much advertising you can buy on television and radio. And so the richest candidates prevail . . . the United States has a very inadequate election procedure.[31]

FAKE ELECTION ACCESS

Well, can we run for office? I tracked down the guidelines and forms to run for office from the secretaries of state of Texas, California, Maryland, and other states. California was the clearest: the guidelines were written so anyone with a high school education could understand them. But other states' materials were extraordinarily unclear.

There must be an organization to help me and my readers learn to run for office! I thought. Where was a national government agency devoted to this kind of education or to publishing clear materials, or even a central database of training programs that was readily accessible to citizens?

I called the encouragingly named American Democracy Institute in Washington, D.C., and spoke to a program director. After explaining that I wanted to help a friend run for office, I asked brightly, "Do you publish materials to help people run for office?"

"No," responded my hoped-for guide and mentor.

"Does any government agency?" I persisted.

"The secretary of state of each state publishes guidelines."

"Many of them are incomprehensible."

"Yes. They have to follow the letter of the law. They *would* be incomprehensible."

I tried not to laugh. "How else can a citizen find out how to run?"

"There are many ways citizens can run. There are many organizations out there. But they are partisan."

"What if you just want to run without going through party gatekeepers?"

"There are issue-oriented groups too—gay, environmental."

"Is there a central listing of such groups that help or train citizens to run that I can refer people to?"

"No."

"Is there a national or government organization that is nonpartisan and not single-issue that just shows citizens how to run?"

"No."

"So if you want to engage, you generally have to be in-debted to a party structure or become a single-issue candidate?"

Silence.

Eventually, he said, "Well, people who want to run tend to be strongly partisan."

This statement was not confirmed by my experience crisscrossing the country in 2007–8. Well, maybe the ones who want to run under these conditions are strongly partisan—they would have to be! But the ones who would want to run in a truly transparent republic would not be. The ones I met who wanted to run but felt daunted were citizens who for the most part simply wanted to serve their larger communities.

"You are a democracy organization, and this discussion illuminates exactly the frustration citizens feel when they think about how to actually do something," I remarked. "It's important. Can I quote you by name on all of this?"

"No," he said politely.[32]

I decided to find out about helping my friend John—a real person I have put in a hypothetical situation—to run for the U.S. Senate in Virginia. John would make a terrific senator: he is a second-grade teacher and longtime education activist who has initiated many reforms in the public schools where he's taught. He has a passionate commitment to helping his area grow in a sustainable way while still protecting investment and development. He has served for years in local community organizations, especially those devoted to after-school education programs and green spaces, and he has a strong record of achievement in forging consensus, problem solving, and building coalitions. He is an innovator, has a great management style—and he still knows the strengths and challenges of every child in his class every year, as well as the name of every character on *SpongeBob*. John deserved to be considered by his peers.

So I went online. This is the beginning of the actual set of instructions for how you run for the Senate of the United States for the state of Virginia, home of Thomas Jefferson:

> November 4, 2008, Election
> **Candidacy Requirements for U.S. Senate**
> If you have questions, call: 804-864-8901
> TTY Toll-Free: 800-260-3466
> Voice Toll-Free: 800-552-9745
> Fax: 804-371-0194[33]

Okay: lots of the initial material was reasonably clear. First John needs to look at the 2008 ELECTION CALENDAR for the U.S. Senate. There is a DEADLINE PERIOD FOR FILING the papers for his candidacy. There is a deadline for his CANDIDATE DECLARATION to be turned in and his PETITIONS to be filed. Then there are other candidate forms he must fill out. There is a date for PARTY CHAIRS to CERTIFY CANDIDATES, if John is running for a party.

Eventually this year John will face a LAST DAY TO REGISTER TO VOTE. The primary for his state is June 10. If he is not running in a primary, his PARTY NOMINATIONS can't be made any EARLIER THAN MAY 9 AND MUST BE COMPLETED BY 7:00 P.M., JUNE 10.

The general election John will be running in will be decided on November 4 by 7:00 p.m. The bulletin and forms John needs to do all this are available at http://www.sbe.virginia.gov, or he can send ten bucks to the State

Board of Elections. On the site mentioned above, John would find the filing deadlines for all the forms and the officer whom he needs to reach in order to file each form correctly.[34]

The information is broken down for the kind of candidate he might be—that is, "Primary Candidate," "Party Candidate Nominated by Method Other Than a Primary," and "Independent (Non-Party) Candidate." John would run as an independent—not connected to an existing political party—but he could, if he chose, run as a Democrat or a Republican candidate. He could also run as a Green, Libertarian, or other party candidate.

John should write his check to the State Board of Elections and include the office he was seeking—in his case, Senator.

If he were running in a national-party primary, the forms John filed would, the site asserts, be mailed to the party chairs by the State Board of Elections. Or so it claimed. Now, John is continually telling his second-graders not to delegate to others what they themselves should make sure gets done. So he may be nervous about this. But he has no choice. He can hope for the best.

When John has questions, he can call toll-free 800-552-9745. (A real person answers that phone.) He can also reach government officials who have answers for him at 804-864-8901. To qualify to run for Senate, John must simply be "At least thirty years of age by the time of taking office; a citizen of the United States for at least nine years; and an inhabitant of the State [he] seeks to represent." All that is good to go: John is thirty-one; he was born in Kansas; and he can serve Virginia.

So now John has to file a CERTIFICATE OF CANDIDATE QUALIFICATION, which he can get from the State Board of Elections as well. Then he has to file a document called his DECLARATION OF CANDIDACY. He can get this too from the State Board of Elections. He has to file this Declaration of Candidacy at the same time that he files his petitions signed by all his friends, neighbors, and supporters. Then John needs to circulate his PETITION OF QUALIFIED VOTERS. He gets this too from the State Board of Elections.

John's petition should have signatures from at least four hundred voters from each of Virginia's eleven congressional districts. The requirement is not so bad; he can use his contacts and friends to reach out to their LISTSERVS, and they can describe who John is, what he has done as a teacher and community member, and how much he wants to improve Virginia's schools. Many of his group of friends are parents from his school community, and they care about the same issues he does. They also know John personally and can vouch for him.

When he gets the magic number of petition signatures, John must file this petition too along with his DECLARATION OF CANDIDACY. John will need to begin circulating his petition for the upcoming election no earlier than New Year's Day 2008, when he and his friends and family will be a bit hungover but excited and ready to go.

On the rest of the site, John will find the REQUIREMENTS OF THE FEDERAL ELECTION CAMPAIGN ACT, which is the material that I will soon discover is the ever-vanishing Holy Grail. He will find SAMPLE BALLOTS. He will learn the rules for his supporters for POSTING CAMPAIGN SIGNS and OTHER MATERIALS. It turns out that John doesn't even need a big investment to get the word out; he can hand-letter his signs—his supporters can do them in chalk, paint, ink, or sparkly sequins, whatever they like—but rules forbid, for instance, posting them over traffic signs. John can learn about CAM-

PAIGN VIOLATIONS he needs to avoid. He can review his QUAL-
IFICATIONS TO BE A CANDIDATE and check the DOCUMENTS
REQUIRED TO BE FILED. He needs to raise his PRIMARY FILING
FEE, which is an exorbitant $3,000-plus. Yikes: He has to
pay this chunk of cash just to file.

But wait. Where in the Constitution did it say that
there is supposed to be a hefty price tag just to file to run
in a primary? Actually, the founding documents don't
mention primaries or parties at all—because that whole
system was invented and imposed on citizens later. We are
not necessarily stuck with it.

But he can pass the hat to raise the cash among the
people who believe in his vision, vowing to try to clear away
that hurdle for other Americans to follow him if his candidacy is successful. He can learn how many signatures he
needs on his petition; he can scan DEADLINES AND FORMS FOR
PRIMARY CANDIDATE document—that's not applicable to him;
he checks DEADLINE AND FORMS FOR CONVENTION/MASS MEETING
CANDIDATE; and finally he closely examines his own category's requirements list, DEADLINE AND FORMS FOR INDEPEN-
DENT (NON-PARTY) CANDIDATE. Then there is REQUIREMENTS FOR
INDEPENDENT CANDIDATE TO USE PARTY ID ON THE BALLOT—again,
blood pressure! Why should he be forced to do that? NO-
TICE OF DEFICIENCIES IN DECLARATION OR PETITIONS (NON-PARTY)
CANDIDATE lets him know how he can be sure to comply with
making his declaration and petitions kosher; he studies the
PUBLIC FINANCIAL DISCLOSURE STATEMENT; he sees what they
mean by ORDER OF NAMES ON BALLOTS—he doesn't care that
much, he figures his supporters will find him and he flips
to FREQUENTLY ASKED QUESTIONS: HOW TO RUN FOR SENATE IN
VIRGINIA.

Cool! Here we go!

But the first thing we learn is that "the Federal Election Campaign Act imposes various rules and regulations on candidates and committees. This Act requires candidates and committees to register and disclose campaign receipts and expenditures and to abide by certain contribution limits and prohibitions. A copy of any campaign report required by Federal law also must be filed with the State Board of Elections. The Act further requires that an *Authorization Notice* appear on any public political advertising." Okay—we read on: the information, we are told, is published in the CAMPAIGN GUIDE FOR CONGRESSIONAL CANDIDATES AND COMMITTEES.

Great! Finally! Just what John needs—the gold mine of information he has been looking for. We can move forward because he has found the place where all will be explained. "This document is published by," we read, "and available from the Federal Election Commission, 999 E Street, NW, Washington, D.C. 20463, 800-424-9530, or on the Web at http://www.fec.gov."

So I went to the FEC website as directed. While I could find out there about the other candidates who were in the running, there was in fact *no* information directed to me or to my neighbors or to John to actually prepare us to be candidates ourselves.

Could this be?

I looked back in bafflement at the instructions in the paragraph on the website cited above: "This Act requires candidates and committees to register and disclose campaign receipts and expenditures and to abide by certain contribution limits and prohibitions," and to file a campaign report, as well as to make sure John's authorization notice is visible on his political ads for his campaign for Senate. Then it directs me to—yes—the fec.gov website, where I am now. It directs me . . . as if the one thing led to the other. This is what you need, this is where you find it.

But was I hallucinating?

No matter where I looked, I couldn't get the information from the fec.gov website about how John could do what I saw with my own eyes the Virginia website had told me it would tell him to do. I went several clicks down the rabbit hole of bureaucratic language, into laws and regulations. Then I got this, which I would need to understand before I could raise any money for John or help him start to think about ads, let alone about the policies he would offer people.

> FEDERAL ELECTION CAMPAIGN LAWS
> Compiled by THE FEDERAL ELECTION
> COMMISSION
> OCTOBER 2005 THE FEDERAL ELECTION
> COMMISSION
> Washington, D.C. 20463

Okay: they exist. And the commissioners start out bravely: "The Federal Election Commission (FEC) has prepared this new compilation of Federal campaign laws as an informative service to the general public."[35] Great! That's us. John and I are certainly members of the general public— and feeling more so every day. Let's go.

But then, oh dear:

> 1. FEDERAL ELECTION CAMPAIGN LAWS: The text of the "Federal Election Campaign Act (FECA) of 1971," as amended, the "Presidential Election Campaign Fund Act," as amended, and the "Presidential Primary Matching Payment Account Act," as amended, contained in titles 2 and 26 of the United States Code. (See Amendments in 1974, 1976, 1977, 1979, 1981, 1983, 1984, 1989, 1990, 1991, 1992, 1993, 1994, 1995, 1996, 1999, 2000, 2002 and 2004: Pub. L. No. 93-443, Pub. L. No.

94-283, Pub. L. No. 95-216, Pub. L. No. 96-187, Pub. L. No. 97-51, Pub. L. No. 98-63, Pub. L. No. 98-355, Pub. L. No. 98-620, Pub. L. No. 100-352, Pub. L. No. 101-194, Pub. L. No. 101-280, Pub. L. No. 102-90, Pub. L. No. 102-393, Pub. L. No. 103-66, Pub. L. No. 103-272, Pub. L. No. 104-79, Pub. L. No. 104-88, Pub. L. No. 104-287, Pub. L. No. 106-58, Pub. L. No. 106-346, Pub. L. No. 107-155, Pub. L. No. 107-252, Pub. L. No. 108-199 and Pub. L. No. 108-447 respectively.)

2. APPENDIX: The text of additional provisions of the United States Code, which are not in the FECA but may be relevant to persons involved with Federal elections, current through September 2005.

3. INDEX TO TITLES 2 and 26: A special index prepared by the FEC.

This compilation is presented in codified form, with FECA section numbers converted to United States Code section numbers, in order to facilitate cross-references between this pamphlet, the United States Code, and the United States Code Annotated.

Readers should be aware that some terms in the law are defined differently in different titles. Thus, the meaning of a particular term may not be consistent throughout this pamphlet. Note, therefore, the definitions provided in each title or section.

Copies of this compilation are available from the Federal Election Commission, Washington, D.C. 20463.

TITLE 2. THE CONGRESS

Chapter 14—Federal Election Campaigns

Subchapter 1—Disclosure of Federal Campaign Funds

§ 431. **Definitions**

When used in this Act:

(1) The term "election" means—

(A) a general, special, primary, or runoff election;

(B) a convention or caucus of a political party which has authority to nominate a candidate;

(C) a primary election held for the selection of delegates to a national nominating convention of a political party; and

(D) a primary election held for the expression of a preference for the nomination of individuals for election to the office of President.

(2) The term "candidate" means an individual who seeks nomination for election, or election, to Federal office, and for purposes of this paragraph, an individual shall be deemed to seek nomination for election, or election—

(A) if such individual has received contributions aggregating in excess of $5,000 or has made expenditures aggregating in excess of $5,000; or

(B) if such individual has given his or her consent to another person to receive contributions or make expenditures on behalf of such individual and if such person has received such contributions aggregating in excess of $5,000 or has made such expenditures aggregating in excess of $5,000.

(3) The term "Federal office" means the office of President or Vice President, or of Senator or Representative in, or Delegate or Resident Commissioner to, the Congress.

(4) The term "political committee" means—

(A) any committee, club, association, or other group of persons which receives contributions aggregating in excess of $1,000 during a calendar year or which makes expenditures aggregating in excess of $1,000 during a calendar year; or

(B) any separate segregated fund established under the provisions of section 441b(b) of this title; or

(C) any local committee of a political party which receives contributions aggregating in excess of $5,000 during a calendar year, or makes payments exempted from the definition of contribution or expenditure as defined in paragraphs (8) and (9) of this section aggregating in excess of $5,000 during a calendar year, or makes contributions ag gregating in excess of $1,000 during a calendar year or makes expenditures aggregating in excess of $1,000 during a calendar year.

(5) The term "principal campaign committee" means a political committee designated and authorized by a candidate under section 432(e)(1) of this title.

(6) The term "authorized committee" means the principal campaign committee or any other political committee authorized by a candidate under section 432(e)(1) of this title to receive contributions or make expenditures on behalf of such candidate.

(7) The term "connected organization" means any organization which is not a political committee but which directly or indirectly establishes, administers, or financially supports a political committee.

(8) (A) The term "contribution" includes—

    (i) any gift, subscription, loan, advance, or deposit of money or anything of value made by any person for the purpose of influencing any election for Federal office; or

    (ii) the payment by any person of compensation for the personal services of another person which are rendered to a political committee without charge for any purpose.

(B) The term "contribution" does not include—

    (i) the value of services provided without compensation by any individual who volunteers on behalf of a candidate or political committee;

    (ii) the use of real or personal property, including a church or community room used on a regular basis by members of a community for noncommercial purposes, and the cost of invitations, food, and beverages, voluntarily provided by an individual to any candidate or any political committee of a political party in rendering voluntary personal services on the individual's residential premises. . . .

Five pages in, I couldn't tell if I was still reading the table of contents. No! It was actual content. It went on and on, only worse, for a total of 211 densely typed pages. I would have to tell John not to make a move till we got some expensive help. Damn.

I showed a friend who wants John to run the troubling and massive text we would need to help John figure out. "That is surely in response to all kinds of abuse," said he. Indeed. I get it that the FEC rules came about as reforms to abuses and to help us adhere to the letter of the law. But there is no translated version readily available to laypeople—and no clear way to understand them.

I imagine you can if you are a lawyer. And I get it that lawyers can't write—except for other lawyers. But isn't there something more fundamental at stake than a horrifying prose style? This 211-page text with which I could make your head spin if I were merely to read it to you over the phone—this is the Holy Grail, the key to power, the New Testament and the Five Books of Moses. It is the only set of the rules of the only game. And it is in Latin, but we speak the vernacular. *Everyone else speaks the vernacular.*

Martin Luther got a reputation as a heretic for having had the New Testament translated from Greek-Latin into his people's language—German—thus sparking a revolution. But no one has yet translated the essential codes of using the Republic into the people's language for those of us who speak the vernacular.

John needed right away to hire a lawyer to make sure we didn't break the law before we could raise any cash at all for his run; but would we be breaking the law while we planned our bake sale to raise our cash to hire a lawyer? So, unsure if I was breaking the law already if I looked at a cookie recipe, I took an aspirin and made some calls.

I called Curtis Ellis. Ellis is a straight-talking, sometimes profane dynamo who has a bit of the air of a pirate—a pirate for liberty. Raffish and charming, he projects a combination of hard-boiled pragmatism and, underneath it, a certain idealism, which together generate confidence.

As he explains all the things there are out there in the political process that should not be trusted, you actually trust him.

Raised by middle-class parents in New Jersey, Ellis has always been driven by the dream of getting some of the power back into the hands of the people. He used to work for CNBC as a producer on political TV shows; then he crossed over into politics, becoming a communications director for a congressman, where he saw firsthand how things are done on Capitol Hill. Wishing to drive citizen democracy more directly, he changed roles yet again and joined a dynamic group of political consultants who actually care about helping to get more ordinary people—truly talented leaders, not party hacks—elected to public office. This group, the Campaign Network, specializes in helping first-time candidates, ordinary, idealistic American citizens who, as Ellis put it, "never thought five years ago they would run for office."

We met at a coffee shop; his BlackBerry continually buzzed with questions for him from the various campaigns he was advising. But he took time to speak with me because he cares so much about helping ordinary Americans confront the process and make it work for their communities.

I told him about all the trouble I was having trying to figure out how to run for office. I asked how John or, say, my New Jerseyan friend Mary, who works in a research lab and has fantastic ideas that would help women move out of low-paid work, could realistically run for office and win. And what had happened to guarantee that our access to the system remained so impenetrable?

First, mincing no words, Ellis told me the nasty truth about how much time I, or my fellow citizens, would have to spend raising money.

"Congresspeople," he said, "can spend four hours on the phone every day raising money. In the morning there are breakfast fund-raisers. At night there are reception fund-raisers." I felt myself go pale.

I told Ellis about my inability to understand the wording of a lot of the material online about civic participation.

"You are right to suspect that there is a priestly caste," he said. "They guard the secrets of the temple— jealously.

"It gets even deeper than that: the political parties are part of this. A lot of the political consulting firms also advise corporations. That's where the money is. They advocate for their corporate clients *while* they advise candidates."

"Don't they have to stop when they go back to the political side?" I asked.

"No. Look at Mark Penn, who represented Blackwater. That's the rule, not the exception."

Ellis also explained how the legislative process is swayed by considerations outside of even these. "The staff are very young and are paid low salaries. They don't just tell him how to vote, they write the legislation: 'vote recs'— vote recommendations. They give him a list.

"The e-mail comes in from the leadership about how he should vote. There are five vote recommendations from the leadership. But the kids say, 'Yes, yes, yes, no, yes.' There are several problems with this situation. First, I think you need people with real-life experience to write the rules for real life. You've got these kids who are twenty-four, twenty-five—living on forty thousand a year. Or they are kids with money.

"They're going to move up, move up, move up—to become chief of staff and then leave to become a lobbyist. That's the revolving door. One lobbyist who made half a million [a year] wanted to come back to work on the Hill for a year—it's worth his making fifty thousand a year short-term in order to refresh his lobbying Rolodex."

"Therefore if that's their career path, there's an incentive to please their future employers—the lobbyists—and less incentive to represent the people?" I asked, clarifying the obvious.

"Thank you very much. Exactly. Even if it is an unconscious incentive. They will be leaving the job in a few months—there are people, potential future employers, all around them saying, 'Do this for me,' 'Do that,' 'I need this contract.' The staffer is going to say to the lobbyist, 'What do you think of this legislation?' "

"But isn't there a two-year limit before working as a lobbyist after you leave the Capitol?" I asked.

"That applies to certain senior staff members and there are ways to get around it. There's always some workaround; they pay you, put you on staff, you say, 'Call him, call her.' There are ways to get around the rule."

"I did not know that. That 'work-around' situation feels like yet another example of a fake democracy. Okay, now I am depressed. Is there any point to my telling people to run for office themselves?"

"Absolutely. In spite of this, you can make an incredible difference. I have helped people like that—Steve Kagen, a doctor from Wisconsin who is up there now working on getting health insurance to people." Kagen is an allergy doctor from Appleton, Wisconsin, who used his own money to run for Congress so he could deliver health insurance to his patients who often couldn't afford the asthma medication he had prescribed for their kids. ("I saw that politicians had the keys to life or death," he explained to me when I contacted him later. "Of course ordinary people should run.")

"The only way to break this stranglehold on power," said Ellis, "is to get decent people who are not party or political hacks to run and to win."

I gathered subsequently, from various sources in that world, that the political parties do have a stranglehold on the process. "A candidate of ours ran for Senate in Florida," said one source. "A Democrat—but not the party's Democrat. They kept him off the Democratic Senate Campaign Committee website—it was like he didn't exist, though all the polls showed him and the party's candidate running neck and neck."

Curtis explained this situation when I asked him about it. "The parties want their people in. They don't want somebody independent of them playing in their sandbox. They're gatekeepers.

"The practical outcome? A candidate who is not a party candidate calls for money—people say, 'Let's see what the national party says about the race.' They go on the website—*you're not there*. They're not going to write you a check. The candidate goes to raise money from gay people. The first thing the voter is going to do is say, 'Do you have the endorsement of the Victory Fund?' He says, 'No.' Because they're an inside-the-Beltway type of group. The outcome: the gay guy is not going to write a check so easily."

I said, "So it's like the Mafia. Between lobbyists, interest groups, and the parties, they are all standing at the gates keeping ordinary people out."

"As Bob Dylan said, 'The cops don't need you, and man, they expect the same.' "

Then Curtis explained one major reason our political leadership is so often so inadequate. Though he confirmed a situation I had suspected was true, I was still horrified.

"The parties and issue groups," he said, "want candidates to follow a certain track: city council; state rep; state senator. Then they think you are ready to run for Congress. They say, 'We don't endorse ordinary people to run for Senate because we think it has to be a seasoned politician.'"

I was agog. What a stupid system. "Do you think that's the best way to get the best people?" I asked. "That career path seems like death."

Curtis said, "It creates organization men. Twenty years in the system—it ossifies you. You become a professional politician, not a tribune of the people." There it was in a nutshell. The political parties versus the founders' vision of citizen leadership.

"Do you agree that if an ordinary person could realistically run for Senate and win we'd get more talent?" I asked.

"Absolutely."

I took a deep breath. Okay then. "Tell me," I said, "how an ordinary citizen—say this friend of mine—can run and win."

"My advice to someone who wants to run is find a consultant," Curtis said.

"I hate that."

"Nonetheless, that will help your friend level the playing field. It's a simple game if you know the rules. Someone once said it is checkers, not chess."

"Isn't that prohibitive? How much is a consultant? How would we do that?"

"It's not necessarily so expensive. Your friend can

make a deal to hire someone. Okay. First, he should hire a general consultant. Then a campaign and elections manager. The American Association of Political Consultants can get him names."

"How much would that cost?" I asked.

"It depends—they could be paid on a monthly retainer or it could be a one-time fee. You can negotiate.

"The first thing they'll say to you is how much you'll have to raise. Every race is different. These days a congressional seat is going to cost a couple of million dollars."

I said, "But no regular citizen can raise that kind of money!"

"You're not right. Technology is changing things, leveling the playing field. An ordinary citizen *can* raise it these days, through a bunch of small contributions gathered online. The netroots *do* make a difference. Because of the Internet, campaign finance reform is basically already here. The technology created campaign finance reform before the law did: look at Barack Obama. A number of our candidates didn't have their own money but have raised their money in this way.

"So, you decide a year or more in advance—one and a half, two, depending on the office that you want to run for. The key with elections is that time is your enemy. God willing, you can find more money, more volunteers, but you can never find more time. In politics, opening night is closing night. The show is over on opening night.

"First, you raise your money. Your campaign consultant will send you to a fund-raising consultant.

"You start your fund-raising with friends and family. Go through your Rolodex: everyone you've ever done business with in your life. Then go to everyone they know. Who's your dentist? Who did you buy your car from? Your cousins, uncles, neighbors. Those will be the people you make the first 'ask' to.

"What a fund-raising consultant will ask you to do—if you're a salesman this will be easy, if not, more difficult—is to develop your 'pitch,' your 'ask.' It's short. You're on the phone for two minutes. You've got to have your elevator speech—what's the two-minute rationale for 'Why me? Why now?'

"The candidate is always the one to make the pitch. The first several months what you're doing is raising money. Money, money, money."

"Four hours a day asking for money?" I said.

"Every day. There are all kinds of tricks. The fund-raiser is sitting there with you. Giving you cookies, whatever it takes. They pick up the phone, they dial; you make the ask. The candidate becomes a machine. They check the response off the list. Then all that information is entered into software—who gave, what they gave, who didn't give, who needs to be called back. There are limits, reporting requirements for the FEC—NGP is the software you would use."

"Where would you get that software?"

"Through your consultant. There's a process for everything. To file for deadlines, to report to the FEC. Because campaigns are chaos. If you don't have a process, you'll never keep track of millions of details coming toward you.

"Second, you figure out the magic number: how many votes you need to win. Where are these people? How do I reach them? What's the most effective way to reach them—will I be knocking on their door or reaching them by radio, TV, or mail? Internet? House parties?

" 'Media' is radio, TV, newspapers. We divide that into

earned media—news coverage and commentary—versus *paid* media, that is, advertisements. In contrast to *media* there is *field*. *Field* is home parties, knocking on doors, town meetings.

"The endgame of all this? GOTV—get out the vote.

"You're going to divide that universe into people who continually vote in off-year elections and those who don't. The ones who do are most important to you.

"Then there is NCEC—statistical work. This info is usually given to you by the party."

"Another stranglehold," I said. "How would I get it if I am not a party candidate?"

"They are supposed to give it to you anyway. But if you don't know to ask, they won't give it."

"A rigged game."

"Totally. Rigged at every level. It's politics. That's why citizens have to know the rules, so they can get some of that power back.

"The data break the voting universe down into who is for me, who is against me, and who is persuadable.

"There is a percentage of each category in every precinct, on every block.

"The people who are for you—you don't need to talk to them. You need to let them know you're there. They need to know your name and that's it.

"The people who are against you—same thing.

"All of your communication and voter persuasion you really want to focus on the persuadables. These are the ticket splitters. Every time you make a contact—say on phone banks—you have a scale of one to four, or sometimes one to three.

"One is: 'I'm definitely for you.'

"Two is: 'I'm considering it.'

"Three is: 'I'm leaning toward the other guy.'

"Four is: 'I'm definitely for him.'

"Ones and fours you set aside.

"You keep the names of the ones. You contact them in the last seventy-two hours—knock on the door, drag 'em off to the polls. Fours—purge them from your mailing list. Whatever you do, don't remind them to go vote! You don't try to persuade them to vote for you, 'cause you never will. The nasty extreme is those who do voter suppression."

"How?" I asked.

"Some guys love this stuff, they do it all the time: confuse the voters—tell them Election Day is Wednesday, not Tuesday; tell them they're not registered and they need to reregister; or tell them that the polling place has changed, send them to the wrong polling place, where they stand in line for three hours; 'robocalls'—the voter thinks the call is from the candidate—they hang up and call the voter back incessantly, usually at dinnertime. Consultants who want this done will find people to do it. They can't do it themselves. Create confusion."

"How common is this?"

"Very common. In an ideal world you don't do anything like this; you just set aside the fours.

"You keep track of the voters through VAN—Voter Activation Network software. State parties have it. It lives on the Internet; it is available to you. With VAN you put in a neighborhood and it prints out a list of names. How often they've voted, et cetera. A bar code next to each name. You can put notes in there. If that person has a dog!"

"Wow."

"Yeah. It's shared information. So all day your team calls: 'Hi, Jim Jones. . . .' 'Yeah, I'll vote for your gal.'

"The last seventy-two hours, you print out all the ones. You have several teams. You'll have your lawyer in case there are any problems: voting machines not working, your name is not on the ballot in some places.

"You'll have your bellwether districts. You will need to determine what your vote goals are at particular precincts—I need fifty-seven votes in this precinct. If I don't get them, there is no way I can win. If I don't hit fifty-seven or come close, the election is over. Or, in different precincts the other guy can take the precinct, but I can still win.

"Throughout Election Day, at headquarters, you keep entering info: they're a one, three, four . . . you're keeping track of who voted and who didn't."

"Is it true to say at certain times every vote really does count?" I asked.

"Yes. You have a volunteer at the polling station—the bellwethers—writing it all down. On Election Day you want someone there doing this, looking at the rolls.

"You also get ready to have a party. You'll have two speeches ready—victory and concession. You'll thank your volunteers. If you're not superrich, have it at a bar. They're happy to get a crowd on a Tuesday night and they'll give you a deal. Maybe cut-rate drinks.

"I go to the polling stations at nine, eleven, two, four. I compare my list of fifty people who said they would vote to the rolls to see if they voted, because you have to sign in. Say twenty haven't voted. They get phone calls: 'Do you need a ride?' 'Can I walk your dog?' A car gets sent."

"I am amazed that it comes down to that. This is inspiring because it means it does matter if you vote."

"Absolutely it matters," Curtis said. "How many, how many, how many. And it matters what you say to your neighbors and that you register them and you organize them so you can show the campaign that they will vote.

"People don't understand: why is money so important in campaigns? The only reason money is so important in campaigns is to pay for TV time to persuade voters. If you can persuade voters and deliver voters yourself, you have power to counter that influence."

"What would you say to a twenty-three-year-old staying home on Election Day because he feels there is no point?" I asked.

"I would say—I would want to say—the truth is that he's being used. I would want to say, 'The people in control don't want you to vote. You're a sucker—congratulations.' "

I tried out on Curtis my theory about the draining of democracy's magic:

"I feel that people are being acculturated to think it doesn't really matter and to give up."

"Absolutely they are," Curtis agreed. "For twenty-eight years, since Reagan, the message has been 'Government is the problem. It's bad, so don't bother to get involved. The government has absolutely no ability to solve your problems, so why bother, it can't do anything for you anyway, just give up.' "

"So you think people are getting subtle and overt messages to stop trying, give it up, don't participate in civic life? What is the reason for that? Whom does it serve?"

"It serves the moneyed interests and the political elite that have been bought and paid for by the moneyed interests. Their mantra is 'Government shouldn't spend your money, you should, so I'll give you a tax cut.' The message is brilliant because on a meta-level it encourages people not to participate.

"But who *is* the government? Curtis said vehemently, grabbing the edge of the table and just stopping himself from pounding on it. The water glasses jumped. Other diners looked up from their lattes. "It's supposed to be *us*," Curtis said impassionedly. "It's *us*. *We* are the government. It didn't come from Mars. It's not the British crown. *We're a democracy.*"

I felt elated that someone who saw the process in all its shortcomings could still feel so moved by the hope of its working as it should. But wasn't there a contradiction?

"But you've just made a very persuasive case that it's *not* us—that our representatives are no longer beholden to the people," I argued.

"Because we've *abdicated*."

"So the people have some power but they've been persuaded by the powerful to walk away from the table?"

"Exactly yes," said Curtis.

"So it's fair to say people have power they are not using?"

"Yes."

"Okay. Apart from running for office ourselves, how do we use it?"

"Well," said Curtis, "start a revolution. Look at what citizens did in Boston: they changed the city charter. If you really want to take power back, infiltrate the party! Take it over! This is what the Ron Paul people did; the antiabortion people did this. Go to any Democratic Party meeting. It's all seventy-year-old people. Get ten of your friends to go down there; you have taken it over!

"When you or one of your friends want to run, then it will be hard for them to throw the sharp elbow.

"What gets candidates pissed off is that do-gooders call: 'Get us out of the war!' But you call that same group back on Election Day, they say, 'We don't get involved in electoral politics.' Then he feels: why should he help you? Horse-trade. *Get in the game.* Use your power. Volunteer.

"Start an affinity group: Democracy Commandos. Call it something. Meet every month or couple of months. Register everyone—even twenty people—and show the list to the Congressperson's district office. That makes you a power broker. No one knows this. Then have debates, set up a website to track your leaders and keep your community informed. Get your team out to help during elections. Make it known to the candidate that you are volunteering: 'I was there for the congressman. I will let people know the congressman is doing his job; I will tell people he is listening.' Tell your Facebook community about the candidate and let his people know you did so. This makes a huge difference to the representative. That congressman will listen to you and respond and act when you make your issues known. It gives you the power that big donors have. It levels the field."

"So you don't need to be a millionaire or a big donor to have an impact on your congressman."

"No. Votes count. Organizing counts."

"You are saying you do have to act in order to take back your power as a citizen. You are saying, 'Play the game—and take it over'?"

"*Yes,*" said Curtis quietly. "So they can't fuck with you anymore."[36]

PART II: CORE VALUES

WE ARE REQUIRED TO
SPEAK FREELY

*I have always been among those who believed that
the greatest freedom of speech was the greatest safety,
because if man is a fool the best thing to do is to
encourage him to advertise the fact by speaking.*
—Woodrow Wilson

The founders knew that life without freedom was not worth having. Freedom to think is followed by freedom to speak.

I analyzed in my last book, *The End of America,* what happens to a citizen psychologically when he or she is systematically lied to, controlled, intimidated, stripped of rights, and even physically threatened or incarcerated. People's adaptations to this kind of oppression snowball: the more scared you are, the more you silence yourself; then, the more the silencers are emboldened; then, the freer they feel to scare you; then, the scarier the methods they use become. And so on.

A psychological process goes in the opposite direction as well. The founders understood this. This process is just as powerful a force for good as the other process is for evil: the more freedom a citizen has, the more he or she believes in his or her capacity to take great risks and make great change; the more he or she sees the results of these great risks, the more courage that citizen will show; the more courage that citizen shows, the more psychological space opens up in the mind and heart of that citizen and in those of his or her neighbors. Before there can be freedom to act, protest, or legislate, there must be freedom to think and then freedom to speak.

I found that true patriots seem driven by a personal, burning sense of responsibility to act in the face of a great wrong. True Americans—domestically or globally—seem to take it personally when faced with injustice; they burn. They can't sit in the bleachers even if they want to, even if it would serve them. A violation of the American premise is not abstract to them. It sticks in the gut.

When a judge refused to allow the Reverend Martin Luther King bail when he was imprisoned for marching without a permit, Robert Kennedy at first agreed with his campaign advisers that he should stay away from the issue altogether. But Bobby Kennedy couldn't stop thinking about what the state court had done. "Without telling anyone on the campaign," reports his son Maxwell, "RFK called the judge."

"It just burned me all the way up here on the plane," RFK confided later about what had led him to change his mind.[1] "It grilled me. The more I thought about the injustice of it, the more I thought what a son of a bitch that judge was. I made it clear to him that it was not a political call; that I am a lawyer, one who believes in the right of all defendants misused in various ways . . . and I wanted to make it clear that I opposed this." The following day, Maxwell Kennedy writes, the Reverend King was let out of jail.

When Abraham Lincoln first gave his speech about America not being able to survive "half slave and half free," it was violently controversial. When Lincoln was running for president, an adviser urged him not, at any cost, to repeat it. At first he complied, but then he gave the speech again. When confronted, he responded, "Upon my soul, I think it is true."[2]

"It just burned me"; "it grilled me." "Upon my soul, I think it is true." This is not political language, and these remarks weren't intended to generate public approval.

When you are a real American, the desire for liberty of thought and action, the desire for justice, burns in you as it did for the founders and as it does for dissidents. And when it burns, you need to speak out in protest and assemble.

Freedom to think, speak, and criticize make possible everything else you love in your life in this nation. Thomas Jefferson was a free-speech apostle; though he was personally vilified in the press—and the colonial and revolutionary press was, if anything, more nasty and mudslinging than today's—he often said and wrote that it would be better to have "newspapers without a government" than "a government without newspapers."[3] "I would rather be exposed to the inconveniences attending too much liberty than those attending too small a degree of it," he wrote.

"Debate and dissent are the very heart of the American process," wrote Robert Kennedy. "We have followed the wisdom of Greece: 'All things are to be examined and brought into question. There is no limit set to thought.'"[4]

The First Amendment rights underlie everything else:

> Congress shall make no law respecting an establishment of religion, or prohibiting the free exercise thereof; or abridging the freedom of speech, or of the press; or the right of the people peaceably to assemble, and to petition the Government for a redress of grievances.[5]

A translation for the modern reader: Congress must not pass any law that formally establishes a given religion in America, nor may it pass any law that keeps people from freely practicing whatever religion they wish to. Nor may Congress pass any law curtailing people's freedom of speech, nor may Congress pass any law curtailing the freedom of the press. Nor may Congress pass any law that limits the right of people to gather together (unite, march, or protest) peacefully, nor may Congress pass any law that limits people's ability to petition (submit petitions to, but also ask, demand, require, confront) their government to address and deal with their grievances (complaints, accusations, issues, concerns).

At many times in our history the First Amendment was weakened or eclipsed. As America was heading into the Great War, many laws began to suppress civil liberties. One was the Espionage Act, which reads, "Whoever, when the United States is at war, shall willfully cause or attempt to cause insubordination, disloyalty, mutiny, or refusal of duty in the military or naval forces of the United States, shall be punished by a fine of not more than $10,000 or imprisonment of not more than 20 years, or both." The law is still on the books, and in the last few years the Bush administration has tried to invoke it to silence Americans by threatening them with long prison terms. A year after the Espionage Act was passed, labor leader Eugene Debs was arrested because an attorney general in Ohio felt that a speech he made was antiwar. In that speech, Debs declared, "They have always taught and trained you to believe it to be your patriotic duty to go to war and to have yourself slaughtered at their command. . . . Do not worry over charges of treason to your masters, but be concerned about the treason that involves yourself. . . . Be true to yourself and you cannot be a traitor to any good cause on earth." Debs was given a ten-year jail sentence and his U.S. citizenship was stripped. (Nonetheless, he won almost a million votes while campaigning for president from his jail cell—and was released in the third year of his imprisonment.)

Do patriots still put themselves at risk for the First Amendment? They do. Why does this matter so much? As Natan Sharansky notes, "As important [as an army or secret police in a "fear society"] is a regime's ability to control what is read, said, heard, and, above all, thought . . . For those living in a free society, the thought that a state would try thoroughly to brainwash its subjects is difficult to grasp."[6]

Josh Wolf (no relation) is a true American: a blogger who spent seven months in federal prison to defend the rights of journalists to protect their sources. In a fear society, journalists are forced by the state to turn over the identities of their sources or their reporting materials—or else face prison time. That's why Josh fought back.

Josh, twenty-six, was born in Santa Rosa, California, a charming small town north of the Bay Area. As a young child, after his parents divorced, he moved with his mother to another small town—this one in Southern California.

"My mother is a teacher," he told me late one night. "She taught primary school. She was very moved by the civil rights movement. She raised me listening to Dr. King's speeches—learning about McCarthyism. My father works in the tech sector."

Josh went to the local public high school, which was quite homogenous. The young man struggled to figure out what his place there was. "After Columbine, my school [proposed a] dress code that said you couldn't wear all black. This led to people persecuting the Goth kids. I went home and wrote a screed—a call to action—for all students to wear all black, or all white. My friend—named Benjamin Franklin, of all people—had somehow obtained the master key for the copier. We ended up distributing five hundred copies of this screed. We got in trouble, but the end result was that the dress code was never formally adopted. They stopped harassing the Goth kids.

"I started off at UCSB—for the first time I felt I could fit in somewhere. Eventually I moved to San Francisco and went to SF State, majoring in psychology and film.

"I got a video camera and started using it. Made a few short videos, a short film. I was living with a few friends in the Haight.

"We—the U.S.—went into Iraq in 2003. Yes, it was great to be in SF, but it was frustrating sitting in a class-room listening to theory about this or that when I felt that I should actually be doing something to stop this war. It led to a dark depression and to me not succeeding in my classes.

"I was involved in civil dissent—documenting protests with my video camera as well as participating. I felt it wasn't stopping the war. I started a public access TV show with my dad—*citiZine*. We created an imaginary reality in which San Francisco is no longer part of the U.S.

"A dozen or so people in the room, we ended up with this document that was an updated version of the Declaration of Independence; we got it approved by the city attorney as a ballot measure. We needed ten thousand and some-odd signatures to make it happen. It was quickly evident that we weren't going to get ten thousand signatures. But it was a great gesture.

"I transitioned from public access TV to the video blogging platform and started *The Revolution Will Be Televised,* my video blog. I became a journalist covering events, not a participant.

"This had started to become almost routine around the time I filmed this particular demonstration on July eighth, 2005. The goal of the protest was to bridge the divide between the new inhabitants of the Mission and the people living there already. It was also to support those protesting at the G-8 summit in Scotland.

"It was like most demonstrations. The police were low-key up until a particular incident. At some point there was a police car. They had a report for some sort of vandalism. They started to investigate it. But they came across these people marching across the street. They decided they needed to clear the street. They decided to do this by accelerating their car *into* the crowd.

"I see this car accelerate into the crowd. The two people in the very back are carrying a giant Styrofoam sign. As the car gets almost to them, they instinctively drop the sign and jump out of the way. A six-inch piece of Styrofoam falls. It is not going to immobilize the car, but the cops jump out and give chase to the two people who had been holding the sign. According to police statements, the piece of foam stopped their car from being able to move down the street—a Crown Victoria, a police cruiser.

"By the time I catch up to the cop he's got a guy on the ground in a choke hold with his body on the street and his head on the sidewalk—the guy's neck was literally inside the curb. He had no signs of resisting whatsoever. The crowd was keeping a moderate distance—three feet away: 'What are you doing? This is police brutality, you're choking him,' they were saying.

"All of a sudden three police come up pointing what I later learned was a Taser with a laser sight. There's this red dot wherever he's pointing the gun. He's pointing it at the crowd: 'Get back. Get back. Get back! Everyone get back!'

"They arrest this gentle man on the [street], his name was Gabe Meyers. Charged him with an arsenal of charges, but they kept 'felony conspiracy to lynch.' The assistant DA claimed that Meyers was using code words to get his colleagues to 'lynch' him from custody—that means, to break a prisoner from custody. The alleged code words? 'Help me.'

"His case went on for months and months.

"After I filmed this I checked my e-mail. Saw an e-mail from a producer for online TV affiliate KRON. I edited down the video and sold the edited video as a stringer. It aired on local TV.

"Within a day or two I get a knock on the door. I had been relaxing, talking to my mom on the phone. I see this guy in Bermuda shorts and a Hawaiian shirt; a woman in spaghetti-strap tank top and jeans. They don't really look like FBI agents.

" 'Are you Josh?'

" 'Yeah.'

" 'Can we talk for a minute?'

" 'Sure.' Then all of a sudden out come the badges flashing FBI. Oh, shit. 'Mom, I need to go.' I hang up the phone. In addition to the two FBI agents, I see two detectives from SFPD. I proceed to talk to them. At that point I didn't know what my rights with federal enforcement were. I talked about how the police broke their own protocol. It felt safe to me. They said an officer was injured. I didn't witness it. 'Can we get a copy of your full video?' Not wanting to upset the FBI, I decided the smartest thing to do was ask, 'Would you be willing to provide an affidavit that you would only use the material to investigate this particular crime?' I felt that they had clearly overstepped their bounds on numerous points—I wanted to be sure they wouldn't add it to their database of videos of protesters.

"I go inside—the FBI is there, having climbed in. I grab my phone and dial 285-1011—the hotline for the National Lawyers Guild. That's the number at every protest—if you get arrested, this is who you call. I was provided an attorney.

"That seemed as if that was to be the end of it. Six months later I am subpoenaed before a federal grand jury. Another knock on the door. They demand the complete video, ask for all my e-mail communication during that time period, they want the software that I used to do the editing. Legal wrangling followed as we tried to quash the subpoena. What they are investigating now is the alleged attempted arson of the police vehicle. 'Arson' is a bit of a stretch. The damage to the car was listed as 'broken right rear taillight.' More than likely, based on the video, someone threw a smoke bomb four days after the Fourth of July.

"I did have to go in front of the grand jury. They asked if I had brought everything with me. Based on my lawyer's advice, I cited constitutional amendments to resist complying with the demands. The principle behind my not complying was my role as a journalist. Eventually they take me down to the judge—he intones to me that I need to do what the U.S. attorney says. 'You know, son, if you don't do this, you could find yourself in jail.'

"They bring contempt charges against me. At the end of the second hearing I am taken from the front of the courtroom by U.S. marshals, handcuffed, taken up to a holding facility in the building, then driven to the federal detention center in Dublin, California. A jail operated by the Federal Bureau of Prisons."

"Did you have a change of clothes?" I asked.

"No, but you don't get to wear your own clothes in jail anyhow."

"Were you scared?"

"I was terrified. You are in a room by yourself. They search all your clothes, take your shoelaces, take your tie, your belt, then give you your shoes back without laces so you can't really walk. They put a 'three-piece suit' on us—handcuffs in the front, leg shackles, and a chain that connects the handcuffs to [the shackles] so that your hands stay together in front of your pelvic area.

"My mom was absolutely terrified as well.

"My feeling was that I would be there for a couple of days. That's not what happened.

"Here I am, five-four, five-five at best, a hundred and thirty, a hundred and twenty pounds, with all these people who are far more robust than I am. There was this very big, scary guy. A cross between a Hell's Angel and a serial killer.

" 'What are you in here for?'

" 'I'm a journalist and I didn't give up a tape.'

" 'That's an honorable thing to do. Be sure you let people here know—you'll get major props.'

"I was there for a month. Released on bail. By September twenty-first, I was back in federal prison. I stayed there for another six and a half months—two hundred and twenty-six days, in a cell about eight by ten feet. The mattress was a foam pad, two and a half inches thick. I wore green overalls. There were three TV rooms—a white one, a black one, and a Mexican one.

"Sometimes I had roommates: bank robbers, felons with guns, drug dealers.

"I received three hundred letters when I was there."

"What did you miss?" I asked.

"I missed female companionship, my friends. I missed being able to receive phone calls or any kind of incoming communications. I missed my iPod! To hear my own music. I missed being able to open a window when it was hot outside. But really music and companionship were what I missed most. I am very glad that I don't have any children—it would be very hard to explain why Daddy is going to jail."

"Do you think what you did was a service to your country?"

"I happen to be wearing this T-shirt right now. It reads, A PATRIOT MUST BE READY TO DEFEND HIS COUNTRY AGAINST HIS GOVERNMENT. As a child I felt this commitment to our country. I do think this was a service to our country—not to our government. I was doing this for the rights of journalists as well as for the rights of individuals.

"Very shortly after I was released, a journalists' shield law was introduced in D.C. It was a reasonable law. The day after that law was introduced, I went to the Hill to testify. But over the next months the law was changed to define 'journalist' in a way that was based on the money you earned. It now excluded many reporters—bloggers, student journalists. There is something heartbreaking about spending seven months in jail for the need for a law that specifically excludes me.

"Meanwhile, the *New York Times*'s James Risen has received a subpoena for the book he wrote on the war on terror.

"Our nation was founded on people standing up for

what they believe in. Questioning authority has and will always be an American value. I've always felt I was a patriot. And I felt that way since fifth grade, when I put the bumper sticker QUESTION AUTHORITY on my binder.

"Would I do it again—go to jail for this? Absolutely. I think we are given few opportunities to actually stand up and make a profound difference.

"The day I went to jail was the first time I felt completely free since the war started. I was doing what I had to be doing to stop the war.

"I felt free."[7]

How free is our speech now? Can we easily get the big picture today? We are increasingly in a bubble that screens out real news and real debate about what is happening to us. When I traveled abroad, my AOL home page reported on many of these crackdowns on civil liberties in the U.S., and also in detail on the elections in Zimbabwe, democracy uprisings in China, new legislation to combat global warming, and other urgent information about the state of the U.S. and the world. In America? My same AOL page: "Britney Involved in Minor Accident"; "World's Most Expensive Car"; "Twelve Diet Tricks"; "Jen's New Hookup." It was as if they were reconfiguring the same product to produce more stupid or less-engaged people.

I had long heard from citizens, especially those on the left, a critique of the mainstream media—originated by Edward S. Herman and Noam Chomsky in their book *Manufacturing Consent* and subsequently repeated elsewhere, a critique so prevalent in online communities that the shorthand was MSM.[8] The critique states that the mainstream media is thoroughly controlled by corporations and censors itself. I had been reluctant to accede to this view because a number of my contemporaries were now compiling or producing the "mainstream media"; I knew that they didn't sit around censoring what was going in their paper or magazine. However, as my journey across the nation and into this battleground played out, I began to confront that while people I knew weren't consciously saying "This can't get in" or "We can't run that!" there was clearly an unspoken and probably unconscious set of boundary lines about what was and what was not going to be let into the agora of national discourse. It became clear to me that certain kinds of news that would expose the ways in which our story about ourselves was at odds with reality—news that would call naturally for drastic citizen action and a redistribution from corporate to citizen power—just wasn't going to make the cut.

And profoundly important news regarding the crackdown on liberties was *not* making it onto the agenda of national news outlets. I was advised by citizens in Detroit, not by the *Detroit Free Press,* that a leader of Code Pink, the antiwar women's action group, was refused entry to Canada. I heard at O'Hare Airport, from a Republican tech guy who worked for the airlines—and not from the *Chicago Tribune* or the noon news—that once you are on "the list," which he helped to oversee, you may never get off, and they never need to explain why you're on it. In the Chicago suburbs, I heard from a citizen—but never read in the suburban press—that people he knew had opened their luggage after a flight to find letters from the Transportation Security Administration that said that they did not "appreciate" the reading material, critical of the administration in power at that time, that these Americans had carried in their personal possessions. I heard from citizens and not from major media in the Chicagoland area when I was there in 2007 that Blackwater had just that summer opened a facility in Illinois, on the strategically important route of the Mississippi. I learned from citizens in San Diego—and not from the local or regional mainstream press there, which had limited its reportage of the issue and not covered local protests—that Blackwater was trying to open another outpost, along the border with Mexico, seeking to get involved with border security.

We have entered an era when citizens must understand that it is not enough for them to rely on the corporate media; while many talented and hardworking reporters in such news outlets struggle every day to report fully and fairly, more and more such reporters have told me off the record that they have experienced direct intervention in newsgathering or reporting from editors or publishers—for either corporate or political reasons. Nor is it adequate for citizens to spend their time online blogging about their opinions alone, as I have warned elsewhere; electronic venting is not enough when you need to lead a country, expose abuses, warn your fellow Americans of dangers, and set an action agenda. Citizens must now create and disseminate the news themselves, acting as rigorous reporters, critics, opinion leaders, and documentarians.

In Part Three, you will find the tools you need to speak out loudly and clearly—to take back the power of voice and return it to the citizens, where it belongs. As our man Jefferson reminds us, "In every country where man is free to think and to speak, differences of opinion will arise from differences of perception, and the imperfection of reason. But these differences, when permitted, as in this happy country, to purify themselves by free discussion, are but as passing clouds overspreading our land transiently, and leaving our horizon more bright and serene."[9]

WE HAVE A DUTY TO REBEL CONTINUALLY AGAINST INJUSTICE AND OPPRESSION

Rebellion to tyrants is obedience to God.
—Benjamin Franklin

PERSONAL RISK IN DEFENSE OF LIBERTY

Tom Paine risked being hung for sedition in England when he published *Common Sense*. All the signers of the Declaration of Independence knew they would have been hung as well in America had the war against Britain been lost. That is why John Hancock signed his name—his possible death warrant—in such a large, declarative hand. Living in a real America means that you will be willing to sustain risk on behalf of liberty. As poet Ralph Waldo Emerson put it, "God offers to everyone his choice between truth and repose. Take which you please—you can never have both." [1]

Many contemporary Americans do take risks for liberty as well. Jim Spencer, a former columnist for the *Denver Post* who had been critical of the Bush administration, told me that I could use his name in my work on this issue: he has found himself on the Watch List. An attorney, Jesselyn Radack, contacted me in New York to say that she had told her colleagues at the Justice Department not to torture the "American Taliban," John Walker Lindh, and to be sure he had a lawyer present when they interrogated him. She says she then faced a criminal investigation, a professional referral, saw her e-mails deleted—and now she too is on the Watch List.[2] Attorney Jack Goldsmith left his job at the White House after objecting to the secret 2003 John Yoo memo that placed the president in many ways above the law.[3]

As Andrew Jackson said, "One man"—or woman—"with courage makes a majority."[4]

PROTEST: THE AMERICAN LEGACY

What are we supposed to do with that courage? Protest.

The revolutionary-era protesters were far rowdier than we are, and American protest has pushed forward the march to freedom at every stage of our history. That value and right is now under assault.

This nation could not have been founded without ordinary Americans' engaging in raucous, even rowdy mass protest—protest without permits. During the 1760s colonists had engaged in dozens of mass protests and daring, even provocative crowd actions as part of the Stamp Crisis—the hated "stamps" allowed the crown to tax the colonists without their having a voice.[5] Mass action erupted: crowds hung stamp distributors in effigy; held mock funerals for stamp distributors; leveled to the ground the buildings that housed the stamps; built gallows to hang effigies and beheaded them; stoked bonfires to consume effigies; and wreaked havoc in this way with the plans of the crown. The protests and mass actions were effective: "Up and down the coast, people who had never before voted or played any public role surged through the streets to participate in boisterous mock executions, defy royal authority, and initiate themselves into the rituals of revolution."

The Boston Tea Party is usually taught to us as if it were an isolated incident—daring, to be sure, but not part of years of a massive eruption of street protests exploding throughout the colonies: In December of 1773, hundreds of American colonists, wearing face paint and Indian head-dresses, boarded a British ship and tossed ten thousand pounds' sterling worth of the East India Company's goods overboard.

But in fact it was a culmination of dozens of outbursts, protests, and confrontational street theater that colonial people from all walks of life had learned to use as a power-ful tool for speaking up against the oppression of the crown.

Today? Those colonists would never have the chance for such provocative acts of civil disobedience. They would likely be kept five hundred feet away from the British ship, across a main road from it, penned behind barricades, their protests against the Stamp Act barely audible. And they would be expected to tolerate that.

The tradition of noisy, confrontational street protest did not die out with the establishment of the nation. On the contrary. In 1790, Jay's Treaty was a proposed agree-ment of "Amity, Commerce and Navigation" that U.S. lead-ers wished to sign with their former oppressor, Great Britain. The plans for this were conducted in secret.

As news of the proposed deal got out into the commu-nity, it became hugely unpopular. Many U.S. citizens felt it imposed humiliating trade restrictions on the young coun-try. Americans burnt leaders in effigy across the nation.

Historian Michael Beschloss noted that Jay joked that he would eventually be able to "walk through all of the fifteen United States by night, illuminated only by the glow of his effigies burning." The people were so angry that their protests spread across the states. "When Hamilton defended Jay's Treaty in front of New York's City Hall, people threw rocks, leaving his face bloody. . . . In Boston Harbor, mobs set a British ship aflame." In Philadelphia, the crowds speared a copy of the treaty on a pole, took it to the very doorstep of one Minister Hammond, and burned it in front of his house. Then they broke his windows while he and his family were "cowering inside." The new treasury secretary worried that reports of such impassioned protest would suggest to Britain that the nation actually wanted war: "The country rising into flame, their Minister's house insulted by a Mob—their flag dragged through the streets . . . & burnt . . . can they believe that we desire peace?" Washington himself thought it "extremely embarrassing" for Great Britain to witness "the people of this country divided," with such "violent opposition" to "their own government."[6] But George Washington and others supported the treaty in spite of the controversy, certain it would help the fledgling republic avoid a bloody war it could not afford to fight.

Even after Washington was back home in Mount Vernon, the protests and furor of the citizens did not abate. Were these Americans who had so recently thrown off the oppression of a massive empire in pursuit of the establishment of a republic going to keep still in the face of something they passionately believed to be wrong? The nation was in "violent paroxysm" and Washington wrote that "a crisis is approaching," threatening "anarchy" if it is not "arrested." Washington's cabinet called the protests "detestable and nefarious."[7] But Americans were not going to shut up.

Eventually, public opinion shifted in support of the treaty and it passed. Two things became clear: as Beschloss notes, Washington had redefined the role of the true American president—nowhere in the Constitution had it said that the executive must show courage in the face of public controversy, but his certainty that the treaty would protect the new nation led him to ride out the storm and establish this template for standing firm in the face of popular opposition. And the people had shown their courage too: their opposition had made their voices echo loudly, setting the precedent that deal-making in America was not to be quietly tolerated behind closed doors and in the hands of a condescending elite who would not be scrutinized by the people. Their protests ensured a better democratic process.

Rough and demanding and difficult, the powerful and powerless equally matched in terms of voice; that is how democracy is supposed to work. These are the American people when they are in alignment with the ideal: while violence is never acceptable, Americans should and must be free to be angry, disruptive, outraged, loud, confrontational, and obnoxious in expressing their views—especially if their views are being trammeled or overridden in secret. They must be free to shout loud enough for their representatives to hear—and be disruptive enough so that the president himself may fear public perception if the crisis they are provoking is not dealt with. That is how the people maintain a relationship of healthy equilibrium with those who seek to act on their behalf. If the people can't precipitate a crisis through protest, what voice do they actually have when their leaders make secret treaties, or wholly override their will, or act in other ways entirely without consulting them?

In 1932, twenty thousand Americans, most of them veterans of the First World War, and even some of their families traveled to Washington, D.C., from all over the nation in empty railroad cars, in automobiles, and even on foot.[8] They came to protest that the men had not received a promised "bonus"—$1.00 per day served at home and $1.25 per day served overseas. The Depression had set in and their families were hungry; the veterans needed their money immediately. They camped out in the tens of thousands by the Anacostia Flats, and they would go to lobby their congressmen every day, while Congress was debating the bonus bill that would decide their fate. These Americans would sit for hours in the hundreds. Photos show them massed, sitting on the steps, blocking the entrance to the Capitol. The Hooverville—the sprawling city built of poverty and outrage where they camped—was a national scandal. While the president would not find time to see them, many of the congressmen listened to them. Poor and patriotic Americans demanded to voice their grievances. They turned the Capitol into a teeming, noisy, ramshackle sea of bodies, shanties, babies, laundry, and picket signs. No one could escape them. It was a mess.

President Hoover sent out the army to evict the men and their families from the shantytowns. They used fixed bayonets and gas on them, burned their shanties, and forced them to run down Pennsylvania Avenue. Hundreds were injured and one marcher died. But the bonus marchers came back. They *kept* coming back, ragged, hungry, tired, but believing in their rights and using the First Amendment powerfully to assemble. Eventually, they won concessions: twenty-five thousand jobs and finally, with popular support soundly behind them, in 1936 they won the bonus—and this win set the stage for the GI Bill of Rights.

That protest would probably be impossible today. Restrictive permits, Tasers, and rubber bullets make sure of that.

In 1965, thousands of people marched together out of Selma, Alabama. Dr. Martin Luther King wrote his famous sermon "Letter from Birmingham Jail" specifically explaining why he had defied the town's demand for a permit for the march.[9] Could that march, which began the transformation of America around the issue of racial justice, take place today? The Selma marchers marched in the streets. Today, that is illegal in most of the country.

In 1989, thousands of East German citizens marched with incredible courage, facing down guns, to assault the Berlin wall. They brought it down. They defied bans on such marching. That protest, which helped bring about an end to the Cold War? If it were held just about anywhere in the U.S. today, it would be illegal because it stopped traffic.

Also in 1989, students in Beijing faced down tanks in honor of democracy. A famous photograph shows a student standing in the street, face-to-face with a tank's gun barrel. In the U.S.? That student would be arrested in virtually all jurisdictions. In America, you are not to go into the street and stop traffic.

In Estonia, a Baltic state that had been occupied by the Soviet Union for forty years, citizens gathered by the thousands in 1987 to start what became known as the Singing Revolution.[10] Ten thousand people gathered regularly at night to sing forbidden nationalist songs. In 1988, 300,000 gathered at the national song festival to protest. Then, emboldened, they gathered in the capital city, Tallinn, and a guy on a motorcycle drove by waving a forbidden Estonian blue, black, and white flag. Then they unfurled a thousand such forbidden flags.

In 1989, an amazing demonstration took place: two million people joined hands across six hundred kilometers of road spanning Estonia, Latvia, and Lithuania. They parked their cars on the highway beside the human chain for thousands of miles. Nothing could pass. The state media ignored or reviled the revolution—calling it "whipping up hysteria" when they did cover it—but the eyes of the rest of the world were upon the human chain.

Pro-Soviet factions took over the assembly house and thousands of Estonians gathered, crowding right up against the entrances to the building and climbing on the roofs and gables, to defend it. Every single person there, including and especially the speakers, was risking a twenty-year sentence in Siberia. A mass movement of citizens began illegally reregistering Estonians from Soviet to Estonian passports and citizenship. Tens of thousands of Estonians, old and young, signed the books for the new identity cards. On August 20, 1991, Estonia's leaders declared independence. When Moscow sent Soviet tanks to shoot the ringleaders of the movement for liberty and to again crush free speech, thousands of ordinary Estonians surrounded the TV and radio tower so that state propaganda would not block information about the revolution. Soviet soldiers backed off eventually in confusion. Then the people formed an illegal national assembly on camera, even as Soviet tanks rolled toward the assembly hall through the streets. Each legislator was signing his or her own arrest warrant with his or her vote. By December of 1991, the USSR had come apart.

Today Estonia is a democratic nation with free speech, free assembly, and transparent elections. Those protests sparked others throughout the Soviet Union until other Soviet satellites declared their own freedom. Those protests were forbidden in a totalitarian society; the same protests would also be illegal in many jurisdictions in the United States of America.

Protesters in Selma in 1965, in Mexico City in 1968, and at Columbia University, also in 1968, simply defied permits and other demands. In Selma, 650 protesters marched despite governor George Wallace's orders not to. A week later, a police line blocked more marching protesters, saying they "did not have a parade permit." When some crossed the line, they were beaten. But all these massive, effective protests would be impossible in the U.S. today. We cannot defy these demands in the same way, and we fear confrontation with the police or arrest, because it is now too risky. Rubber bullets and Tasers have contributed to our docility.

Many Americans whom I met on my travels asked why demonstrations in the 1960s and early 1970s were effective but today's protests are not. They assume the reason is that "the corporate media won't cover it." Or that somehow conditions of contemporary life mean that cyberactivism is more useful than street assembly.

But real marches—those that stop traffic with thousands of bodies—are immensely potent. When I read accounts of the great U.S. and international marches and protests of the past, three things became clear.

First, the successful marchers of the past often believed in the power of their own reality and the justice of their mission; coverage was secondary to that conviction. When citizens march in this state of mind, it carries an energy field, a moral force that is inexplicable and that impresses onlookers and frightens despots.

Second, they were willing to stand up and be counted personally—to use their names and offer their identities. And they were willing to cause a major, if nonviolent, disturbance of business as usual. They put themselves on the line.

The early patriots were inspired—and sometimes shocked—by the crowds storming the Bastille in the French Revolution. The nation was changed by the march of suffragists down Fifth Avenue in Manhattan, dressed radiantly in flowing white gowns, some young women riding on horseback; by the suffragists who chained themselves to the gates of Congress;[11] by the parades of mothers in sundresses with their babies in strollers before them protesting nuclear testing in the 1960s; and even by the chaotic eruption of citizen protest—people illegally sleeping in parks and climbing statues—in Chicago in 1968.

Third, they had to be able to literally take to the streets and stop traffic and the daily activity of the nation, even defying obstruction from legislators and restrictive permits in order to do so. When Dr. King called for a five-day march and applied for judicial approval, Wallace refused to support the event. Twenty-five thousand people joined the march anyway, and the violence directed at the marchers galvanized a nation. When all three of these elements were in place, mass protest at home and abroad—in the Philippines, in France in 1968, throughout Eastern Europe in 1989, even in Pakistan in 2007–2008—always, *always* led, usually quite quickly, to changes in national outcomes.

That number three is no longer realistic for us here at home is no small point.

Our protest space in America today is closing down. One reason is the enforcement of new regulations that have systematically chipped away at where and how citizens can assemble. Remember the First Amendment: "Congress shall make no law . . . abridging . . . the right of the people peaceably to assemble." That is *no* law. Yet while restrictions on protest have been litigated for sixty years, they have, after the sixties, proliferated at the local level with new force and complexity. And the arsenal used against protesters in the U.S. has grown more sophisticated.

When I read Abbie Hoffman's book about citizen resistance—*Steal This Book*—the sections on how to protect yourself from police violence were out of date.[12] The young people protesting the war in the 1960s and early 1970s were facing discomfort and some danger: tear gas was used on them, sometimes Mace, and truncheons. Protesters of the era were sometimes bloodied by police beatings, and four, famously, died at Kent State. Civil rights marchers faced dogs, the brutal use of nightsticks, and fire hoses. My mother recalls people being washed down the steps with hoses at Berkeley while protesting the Vietnam War.

Today, though, we are reluctant to protest in this confrontational way, in defiance of restrictive permits—for good reasons. Police crowd-control tools have become far more technologically sophisticated. We have enough of a gut sense of this that when we do show up for them, our marches are tame and compliant and almost bureaucratic—guaranteed ineffectual and far from the vital, anything-can-happen energy of the great, often technically illegal marches of the past, with their many arrests.

The Taser alone has the power to undo the First Amendment in practice, even while leaving it intact on the books. Patented in 1974, the Taser—which is legal in many locations around the nation—has, according to Amnesty

International, killed more than three hundred people since 2001.

While older models were cumbersome to manage and heavy, thus posing an obstacle to their widespread use by police officers on patrol, an easier-to-carry model has just been developed that fits readily into holsters. While Tasers used to be carried only by New York City officers in emergency units, as of June of 2008 sergeants on patrol will carry them in their belts in Manhattan.[13] Online, you can see the terrifying effects of Tasers on citizens: the famous video of student Andrew Meyer at the University of Florida screaming, having been wrestled to the ground by Taser-bearing officers after he asked a question of John Kerry about vote fraud in 2004;[14] videos of ordinary Americans pulled over for speeding, then Tasered. One unresisting man in such a video clip was Tasered by an officer just when he asserted that he had rights. He was left in the midst of the highway, having dropped like a stone. Police spokesmen in New York say the Tasers will allow them to stop dangerous suspects who would otherwise have been shot. If you are black and poor, that might be an advantage. But if you are white and middle-class, your danger has increased. Police don't tend to shoot middle-class white people. But the data show they don't hesitate to stun them. For such citizens, a beat officer armed with a gun is far less of a threat than one who is armed with a Taser. When he is policing middle-class crowds who are marching in protest, the officer is far more likely to reach for his Taser than he would have been to reach for his nightstick or his gun.

And in development by the Pentagon now is a new weapon that can effectively *microwave,* and thus bloodlessly incapacitate, American citizens who are demonstrating. In practice trials, this new weapon was used against subjects dressed as American antiwar protesters. A 2008 piece in the *New Yorker* by reporter Alec Wilkinson, "Annals of Technology: Non-lethal Force," shows how the development of new "non-lethal weapons" that may be used against U.S. citizens is a growth industry nationwide. "Recently, [Charles] Heal [a specialist in these technologies] has attended tests of the Active Denial System, or A.D.S., made for the military by Raytheon, which sends a beam of energy that heats a person's skin to a hundred and thirty degrees within a matter of seconds." It is to be used for crowd control in Iraq. Wilkinson says that no current law prohibits its use by domestic law enforcement in the U.S. Rather, he argues that the main deterrent against its use here would be a lawsuit on behalf of someone killed by such technology. According to another expert he cites, the nonlethal weapon everyone desires is "the phaser where you can put it on stun."[15]

Wilkinson notes that the British developed teak bullets to use against colonials; a refinement was the invention of rubber bullets. The British developed these in 1970 to use against the Irish in Northern Ireland. Rubber bullets, he writes, "were lethal often enough to be controversial."

The St. Paul, Minnesota, police bought 230 Tasers and other "sonic weapons" for crowd control in advance of the Republican National Convention in September 2008. The Denver police, with $50 million in federal funds, are stocking up on "nonlethal" rifles—high-powered pepper ball rifles—before the Democratic National Convention in August 2008: Eighty-eight Mark IV models that shoot balls containing a "super-irritant powder" up to one hundred meters. The MK-IV also shoots glass-breaking projectiles and high-impact rounds made of rubber. "MK-IV has knockdown power to spare," claims its manufacturer. In spite of an ACLU lawsuit, the Denver police refuse to say what other weapons they have bought for use on activists.

As I planned to attend my next protest, I was stopped short by the following news: the Center for Constitutional Rights reported, "In November 2003, dozens of law enforcement agencies launched a deliberate and coordinated disruption of lawful protests in Miami, FL, against the FTAA's 'free trade' policies. Hundreds of activists were politically profiled, unlawfully arrested, subjected to pepper spray, rubber bullets and more as part of the 'Miami Model' of policing mass demonstrations."[16] If the Miami Model or the Denver Model spreads further, and we do not defeat them with our own revolution, there will be no more truly free assembly in America, even while the right to assemble is still ours on paper. Today, even protesters in Pakistan don't face such technology.

How do we reconnect with how crucial it is that in the U.S. we are not supposed to fear the state when we assemble—that is, march and protest? How can we feel urgently enough how precious and rare that right is so we fight to protect it while we still have it?

If you understand that "America"—the contract, the psychology of liberty—depends upon a *duty* to protest injustice and overthrow tyranny, you see that we must outlaw the Taser state by state; ban the Miami Model, the Denver technologies, rubber bullets, and violent nonlethal weapons from being used on nonviolent protesters; outlaw paramilitary units such as Blackwater from operating on U.S. soil; and punish preemptive detention.

It is easy for us to look at the diminishing of our common space to assemble and protest as a minor inconvenience; we are overcommitted and protesting doesn't sound like much fun anyway, and, hey, in the Internet era, isn't it beside the point? Can't I do just as well staying safely in my study, clicking a mouse?

No, we cannot do just as well staying in our private rooms and going online; that is how private space becomes the isolation of citizens and in turn eventually becomes a comfortable personal cage. At times we must amass ourselves; this action is not expendable. Its benefit to us is not just stylistic or a matter of nostalgia. Mass disruptive protest is history's time-honored tactic against the suppression of citizens' rights; the assembling of citizens in defiance of wrongdoing also feeds a psychological space that we need to fill if we are to live truly as free men and women. Amassing in the thousands helps us to grasp the power we have unleashed. It heartens us. Because the founders meant for you to be sovereign and to have your own nonviolent but disruptive army; and we are supposed to be your army.

I met Paul Dean, a community college instructor in Spokane, Washington. He confirmed what I had heard on college campuses across the country—that the space for campus picketing is diminishing. "Kids are being constrained in spaces the size of a postage stamp," he told me with frustration. He pointed out that the University of Texas now has a "free speech plaza" for campus protest— and he says you need a permit even to protest *there*. A white-haired gentleman wearing a lumberjack shirt overheard us and laughed sadly at this. He had been a student at the University of Texas when protests overflowed the campus. "There was a free speech plaza then," he said, "but we just ignored it."

The American right to free assembly means that people may use their bodies as proxies for their voices. For assembly to be "free," it must have the potential to stop a town or city from engaging in business as usual. The freedom to assemble is meaningless if it can be so managed that everyone is able to entirely ignore it.

I kept looking at permit regulations in locality after locality, and then at the Bill of Rights, feeling baffled, then angry. The First Amendment is simple. The rights it enshrines are as big as our nation's sky. Those rights mean that our consciousness can be as big as the sky.

The First Amendment does not say "Congress shall make no law abridging the right of the people to assemble, provided that the people have obtained a permit in advance, or half a permit if they can't get a complete one; and if they have paid for registration fees and fines and cleanup costs even if they don't make a mess; and provided they don't obstruct the sidewalk, and as long as they stay away from entrances and traffic, and assuming they move in an orderly way; and by the way, they should be prepared to duck the Tasers or face possibly lethal rubber bullets, or subject themselves to microwave technology used by the state."

I was at a dinner recently at which I was discussing our suffocation by permit. The others there repeated what I hear often: "Isn't protest passé? Isn't it pointless? Can't you do more on the Internet?" That activist citizens have been led to believe this shows how effective the war on liberty has been.

Naomi Usher, an activist who is trying to protect our neighborhood's local character, said that she went out to a peace march in Union Square with her toddler in a stroller—and was about to make a turn when she was faced down by a cop in full black riot gear, armed with guns, a Taser, a face shield, a helmet, and body armor. She said, "I wasn't going to even think of challenging him. I was going to go just where he told me to." She also described how it felt to stand in the protest that *was* allowed in Union Square: "We couldn't move two feet in either direction." Naomi is onto something: "protest" like this is in fact pointless and impotent, while true mass free assembly is among the most powerful forces on earth.

The point of the protest and assembly that the founders intended was to amplify Americans' voices with their bodies so as *to make business as usual impossible*.

That is how public assembly has weight and power; that is how great change happens when people in a democracy gather. The many regulations restricting free movement in our nation have subverted this key part of our liberty. A "march" under conditions now imposed on Americans is assembly without freedom. We are required to accept lifeless, joyless, and finally impotent assembly; assembly that can't stop traffic; assembly that takes place half a football field away from those whom we are trying to confront; assembly with half a bullhorn. In short, fake assembly.

And if the permit process doesn't deter you, check out the costs of your First Amendment rights. According to Marjorie Cohn, president of the National Lawyers Guild, increasingly groups and individuals are being asked to pay for the right to assemble and speak, or ways are being found to prevent assembly or punish them for it. "Although these rights are enshrined in the laws of this country, law enforcement continually erects obstacles to the people's exercise of those rights," Cohn said. "Our most fundamental democratic rights are under attack." [17]

Can the government impose a financial charge on exercising free speech rights? Reading the founders, you'd be sure that could never happen; but according to the National Lawyers Guild, "increasingly, local governments are imposing financial costs as a condition of exercising free speech rights." Local governments have started to bill citizens for the very permits that they must ask for to march or protest; they are demanding that citizens put up security deposits for cleanup before they may speak; and they are charging the citizens who wish to speak the cost of the police presence that the city sends to monitor them!

Do you think this chipping away at our rights to march and assemble is a side issue? I personally went from being willing to march with my fellow citizens—and to bring my children—to being unwilling to do so without a democracy movement protecting me from harm, within the space of one day, when the *New York Times* reported that my city's police sergeants now carry Tasers.

Do you think if we just comply with the permit requirements we can have our free speech back? Think again. On May 3, 2008, the *New York Times* reported that a number of organizations that had wished to protest at the Republican National Convention in Denver had had to file a suit that was making its way through the courts because there had been a complete nonresponse from the Secret Service to their requests for permits, a nonresponse that the citizens involved saw as being both deliberate and strategic: the time needed to allow the protests even to take place was running out.[18] With enough conditioning of Americans to comply with ever-more-onerous permit requirements, fees, hurdles, and ever-more-sinister crowd-control technologies, the anti-citizen interests of the nation have put in place a system that lets them finally ignore Americans' speech rights altogether. These permit restrictions are escalating in severity even as citizens' objections to them are weakening.[19] You can also bet that Americans will, sooner or later, become too worn-out and frustrated—or simply too scared of being hurt—to demand these rights at all.

Our revolution must defeat such forces. We need powerfully to be able to take to the streets. In Part Three, you will find the tools you need to lead your personal army to take what you see as being the right direction.

ORDINARY PEOPLE ARE SUPPOSED TO RUN THINGS

The mass of mankind has not been born with saddles
on their backs, nor a favored few, booted and spurred,
ready to ride them legitimately by the grace of God.
—Thomas Jefferson

T he core ideal of the revolutionary era was that ordinary people in America—those who were enfranchised—could become agents of change. "The Revolution brought respectability and even dominance to ordinary people long held in contempt and gave dignity to their menial labor in a manner unprecedented in history and to a degree not equaled elsewhere in the world," historian Gordon S. Wood writes in *The Radicalism of the American Revolution.*[1] Certainly many elite members of the founding generation had fears and apprehensions about what this might mean. But the current of this powerful idea, reaching as it did into farms, towns, and villages throughout the colonies, swept history forward nonetheless.

This was a complete transformation of the role of common people as the rest of the world had understood it. "These changes" in the way ordinary people thought of themselves "were radical, and they were extensive," writes Wood. We should not, he argues, be blinded because our revolution had "no stormings of prisons" and "no burning of châteaux." Rather, he claims, if we measure the American Revolution by the fact that in 1760 the two million subjects of the king took for granted "that society was and ought to be a hierarchy of ranks and degrees of dependency," but that a mere fifty years later the republic had become "ten million egalitarian-minded bustling citizens," then we can understand that our revolution "was one of the greatest revolutions the world has known, a momentous upheaval." Wood points out that the most profound change it brought to the world was not its transformation of a system of government. The most profound change, rather, lay in its transformation of human beings.

Before our Revolution, men and women, no matter what their political beliefs, generally took for granted that human reality was constructed in a set of fixed dependencies of rank. In such a world there can be no real liberty and no psychology of liberty. But after our Revolution, "in destroying monarchy and establishing republics, [Americans] were changing their society as well as their governments, and they knew it."

Wood goes on,

> To focus, as we are today apt to do, on what the Revolution did not accomplish—highlighting and lamenting its failure to abolish slavery and change fundamentally the lot of women—is to miss the great significance of what it did accomplish; indeed, the Revolution made possible the anti-slavery and women's rights movements of the nineteenth century and in fact all our current egalitarian thinking. The Revolution not only radically

changed the personal and social relationships of people, including the position of women, but also destroyed aristocracy as it had been understood in the Western world for at least two millennia. The Revolution did not just eliminate monarchy and create republics; it actually reconstituted what Americans meant by public or state power and brought about an entirely new kind of popular politics and a new kind of democratic officeholder. . . . Most important, it made the interests and prosperity of ordinary people . . . the goal of society and government. . . . In short, the Revolution was the most radical and most far-reaching event in American history.[2]

The Revolutionary generation believed that "even the reins of state may be held by the sons of the poorest men, if possessed of abilities equal to the important station."[3] They wished to ensure that "all offices lie open to men of merit, of whatever rank or condition" and that a man's merit should "rest entirely within himself, without any regard to family, blood, or connection."[4] In 1806, Philadelphians sent to Congress "farmers . . . a Blacksmith . . . a Butcher."[5] In other words, the revolutionary idea that ordinary people were natural leaders and that the oppression of ordinary people was intolerable spread outward, gaining momentum and force.

This view of the innate worth of ordinary people grew so widespread that a group in Philadelphia in 1784 set free a ship full of indentured servants; soon servants resisted the terms "master" and "mistress." Elsewhere in the young nation, when challenged by foreigners, servants insisted that this was "a free country," that they were as good as anyone, and "that it was a sin and a shame for a freeborn American to be treated like a servant."[6]

Today that self-confident, truly American sense that everyone is significant is in retreat. The powerlessness I heard expressed by contemporary Americans was striking. Most had no confidence that they had a valuable voice or a real role in national deliberations. Many of their questions were framed as complaints or even as whining: why don't *they* do something? Or, why don't *you* do something? Ironically, this was most often the case when I was speaking to some of the most privileged of citizens.

In contrast, revolutionary essayists placed ordinary citizens in a central role as arbiters of the state: "Cato" wrote that they are "the best Judges, whether things go ill or well with the Publick . . . every ploughman knows a good government from a bad one."[7] Ordinary people responded to this confidence in them: in the four decades after the revolution, they formed hundreds of civic and voluntary associations.

When I had dinner in a state college campus meeting room in an exurb near Detroit, this confidence was nowhere to be found.[8] The group included middle- and working-class students and teachers, administrators, and parents from the nearby area. All expressed feelings of hopeless disenfranchisement. Sadly, because under the circumstances it was a reasonable request, some of the citizens present asked not to be identified. I asked why they thought many Americans were so passive.

"We're not having those debates anymore," said teacher Jo Reger. "It feels now as if we *never* really had those debates. We're not talking anymore about when does life begin, what does it mean to go to war, what does it mean to be an American. You always feel that there is a story behind the story when you are reading the news—a story that you are not privy to. Sometimes you feel that there is all this stuff going on behind our backs. *I* feel that, and I *try* to know what's going on."

Sue Rumph, her colleague, agreed: "WMD—we were kept out of the loop!"

"It's depressing," said Reger, "because people are conditioned not to think. I ask my students to name for me some of the countries that are involved in the conflict in the Middle East. I was getting Korea. And Albania.

A student who asked me not to name her, whom I will call Ann, agreed with this: "It's not just that people are being conditioned not to think. It's that they are being conditioned not to be concerned. There are different agencies for change that we don't use. Is it because we are thinking, 'This is as good as it gets'? Like, 'This is America—a superpower—you're here, you're safe, we will take care of you'? The students that I see, they are working full-time, going to school. Protest doesn't enter their minds, or citizenship. Because of lack of time. We just had a peace rally on campus and there were just twenty-five to thirty people who showed up."

"Like me," confirmed student Adam Roberts with feeling. "I'm working four part-time jobs. Going to school and taking care of my eleven-month-old son in the mornings. It leaves you with very little time to do anything. No time to be informed."

Another teacher said, "Pervasive anxiety about the next paycheck creates a huge unwillingness in people to put their necks out very far."

Ann pointed out, "But how much do we know about Britney Spears? And Heath Ledger?"

I mused, "I wonder if the problem is a problem with how we frame our situation. Maybe there is something wrong with the way we are *thinking* about ourselves, something that wasn't wrong with the Americans who were part of the revolutionary generation or, say, the civil rights movement."

Reger disagreed: "The great revolutions came out of communities."

· Her colleague thought out loud, "It's a failure of imagination. When you ask students how it could be done differently, the conversation stops. There had to be some propulsion forward that comes from believing that what *is* doesn't have to be. There *is* a loss. It's the loss of being able to imagine that what is doesn't have to be."

I turned to Reger. "I hear that point a lot, but respectfully, this feels like full-circle reasoning to me. Sometimes it feels almost like an excuse. People say we don't have citizen action because we don't have community—but which comes first? The great revolutionary Americans burned. Nothing stopped them. They would have created community if it had not existed for them."

She said, "Are you saying we have become more accepting of our oppression?"

Danielle Falls, a young part–Native American student leader, spoke about how she has gone to work to help build low-income housing with her own hands and had been doing so since she was a young teenager. She had led others to be involved as well.

I asked her, "What is it then that makes you feel you can still make a difference?"

"I feel empowered," she replied. "I'm young, I haven't been put down a lot. If you can get one person to help you and they can get one person . . . I have gotten four people involved in building housing for those who need it, and they are still doing it."

Adam Roberts said quietly, "Greatness comes from people that are personally invested."

Greatness comes from people that are personally invested. Adam Roberts, a twenty-two-year-old dad who was holding down four jobs, had, along with everything else he was juggling, summarized in a sentence the key American insight. He and his fellow citizens need the tools and blessing of the original revolutionaries.

The founders redefined the idea of who should be running a country. While many of the founding generation argued for a genteel Enlightenment ideal of a small group of elite citizens with liberal arts educations as best suited to direct public life from a "disinterested" (meaning, nonselfish) point of view, the kernel of radicalism in the American ideal quickly energized ordinary "middling," meaning middle- and working-class, men—laborers, artisans, and small craftsmen, then called "mechanics"—to insist that they too were equally, if not better, equipped, to run things than were the local educated and moneyed elites. Ordinary Americans even developed an ideology that disdained the leisure of the ruling classes, celebrated the common man's capacities for leadership, and expanded on the notion of the equal dignity of all: as Andrew Jackson put it a generation later, "the duties of all public offices . . . are, or at least admit of being made, so plain and simple that men of intelligence may readily qualify themselves for their performance. . . . In a country where offices are created solely for the benefit of the people no one man has any more intrinsic right to official station than any other."[9] This republican sentiment also influenced women of the era, and while it would take a century and a half for them to gain the formal vote, revolutionary America expanded the scope of women's participation in public life in an unprecedented way, with changes in law, property rights, and inheritance practices that led to women being far more independent in the young republic than they were anywhere else in the world at that time.

Town meetings had begun with the Puritans. Indeed, the first complete recording of a town meeting dates to 1633.[10] And the revolutionary era saw ordinary people assembling, debating, and deliberating in many kinds of legislative bodies.

The more I learned about the early history of the republic, the angrier I became about the gap between the founders' gift and our reality. Current historians demonstrate that these ordinary people did as good a job leading their communities and their nation as did the elites. But the Americans I heard from doubted that ordinary individuals, not backed by corporate or state power, could be agents of tremendous change. My students generally have not been taught that all that we cherish or even simply take for granted—that African-Americans work and live beside white Americans as fellow citizens rather than being held by them in bondage; that women have the rights to vote and own property; aspects of our lives as basic as weekends, safe workplaces, food that won't kill us; that kids go to school rather than labor twelve hours a day in factories—all came about because of some handful of crazy idealists who simply did not accept that they were powerless to spark great change, who gathered in spite of opprobrium, every kind of ridicule, and every reason to believe that their vision of the future was a pointless, even suicidal, dream.

My sad discussion with the citizens of the Detroit exurb—their doubts echo across the country—shows how we must recall that the point of a democracy as the founders and our greatest leaders have understood it is to produce not a certain system of government, but rather a certain kind of human being. As Robert Kennedy said, "All our great cooperative efforts will come to little if they do not succeed in restoring importance to the lives of individual men." He also noted that "the fulfillment of that objective is increasingly difficult in the face of the giant organizations and massive bureaucracies of the age. Still it is what we must seek, helping men and communities to mark off a corner of the world in which to move, to stretch mind and body in the effort 'not only to equal or to resemble but to excel,' which John Adams told us would forever be 'the great spring of human action'—and which was our goal for ourselves and one another in our compact two short centuries ago." [11]

A National Referendum: Direct Democracy

The Americans I heard from feel powerless not only because they are sure they can't become members of Congress, they are also sure that anything they have to *say* to Congress can't make a difference. As Curtis Ellis's insider analysis makes clear, our representatives can no longer effectively represent us without our own revolutionary behavior engaged in pushing them to push back. We have to face that there is no alternative to a real confrontation by ordinary citizens of a thoroughly corrupted system.

The solution? We must secure legislation to drive a national referendum system. Is this impossible? We would need to amend the Constitution to do so—particularly, as Zach Heiden of the Maine Civil Liberties Union notes, "The presentment clause and the guarantee clause, which are (to put it mildly) significant provisions. The Constitution can be amended—everything except for the guarantee of equal suffrage in the Senate is open to change—but it has only been amended 26 times in over 200 years, so this is not something that could happen overnight." [12] As daunting as that sounds, I would argue that, given the reality of this, a drive for this nature of amendment could happen with far greater momentum and speed than the laborious fights of the past: the combination of voter rage and the technology of the Internet could create a tidal wave of demand for this reform.

Would havoc ensue? Or can we actually trust the American people?

Today, for instance, 61 percent of Americans say we should have stayed out of Iraq, 76 percent say additional troops sent there are having no impact or making things worse, and 63 percent want a timetable for withdrawal. But most of these same citizens often feel they have almost no power to help bring their own troops home.

Our founders left us a republic, which, as voices dating back to the Federalist Papers and before point out, is quite different from the feared "mob rule" of a majority-driven democracy. But when a republic is broken, nothing in our system categorically prevents us from creatively fixing it with some elements of direct democracy.

Some direct-democracy action must be raised to a national level. Congress can't make a difference without a drastic push from us. We must drive a limited national referendum system.

This is not an untried idea on the state level. Twenty-four U.S. states have direct-democracy systems: ordinary citizens can put an initiative on the ballot and drive a referendum. This means that the people themselves can create a proposed law and with a certain number of signatures put it on the ballot for their fellow citizens to vote on. If enough of their fellow citizens vote in support of the initiative, it becomes state law.

Studies of such initiative and referenda states prove that on balance the legislation is self-correcting—ill-conceived, bigoted, or unrepresentative laws drive a countermovement.[13] Studies also show that citizens who participate in the initiative and referenda process become better informed, deliberate more with their neighbors, make better decisions in voting, and eventually vote more frequently. Citizens in states that have this system also, I have informally observed, tend to feel much more hopeful about the possibility of personally making a difference. Others argue that it is possible to use the system to oppress minorities. But I hold that, even given these drawbacks, a fight among citizens is preferable to our current situation, in which the people are being forced out of decision-making processes altogether.

Why not take direct democracy of this kind to a national level? Articles 1 and 2 set forth the exclusive procedures for creation of law—a majority vote of both houses of Congress and signature of the president. Article 4 guarantees to the states a republican (not direct-democracy) form of government. But the Constitution can, as I noted, be changed.

Switzerland has been a "direct democracy" since the late Middle Ages.[14] According to a Swiss website, direct democracy can be defined as a form or system of democracy that gives citizens an extraordinary level of participation in the legislative process and grants them a maximum of political self-determination. Switzerland has a national referendum system. While it has representative bodies—cantons (like our states) and a parliament—all draft federal laws are submitted to a large number of people in a kind of opinion poll. Cantonal governments, organizations, and formalized political parties weigh in. The result is debated by parliamentary commissions, decided in parliament, and presented back to the people. The people then have veto rights. If 50,000 sign a form demanding a referendum, it must take place. A majority of the national electorate is needed to pass a referendum. The people, in a kind of support for the existing check-and-balance system, help pass over a dozen such laws per year in that country. And if 100,000 Swiss citizens (2.5 percent of the electorate) call for an initiative, the federal parliament is compelled to discuss, accept, reject, or change it; but the result goes back to the people in the form of a referendum. Switzerland is stable, peaceful, and rich. Its streets are paved, its public schools first-rate, its industrial development proceeds in areas separated from its protected natural landscapes, and its museums are subsidized.

Has direct democracy on a national level created mob rule in Switzerland? When something crazy is proposed as an initiative, the person can't get fellow citizens to sign it. Recently an initiative was put forward seeking to deny individual foreigners citizenship based on subjective opinions.[15] Didn't pass. And whatever you may think of that nation's tradition of neutrality, when the people of Switzerland don't want to send their children to war, they don't fight a war.

A national network of "democracy commandos" that I will describe in Part Three can quickly ramp up the pressure for a direct-democracy movement, U.S.-style, on Congress. Public awakening drives great change when America is working. The Thirteenth Amendment, which abolished slavery, took decades of movement activity to push the nation to a crisis point. The Nineteenth Amendment, which extended the vote to American women, was also first a sixty-year state-by-state battle. Both of these amendments passed when society had shifted to the point at which it was psychologically untenable for a plurality or majority of Americans to resist the concepts that then drove the law. Nothing in our Constitution prevents us from creating conditions for an American-values version of some direct citizen support for the legislative process.

A national referendum system of some limited kind does require constitutional change. The founders put such mechanisms for change in place. We also need a movement and champions in Congress. Congress can pass a federal referendum bill creating a fourth, supplementary power nexus—the people's. If twenty-four states have citizens' referenda—direct democracy—why not a limited national referendum system? Will Congress accept such an empowerment of the people of its own accord? Of course not; such a bill would break up lobbyists', special interests', and incumbents' hegemony. But if a massive grassroots movement shows that the vast majority of Americans support such a law? Our representatives would be hard-pressed to explain to us why they do not trust the people.

The moment such a law passed, we, the people, would be equal in power in some ways to the lobbyists and the donors. We would be able to sit at the table in direct deliberation with our representatives. This is not a radical revision of the system but rather a corrective, returning a system far distorted from its original, participatory blueprint, back in the direction of the people it was intended to serve.

If we shift our thinking about ourselves and demand that we restore our position in the country as its true leaders and legislators, the nation will shift its thinking, and congressional, lobbyist, and donor constituencies who will fight to defeat or smear this movement for some supplementary, American version of nationwide direct democracy will eventually look like the rearguard, repressive forces that they are.

With a benchmark of a certain number of signatures—say 2.5 percent of the electorate to use the Swiss example—an initiative can be certified to be part of a national referendum. If the referendum comes to the people, yes, a majority can pass it. Overnight, for instance, with a vote on such a referendum, if the majority wills it, you could pass effective campaign finance reform to restore clean democracy to the people—reform measures that will never get passed without a radical intervention such as this, since the people have a vested interest in its passage but the incumbents in Congress do not. For example, you could have a fair fight with Exxon and Halliburton when it comes to national policy. You could cap emissions and save the planet for your grandchildren.

Direct democracy—in a limited context—in the United States of America. Is it so scary? Given how unrepresentative of the people's wishes Congress must now be, is the status quo or is a federal referendum bill (say, the People's Voice Act) closer to the founders' will? Given how high the stakes are of remaining passive in a status quo hurtling us towards an unlivable planet, should we not think as boldly as the founders did? Do you believe Americans should have so direct a voice in the nation's destiny?

What would you do with such a voice?

AMERICANS CHERISH THE RULE OF LAW

*But where says some is the king of America? I'll tell
you Friend, he reigns above, and doth not make havoc
of mankind like the Royal Brute of Britain. Yet that we
may not appear to be defective even in earthly honors, let
a day be solemnly set apart for proclaiming the charter;
let it be brought forth placed on the divine law, the word
of God; let a crown be placed thereon, by which the
world may know, that so far as we approve of monarchy,
that in America the law is king. For as in absolute
governments the king is law, so in free countries the
law ought to be king; and there ought to be no other.*

—Thomas Paine, *Common Sense*[1]

All over the world, what citizens of less open societies envy when they look at America—and long for
in pursuing "America" in their own minds and
nations—is the nation's historical commitment to the rule
of law; what astonishes and stirs others is how respect for
the rule of law is materialized by ordinary people. As Robert Kennedy pointed out, "In a democratic society law is
the form which free men give to justice. The glory of
justice and the majesty of law are created not just by the
Constitution—nor by the courts—nor by the officers of the
law—nor by the lawyers—but by the men and women who

constitute our society—who are the protectors of the law as they themselves are protected by the law." [2]

Before the American Revolution, everyone saw relationships in a fixed hierarchy and they saw access to the rule of law the same way: the people at the top owned the rule of law and everyone else suffered from that ownership. After 1776, something unprecedented came into being and ordinary people owned the rule of law and maintained responsibility for it. This is the true American position.

Even before the country's birth, Americans of all backgrounds clamored to participate in both claiming access to and upholding the rule of law. And the law was fairer in the colonies to white women and the unpropertied than it had been anywhere else: "In colonial courts, wives gained more control over property they brought into marriage than in England or Ireland. They also had broader rights to act for and with their husbands in business transactions," historian Gary B. Nash writes.[3] By the 1730s, colonial women were demanding the right to participate in civic life and even to fight for liberty. "We the widows of this city," New York women declared in 1733, "protest the failure to invite us to court. We are housekeepers, pay our taxes, carry on trade and most of us are she Merchants. . . . We have the vanity to think we can be fully as entertaining [engaged] and make as brave a defense on case of invasion and perhaps not turn tail as soon as some of the men." In 1779, two Philadelphia women posted a broadside declaring that American women too were "born for liberty" and wished to resist bearing "the irons of a tyrannic government."[4] Abigail Adams championed women's sacrifices during the war—indeed, historians now believe that several thousand women served bravely in providing support

to the Continental Army. But, just as the male revolutionaries had done before the war, Adams protested that American women were still "deprived of a voice in legislation
[and] obliged to submit to those laws which are imposed
upon us."[5]

People of color made this profound psychological shift
as well. In 1766, a slave named Jenny Slew went to court
in Salem, Massachusetts, with the charge that her master
had deprived her of her liberty. John Adams noted many
similar cases of what others called "freedom suits."[6] In
1773, "Massachusetts slaves had taken a page from the patriots' book" and presented the governor of that state with
a petition for their liberty. In 1774 slaves tried yet again to
petition the legislature: "A great number of Blacks of the
Province . . . held in a state of slavery . . . have in common
with all other men a natural right to our freedom without
being depriv'd of them by our fellow men as we are a freeborn people and have never forfeited this blessing by any
compact or agreement whatever."[7] Though the petition
for the protection of the rule of law was unsuccessful, this
claim formed the basis of the argument for abolition for
generations.

One thoroughly subjugated patriot who insisted on
claiming access to rule of law as a true American was called
Mum Bett. Mum Bett—later, Elizabeth Freeman—looks
out at us from a portrait painted by a contemporary. She
wears an elegant white cap and a simple dark gown and
has a grave, stern, meditative expression.

Mum Bett was an enslaved woman who grew up in
Sheffield, Massachusetts. She lost her husband to the fight
for the colonies' freedom—but was left in chains herself
nonetheless.

She considered deeply the words of the Declaration of

Independence, even as she was forced to serve the affluent landowner Colonel John Ashley. She said to him once that the Declaration of Independence's words held "that all people were born free and equal, and she thought long about it, and resolved she would try whether she did not come in among them." In 1781 her mistress swung a hot fire shovel at Mum Bett's sister. Mum Bett placed herself to receive the blow and was scarred for the rest of her life: "Outraged, she stalked from the house and refused to return. When her master appealed to the local court in Sheffield for the recovery of his slave, Mum Bett called upon Theodore Sedgwick, a rising lawyer from nearby Stockbridge, to ask if Massachusetts' new state Constitution, with its preamble stating that 'all men are born free and equal,' did not apply to her. Sedgwick took the case."[8]

The jury found that the preamble did indeed apply to Mum Bett. The decision set a precedent—and partly due to the courage of this remarkable American patriot, and others just as brave, whose leadership was wholly omitted from my history lessons, slavery ended thereafter in Massachusetts. Having taken for herself the name Elizabeth Freeman, she later worked for the Sedgwicks. She became an accomplished nurse and midwife, a much venerated citizen of the town. Later she would say, "Any time while I was a slave, if one minute's freedom had been offered to me, and I had been told I must die at the end of that minute, I would have taken it—just to stand one minute on God's airth a free woman—I would."[9]

How the Bill of Rights Keeps Us Safe

How did ordinary people in America like Abigail Adams and Elizabeth Freeman come to so internalize respect for and belief in the rule of law even when they saw that they were not included equally in its blessing? Look at the genius in the construction of our Bill of Rights. It teaches us the mental habits of freedom. It protected ordinary citizens in America from the danger people faced elsewhere. In Europe, men would be kidnapped by the state for military service, as in England, and families would see their lands confiscated, as in Scotland. The Bill of Rights protected the Revolutionary generation from these common terrors. The Second, Third, and Fourth Amendments dovetail with the First and build on it, to give us shelter, space, and safety. Together, they guarantee the psychological and physical space and safety that is "America," a place in which we can disagree with one another, call each other names; form factions, movements, and subcultures; get on each other's nerves, make fun of each other, scheme to persuade or lobby each other; fund-raise to convert each other—but in which neither we nor the state can massacre citizens or hold them hostage, nor steal people's possessions. These first four amendments give us a psychological home in which we need have no fear of being hurt or killed with impunity by one another or by the state.

The First Amendment bears repeating here: "Congress shall make no law respecting an establishment of religion, or prohibiting the free exercise thereof; or abridging the freedom of speech, or of the press, or the right of the people peaceably to assemble, and to petition the Government for a redress of grievances." [10]

The Second Amendment reads, "A well regulated militia, being necessary to the security of a free State, the right of the people to keep and bear Arms, shall not be infringed." [11] This means a free nation, to be secure, needs a well-regulated (orderly, not chaotic, not unleashed from a chain of command and terrorizing people) militia (formal-ized group of armed men). The people have a right to keep and carry weapons.[12] Much ink has been spilled over what exactly this amendment means—whether, for in-stance, it gives every American the right to carry a gun for personal use. But at a minimum the Second Amendment establishes the National Guard or other state militia units, regulated by the rule of law, to keep order domestically. It means that the executive in Washington is not allowed to oppress Americans violently—as the founders knew from their bitter experience with George III.[12]

The Third Amendment establishes safety for us in our homes and streets: "No Soldier shall, in time of peace be quartered in any house, without the consent of the Owner, nor in time of war, but in a manner to be prescribed by law." Think of how soldiers were billeted in the homes of colonists before the Revolution, to the great fear and hu-miliation of their families. Think about how German sol-diers took over the homes of French peasants and farmers during the occupation of France in World War Two— breaking in and slaughtering animals, hunting down refu-gees in hiding and murdering them, menacing women. Think of the occupation of citizens' homes by the violent state militia in Darfur, Sudan, today; of Afghani civilians' homes occupied by Russian troops in that conflict; or of how violent militias took over homes in Sierra Leone dur-ing its civil war. There is no faster way to crush, humiliate, and frighten a people. Hardin Lang, Political Affairs Offi-cer at the United Nations, notes that, "All over the world, if you don't have the rule of law, people turn into tribes or blocs and set up local militias to defend themselves. The rule of law? Without it, no institutions, no personal safety, no economy."[13]

Though no one is sure what the Second Amendment means right now, since *D.C.* v. *Heller,* decided by the Supreme Court, gave private gun owners new rights, what is certain is that the founders sought to protect U.S. citizens from a situation in which they were at the mercy of violent, unaccountable agents of the state preying on them.

In this vein, add the Fourth to our blessings: the Fourth Amendment guarantees that we have a private life protected from state intrusion, where we can think what we want, love whom we wish, speak to our families, and write to ourselves as we please.

It guarantees that the state can't break down your door, barge in, and mess with your stuff, whether it is peacetime or wartime:

> The right of the people to be secure in their persons, houses, papers, and effects, against unreasonable searches and seizures, shall not be violated, and no Warrants shall issue, but upon probable cause, supported by Oath or affirmation, and particularly describing the place to be searched, and the persons or things to be seized.[14]

Translation for a modern reader: The people have a right that must not be violated to be secure (safe) in terms of their bodies, their houses, their papers, their computers, and their possessions. They have a right to be safe against unreasonable searches (of their bodies, houses, papers, computers, and possessions) and against the state's unreasonably seizing (taking possession of) their bodies, homes, papers, computers, and possessions. The state must not issue a warrant (a document calling for the search or seizure of bodies, homes, papers, computers, or possessions) unless it can persuade a magistrate that there is "probable cause" that a crime has been committed. This assertion that there must be probable cause that a crime has been committed, which would justify the magistrate's issuing a warrant for search or seizure, must be backed up by a sworn oath or affirmation (that is, the state can't just idly make a false or random charge that a crime has probably been committed). Finally, the state must limit its request for a search warrant to a *specific* place that it wishes to search, or to *specific* people or things to be seized (that is, taken possession of).

What does this mean in real life?

Say the government is worried that some antiwar activists at Ohio State University set fire to a weapons-development lab on campus.

Because of the Fourth Amendment, the state can't say "Let's just confiscate all the computers at Ohio State University," or "Let's tap all the phones at Ohio State University." You won't come home to your dorm to find your computer gone, as you would in China or Russia. The Fourth Amendment means that your government has to show a magistrate (translation: judge) that it has reason to believe that John X, a sophomore at Ohio State, probably committed a crime, and to ask for the judge's written okay to take only John X's computer, and not yours—or those of his roommate or his dorm adviser. When John X's classmates are free from the fear of intrusion—when all of John X's classmates are safe to rest their papers and journals, their Web searches and love letters, their Che posters or their annotated Bibles, secure in their locked dorm rooms and in true psychological private space, they can develop at liberty as real individuals.

• • •

The founders left us the gift of the law. But lawlessness is being released in our homeland.

Donald Vance, who blew the whistle on irregularities involving arms sales in Iraq, was taken hostage *from* the U.S. embassy *by* U.S. soldiers and kept illegally without recourse to a lawyer in a U.S.-held prison, abused and terrified, for months—and scared to talk once he got home.[16] In 2007 U.S. military contractors, who were positioned by Paul Bremer, with his Order 17, to essentially operate outside the rule of law in Iraq, butchered seventeen Iraqi civilians.[17] The FBI, upholding the rule of law, tried to investigate; but the State Department obstructed the investigation. The 9/11 commissioners, upholding the rule of law, asked the CIA for all tapes or evidence relating to the interrogation of prisoners connected with the attacks on the World Trade Center; the CIA acknowledged under pressure that they had destroyed tapes of the abusive interrogation of Abu Zubaydah—which is illegal.[18] Military JAG lawyers, upholding the rule of law, tried to get evidence about whether their clients had been abused in custody. But the White House denied them access to that evidence—which is illegal.[19]

The Center for Constitutional Rights upheld the rule of law by filing charges against Donald Rumsfeld for torture. But the directives to torture prisoners came out of the White House itself. In directing torture, Dick Cheney, Condoleezza Rice, and Donald Rumsfeld have all committed crimes as defined by U.S. and international law.[20]

In 2008, the ACLU revealed a secret memo by Justice Department counsel John Yoo that argued the president has the power, based on his role as commander in chief, to authorize interrogation techniques generally regarded as torture and that a war context put the president above many international and U.S. laws.[21] Congress passed legislation in 2005 granting the executive expanded powers to suspend the law in building a fence with which the Department of Homeland Security plans to close off the U.S.'s southern border and eliminating overt judicial review.[22] This all happened as Americans went about their business.

This principle—America defined by its respect for the rule of law—seems on its face too obvious even to call attention to. Yet how fundamental it is, at a time when the rule of law is under threat.

I wrote about this issue in a friend's house on an island off the Massachusetts coast; one side of the island is exposed to vicious nor'easters. An ocean rain was crashing down.

I had been up late the night before reading John Adams—a man who defended a hated British soldier in court, and risked his career, out of his reverence for the rule of law. So recently having absorbed the founders' thoughts, I felt the storm driving in against the American homeland. I had been reading about other storms driving against the nation in earlier parts of its history. It became obvious to me that the worst storms in our past were not crises in which we suffered and sacrificed in alignment with our ideals, but rather those hurricanes that we brought against ourselves when we acted athwart our own ideals ourselves.

A storm is raging against us now from Guantánamo Bay, one fully capable of extinguishing our psychological light and breaching the protection of personal boundaries represented by American respect for the rule of law.

John F. Kennedy wrote in *Profiles in Courage* about

Republican senator Robert Taft, who was for him a hero in his support of the rule of law. Against the wishes of Taft's party, and much against the popular national will, Taft objected, in 1946, to the structure of the Nuremberg trials. He argued that they "violate the fundamental principle of American law that a man cannot be tried by an *ex post facto* statute"—that is, by a law that did not exist when the crime was committed.[23]

He took this grossly unpopular position at a time when hated enemies were in U.S. custody and Americans had an overwhelming desire to make the enemy pay with blood. But Nuremberg, Taft argued, "was a blot on American constitutional history, and a serious departure from our Anglo-Saxon heritage of fair and equal treatment, a heritage which had rightly made this country respected throughout the world."[24]

Taft wrote, of the greatest criminals the world has ever seen, "We cannot teach them government in Germany by suppressing liberty and justice. As I see it, the English-speaking peoples have one great responsibility. That is to restore to the minds of men a devotion to equal justice under law."[25]

Why should illegal mistreatment of prisoners in our custody matter to us? Because it shreds not only our pride in our nation but also our security as guaranteed by the rule of law. Senator Bob Taft was a staunch conservative. He hated the enemy in the dock in 1946 as deeply as George Bush or John McCain hate the enemy now held at Guantánamo. But as Senator John Kennedy wrote of Taft, it was "the Constitution . . . which guided the policy decisions of the Senator from Ohio. It was his source, his weapon and his salvation. And when the Constitution commanded 'no *ex post facto* laws,' Bob Taft accepted this precept as *permanently wise* and *universally applicable*" (italics mine).[26] To an astonished Ohio audience, Bob Taft said:

"The trial of the vanquished by the victors . . . cannot be impartial no matter how it is hedged about with the forms of justice." He went further: "About this whole judgment there is the spirit of vengeance, and vengeance is seldom justice. The hanging of the eleven men convicted will be a blot on the American record which we shall long regret.

"In these trials," he went on, at great risk to his own career, "we have accepted the Russian idea of the purpose of trials—government policy and not justice with little relation to Anglo-Saxon heritage. By clothing policy in the forms of legal procedure, we may discredit the whole idea of justice in Europe for years to come." "Robert Taft had spoken," wrote Senator Kennedy, "not in defense of Nazi murderers," as his accusers had accused him of doing, but rather in defense of justice itself: "To [Taft], justice was at stake and all other concerns were trivial."[27]

Today patriots across the political spectrum are standing up for the rule of law, sometimes at great cost to themselves.

Former deputy attorney general James Comey said yes to the rule of law: he refused to go along with illegal spying on Americans, and he told colleagues that they would someday be ashamed when the world learned about the administration's warrantless wiretapping.[28] Military JAG lawyers have publicly come out against the corruption of the rule of law represented by the military tribunal system—and some have suffered career setbacks as a result.[29]

How exactly does reverence for the rule of law protect us? Think about how fragile liberty can be once the state starts to punish, dismiss, harass, or even round up those who are the vanguard of the rule of law—lawyers, judges, and justices of the peace.

The *Australian* reported that New South Wales (NSW) justice of the peace Mamdouh Habib is suing the Australian federal government, which had colluded with the U.S. in committing various abuses against detainees and due process, for having allowed him to be kidnapped in Pakistan in 2001 and sent illegally to Egypt, where he was imprisoned and tortured for six months. After that the United States held him for *four years* in Guantánamo. His complaint notes that he is a law-abiding citizen who was swept up under false pretexts. "It turns out that Habib has incontrovertible proof of his good standing," the *Australian* noted. "He is a fully accredited Justice of the Peace in NSW. A search of the NSW Attorney General's Department website reveals that not only Habib, but his wife Maha Habib, is a JP." To become justice of the peace in New South Wales, the *Australian* added, "you have to be nominated by a member of the NSW parliament and submit to a full character inquiry, including a criminal records check by NSW Police."[30]

A justice of the peace—detained wrongfully by us. Had you heard of that? Neither had I. So how can we be sure there is something so sacred about an American justice of the peace or even a judge?

This kind of leap to the next level of threat to us as citizens seems implausible to many people because they assume that there is an orderly and effective democratic response to this kind of eruption of lawlessness. But what would indeed happen as a countermove if a U.S. justice of the peace or a judge were rendered? Would the Bar Association protest?

What would we do in America if confronted by an even more sudden undermining of the rule of law than that which we have faced? In Pakistan, it was clear from interviews that, in spite of a powerful grassroots movement, when Pervez Musharraf declared a state of emergency and began rounding up the lawyers and arresting the judges, no one in the democracy movement there had a clear plan B.[31]

In a sudden sharp move against democracy and the rule of law on the part of the U.S. government—any U.S. government—there is nothing a democracy is prepared effectively to do; that is the nature of democracy. The Bush years merely illustrate a test run for the future. The lesson is timeless: there is no war room for democracy; no one has an organizational chart detailing who would do what in a final crisis. That is why other nations envy the reflexive American reverence for the rule of law—such reverence itself if we engage it is a guarantor of stability; such reverence itself if we engage it is preventive.

As we saw from the blackout surrounding the Yoo memo until almost five years after it was written, such a leadership develops, in secret locations and intellectual spaces unavailable to the citizens, the basis for the events and actions it wishes to set in motion. In the event of a contemporary radical suspension of the rule of law, many people I heard from in my travels expressed faith in the U.S. military. Of course, most of our military men and women are patriots and cherish freedom; but they take an oath to obey the commander in chief. Who would direct a resistance to such an edict? What would be the chain of command? From 2007 to 2008, Pakistani citizens, led by lawyers and judges, thronged the streets of their nation and brought the country to a crisis point because they refused to accept a blasted constitution, an intimidated judiciary, and an illegal leadership. With American policy—unbelievably—opposing this democracy movement and seeking to prop up Musharraf, the man who has stamped out the flames of liberty that our own founders would have cherished, these citizens nonetheless succeeded in pushing back. They would not sit quietly as the rule of law was dismantled.

In Part Three, we will see how to take action to push back and restore the rule of law here at home. We too must become once again, as the founders intended us to be, intoxicated with our own right to the rule of law. We must become once again as "American" as are these Pakistani lawyers, judges, and ordinary freedom-loving citizens. Their fight and ours were both given to us by the founders.

The stability we have enjoyed for over two hundred years comes from a place within ourselves that reflexively reveres the rule of law and claims it for our own. We need to live once again from that place.

PRINCIPLE FIVE:

AMERICA ESTABLISHES NO GOD

The wall of separation ensures the government's freedom
from religion and the individual's freedom of religion.
The second probably cannot flourish without the first.
—Leonard W. Levy

America was founded by religious refugees: men and women who had been persecuted for their religion, often by the state. Most of them were Christians: Puritans, Quakers, and Huguenots. All had fled violent oppression directed at them by nation states in which established churches were essentially extensions of consolidated state power. The founders and their forebears knew intimately how bloody and terrifying it was to be a religious minority in Anglican Britain or in Catholic France. They knew how precious freedom of conscience was, and how impossible it was to have such freedom when the full power of the state claimed a certain version of God and would force you out of a livelihood—or imprison, torture, or kill you—if you did not sign on to that version.

That is why "America" is inseparable from religious freedom. There is meant to be no theocracy here, ever. An American theocracy would be a heresy against the vision of many of our nation's founders. America was established as a haven for a plurality of religious beliefs—and many of the founders saw freedom of religious conscience as *the* sacred American precept.

It is not that the nation's forefathers and foremothers wished for an America where people did not believe in God. Many were people of devout Christian faith. It is, rather, that they understood a government "conceived in liberty" to be one that by definition could not and would never dictate beliefs in God. In a famous 1776 sermon before the Council and House of Representatives entitled "The Duty to Rebel," Samuel West, one of New England's most admired clergymen, preached, "For the civil authority to pretend to establish particular modes of faith and worship, and to punish all those that deviate from the standard which our superiors have set up, is attended with the worst pernicious consequences to a society. . . . I cannot but look at it as a peculiar blessing of Heaven that we live in a land where every one can freely deliver his sentiments upon religious subjects, and have the privilege of worshipping God according to the dictates of his own conscience without any molestation or disturbance—a privilege which I hope we shall ever keep up and maintain." [1]

According to many scholars, including Steven Waldman, who wrote the comprehensive *Founding Faith: Providence, Politics, and the Birth of Religious Freedom in America,* the core conviction of the founders was not to create a Christian America; their true religion was religious liberty. [2]

Thomas Jefferson and Benjamin Franklin were especially passionate in articulating this value. Benjamin Franklin's biographer Walter Isaacson calls Franklin "an apostle of tolerance." [3] Franklin derided religious intolerance and even wrote a blistering satire of it in the form of a biblical parable: Abraham, he wrote, became enraged at a visitor to his tent because the man worshipped another God; the patriarch drove him away with blows. "And at Midnight

God called unto Abraham, saying, Abraham, where is the Stranger?

"And Abraham answered and said, Lord, he would not worship thee, neither would he call upon thy Name; therefore have I driven him out before my Face into the Wilderness.

"And God spake again unto Abraham, saying, For this thy Sin shall thy Seed be afflicted four Hundred Years in a strange Land."[4]

Thomas Jefferson said that America must be free of established religion in as many ways as he could. Jefferson "consistently advocated the separation of church and state," writes historian John P. Kaminski.[5] To a correspondent, Jefferson wrote, "However, religion is not the subject for you & me; neither of us know the religious opinions of the other; that is a matter between our maker and ourselves." And yet again: "The subject of religion, a subject on which I have ever been most scrupulously reserved, I have considered it as a matter between every man and his maker, in which no other, & far less the public had a right to intermeddle."

"Jefferson," explains Kaminski, "believed that religion was a highly personal thing between each person and God. He steadfastly supported the free exercise of religion without government interference. He lived by a strict moral code regulated by his conscience—the moral compass given to all by God. . . . 'History,' wrote Jefferson, 'I believe furnishes no example of a priest-ridden people maintaining a free civil government.' "[6,7]

Gordon Wood argues that this respect for religious freedom was generally held by the founders:

"At the time of the Revolution most of the founding fathers had not put much emotional stock in religion, even when they were regular churchgoers. As enlightened gentlemen, they abhorred 'that gloomy superstition disseminated by ignorant illiberal preachers' and looked forward to the day when 'the phantom of darkness will be dispelled by the rays of science, and the bright charms of rising civilization.' At best, most of the revolutionary gentry only passively believed in organized Christianity and, at worst, privately scorned and ridiculed it. . . . Even puritanical John Adams thought that the argument for Christ's divinity was an 'awful blasphemy' in this new enlightened age. When Hamilton was asked why the members of the Philadelphia Convention had not recognized God in the Constitution, he allegedly replied, speaking for many of his liberal colleagues, 'We forgot.' "[8,9]

I do not reproduce this remarkable graf in order to take a position on the divinity of Jesus, or to assert the truth or falsehood of any one religion. I personally do have religious belief. I just agree with the founders that my personal religious belief is not the business of the state.

I reproduce this graf to remind us that America was founded without the founders themselves in general resorting to claiming a specific divine authority to sanction the republic's ideals. Indeed, the great American innovation was religious privacy.

With the guarantee of religious freedom—a guarantee that, as we will see, is being stripped from brave servicemen and servicewomen today—individuals in the revolutionary era were told that each was "considered as possessing in himself or herself an original right to believe and speak as their own conscience, between themselves and God, may determine."[10] This freedom, paradoxically, became a spiritual gift of liberty: it led Americans to become far more religious than were their counterparts in Europe, where people knew there was no separation between the established churches and the state.

At that time, the importance of freedom of conscience—freedom of worship—was so well understood that Jefferson wrote about the importance of it to the Baptist Association of Danbury, Connecticut. Rather than pandering to some idea of a "Christian"—or even a Baptist—America, Jefferson wrote, "*Believing with you* [italics mine] that religion is a matter which lies solely between Man & his God, that he owes account to none other for his faith and his worship, that the legitimate powers of government reach actions only, & not opinions, I contemplate with sovereign reverence that act of the whole American people which declared that their legislature should 'make no law respecting an establishment of religion, or prohibiting the free exercise thereof,' thus building a wall of separation between Church and State." [11]

But today fake patriotism is using God as product placement. Even Americans in the military academies, and candidates on the campaign trail, are being asked to profess faith in a certain religious belief as a condition of participating in what most of the founders intended to protect as secular civic institutions. In 1996, then-first lady Hillary Rodham Clinton's Methodism was placed under a media spotlight. Republican contenders regularly make pilgrimages to Pat Robertson. In 2000, George W. Bush secured his base by speaking about having been "born again" as a Christian. In 2008, the Democratic nominee for president, Barack Obama, faced a disinformation campaign intended to persuade Americans that he is Muslim. He has declared, perhaps in response, "I pray to Jesus Christ," and talked about the church where he "found Jesus Christ." [12]

This religiosity may all be deeply felt. But we have forgotten what a blasphemy this kind of scrutiny represents to the civic religion of most of the founders. A "Christian America"—or any America in which the state purports to speak for any version of God—is one of those aspects of today's fake patriotism that is simply un-American. The church-state wall is essential to the establishment of a ground of common discourse and action that allows neighbors to deliberate and to disagree with one another openly, on a level playing field.

This posture is not just meant to maintain a level of purity regarding what happens between God and man, and between man and the state in America. It also safeguards the benign nature of conflict between individuals in a republic.

That wall the founders left us for our protection is being dismantled. In 2008, a young soldier in Iraq, Specialist Jeremy Hall, stood up for Jefferson and Franklin's America.

Raised a Baptist, Hall began to question his assumptions about what he had learned about his faith. He did not announce his questions. But at a 2006 Thanksgiving meal in Iraq, Hall declined to pray. A sergeant angrily ejected him from the table. Over the ensuing months, Hall was threatened by other soldiers and sent home early. Sergeant Major Kevin Nolan wrote an unsettling e-mail "counseling" Hall: "I caution you that although your 'legal' issues are yours and yours alone, I have heard many people disagree with you, and this may be a cause for some of the perceived threats." Later another sergeant threatened to "bust him in the mouth." Yet another told Hall he was not entitled to religious freedom "because he had no religion." [13]

Experts say the official numbers of such complaints

in the military vastly undercount such incidents because service members are afraid of retribution if they do come forward.

Mikey Weinstein of the Military Religious Freedom Foundation told the *New York Times* that he has been contacted by more than fifty-five hundred service members, the great majority of them Christian, about incidents of religious discrimination, ranging from prayers "in Jesus's name" at mandatory functions, which is a violation of regulations, to the proselytizing of subordinates by their superiors. "Religion is inextricably intertwined with their jobs," warns Weinstein. "You're promoted by whom you pray with."[14]

Specialist Hall did not only serve as a true patriot by risking his life in Iraq; he served as a true son of Jefferson and Franklin by speaking out. Though the Justice Department has as of this writing simply ignored the lawsuit he has filed, Hall believes his speaking out is ultimately worth it. "Even if it [the lawsuit] doesn't go through, I stood up," he says. "I don't think it is futile."[15]

Many brave men and women from all political and religious backgrounds in the military are taking risks themselves to speak up in defense of this principle of the separation of church and state. One is David Antoon.

Even if you didn't know him, it would still be hard not to guess that David Antoon was trained as a soldier. Now sixty years old, Antoon still looks years younger, a slim, handsome man with salt-and-pepper haircut regulation-short. Antoon had traveled across the country from his home in Ohio—taking time from his work as a commercial pilot—to speak out on behalf of liberty.

He joined me for our conversation wearing a dark shirt and khaki slacks, both without a wrinkle. He stood to greet me, then sat down with the composed posture and bearing of a former combat pilot.

Antoon put his career on the line because he believes in standing up against what he sees as the taking over of the military academies by evangelicals.

He descends from a military family. Antoon's father served in World War Two, then stayed in the military after the war. Young David grew up on army bases around the world. His mother is Protestant; his father, Catholic. He was, he said, "positively exposed to religion" as a child and as an adolescent.

Ever since he was a boy, Antoon knew he wanted to fly. As a young man, he applied to the Air Force Academy. Antoon not only got his wings, he served two separate tours as a combat pilot. "In 1970 I graduated from the academy. Then pilot training; then Vietnam.

"I flew C-130s in Vietnam, in Cambodia. I thought, 'My government is right. I do what my government tells me and I trust my leadership.'

"Then, you realize your classmates who died in Vietnam died for a lie. It's all a fraud.

"So when this war kicked off, they're talking about WMD. I am thinking about the Gulf of Tonkin. I went through an evolution from believing to questioning. There are so many connections I saw between Vietnam and this Iraq war. Connections between the atrocities of My Lai and those of Abu Ghraib."

Nonetheless, in spite of his misgivings, Antoon fought bravely and was decorated for his courage in Vietnam. He received three Air Medals and the Distinguished Flying Cross—"for getting shot at," he says, laughing.

"After Vietnam they came out with 'The Soldier's Creed,'" he said, "as a direct result of My Lai. The goal was to put a stop to atrocities. But 'The Soldier's Creed' has now been replaced with something called 'The Warrior's Creed.' 'The Soldier's Creed' was about loyalty to unit, to victory, to ethics, and to honor. 'The Warrior's Creed'? Victory at all costs. Nothing about honor. A commitment to engage and completely destroy the enemy in close combat."

Antoon described how his teenage son also wanted to attend the Air Force Academy. His pride in his son, indeed, his delight in each of his four children, shone out from his face as he told his story. The young man was accepted to his father's alma mater with a full scholarship.

"I went out to the Academy with my son," he said. "We got out to orientation. At that time he was eighteen: a private pilot, glider pilot, skydiver, technical rock climber, National Merit semifinalist." I smiled; his pride in his son was contagious. "My son was admitted; he was going to attend the Air Force Academy. His dream.

"We walk into the orientation—General Johnny Weida is walking on the stage. Every other word he is saying is 'warrior.' Nothing about honor.

"Then we go to the chapel. Ten chaplains are standing shoulder to shoulder. All of them are evangelicals. They are led by Chaplain Watties.

"Chaplain Watties was boasting about having half the cadet wing attending Bible studies in the dormitories on Monday nights. He told the incoming class that he hopes to expand those numbers with their participation.

"When I went to the Air Force Academy, there was mandatory chapel. But the Supreme Court said it was unconstitutional and did away with it.

"What's happened in the military now is that there are cells of evangelicals who are being placed in key positions and advanced. Military leaders are attending prayer services in uniform. They used to teach the Constitution in the military academies. Now they no longer do so. Yet we have these religious fanatics—from Jim Dobson's church in Colorado Springs, Focus on the Family— invited to actively teach and evangelize in the dormitories. We see the results of that right now: officers whose loyalty is to a religion first.

"Military leaders [such as Air Force general and Academy graduate Jack Catton] saying in public, 'We don't have enough Christians in Congress.' Military leaders who say, 'My primary responsibility is to proselytize to the Joint Chiefs of Staff.' West Point Commandant of Cadets Caslen said, 'We are the aroma of Jesus Christ here at the Pentagon.' The loyalty of these men was to the religious ideology, the political party—not to the Constitution.

"People serving in the military now know that their careers are jeopardized unless they sign up to be evangelized. Religious loyalty is more important than the Constitution now; religious loyalty is more important than the oath of office."

"Soldiers take an oath of office? Like presidents?" I asked.

"Yes, it is very similar to that of the president. Every soldier promises to 'preserve, protect, and defend the Constitution from all enemies, foreign and domestic.' The first loyalty of a U.S. soldier, of every American in uniform, is to the Constitution."

"Why is it important for a U.S. military officer or soldier to defend the Constitution first and not place first loyalty to a religion?"

Antoon said, "You can see what is happening: our form of government is being shredded by religious zealots. At the Academy, I saw this warrior mentality and this religious mentality coming together at the expense of our service to the Constitution.

"The more I investigated, the more I realized the religious thing was not just in the academy. I came across the Christian Embassy: it is all these general officers making all these outrageous statements about their first loyalty being to Christianity, not to the Constitution.

"I am now part of the Military Religious Freedom Foundation—Mikey Weinstein and I founded it. I went to the Academy grads with this message. I got lambasted. Not one Academy grad stood up with me and Mikey and said, 'This is wrong.' One chaplain stood up and said it: Chaplain Melinda Morton. She was immediately reassigned to East Asia someplace. She resigned and she went public.

"I wrote articles in [websites] Truthout, Truthdig. I wrote about the evangelization in the military academies. What happens when you have church and state mixed allows what is going on now: U.S. soldiers offending Iraqis by handing out religious medallions; General Weida sending out e-mails with biblical passages in them.

"The danger is like what we have now with Blackwater. You are going to have your military being controlled through ideological means and reinforced with religion. Your democracy is gone. The rule of law is gone. We see it in what's happening now."

I said, "What if there's a coup? I have to ask. Is there any training for the military in the event of a coup?"

"I don't know of any. Your loyalty is to the commander in chief. If the commander in chief is leader of the coup, what are you supposed to do? Have him arrested? By whom?

"This is exactly why it is so important that the military's allegiance as citizen soldiers, not warriors, be to the Constitution and not to a religious or political ideology. As a soldier, I was taught individual responsibility. That was part of 'The Soldier's Creed.' If your commander orders you to do something and it is a war crime, you will be held accountable. So it is your responsibility not to follow illegal orders. That training keeps us safe—from committing atrocities like those we are seeing now, but it also keeps us safe from being overtaken by a coup.

"Why is there a separation of church and state? To keep us safe in this way from a militarized religious force or a militarized political party.

"We now have a right-wing cultish political group that has gained control of the military.

"It's not about their God," Antoon said. "It's not about our God. It's about the Constitution. It's about international law. As a soldier, you cannot give your primary loyalty to a specific religion and give your primary loyalty to the Constitution at the same time.

"Our Constitution is based on loyalty to rule of law, not faith-based ideology. What we see in Iraq is the demonizing of people based on religion. What is precious about the United States is our not demonizing.

"I think history will bear out that when you have a culture that is so intolerant of others—a religious culture taking over a secular institution—this intolerance breeds contempt. It allows what we are seeing today: we are seeing the demonization of Muslims across this country."

"Why is that un-American?"

"Why?" Antoon looked at me as if I'd asked the most obvious question in the world. He raised himself to his full height and squared his shoulders. " 'All men are created equal,' " he said. "Regardless of race or religion.

"My issue is not just religious freedom. It is the separation of church and state. I have no problem with anyone expressing their own religion in their own church. But when you have a prison guard in a prison—that's what the military is like—and your boss says, 'I want you to come to my church with me' or 'You're not Christian enough'—or you realize that in order to succeed, to be promoted, you have to toe the religious line . . . I have had officers come to me and say they have not been promoted for that reason.

"Chaplain Melinda Morton wrote to me saying, 'I can corroborate everything you said. I wasn't allowed to be up-front at your son's Air Force Academy orientation [with the evangelical chaplains] because I am Lutheran. I had to observe from the choir loft.' All the other chaplains got promoted for being silent. Loyalty pays. Loyalty to unit or party pays. Loyalty to the Constitution does not pay. Except for Chaplain Morton, not one Academy officer challenged this extreme religious fundamentalism, which now permeates the Academy and the military.

"These kids coming back from Iraq—they are all wounded. It is psychological damage." Though he is clearly a man of emotional restraint, Antoon's eyes began to well up. "Can you tell any one of those kids they have supported and defended the Constitution by their actions in Iraq? You cannot. That is where the grieving really sets in, the post-traumatic stress disorder. I think people can bear sacrifice if it is justified—if there is a valid cause.

"You show me the valid cause for what we've done to Iraq. When you come to the reality of over one million dead, over four and a half million refugees—we are having all these suicides among returning soldiers—I think when your government has put you in a situation that results in over a million deaths of Iraqis, most of them innocent, and your buddies are dying—how do you reconcile that? You can never reconcile that.

"Our military actions in Vietnam resulted in over three million dead, mostly civilians. It resulted in the destabilization of the region and the resulting genocide ("killing fields") in Cambodia. As a Vietnam vet, I contributed to what I now consider a war crime. I have some spirituality. When my preacher stood up in my [Christian] church and promoted this Iraq war, I committed to my family that I would never attend church in this country again. When the drumbeat for this war began, if I had said or done nothing, I would have been guilty.

"One of the toughest things I ever did was to discuss all of this with my son. He decided not to attend the Academy. Giving up his lifelong dream to attend the Academy also meant giving up a scholarship of hundreds of thousands of dollars. My son would have been a fantastic fighter pilot. But I did not want him to be a murderer. I did not sleep for several months after my son turned down his scholarship.

With his airline retirement pension now terminated, Antoon is still working full-time as a commercial airline pilot, even though he is actively fighting prostate cancer. Vietnam veterans exposed to Agent Orange have a very high rate of cancer, including prostrate cancer. "The legacy of cancer and mutagenic birth defects we have left in Vietnam is now being repeated with the poisoning of the Iraqi landscape with depleted uranium from American weapons," Antoon says.

"I turned to my son and said, 'Torture, occupation, Gitmo, Haditha, Fallujah. I can't do this.' Instead: 'Constitution. International law. Decency. Humanitarianism.'

From a citizen soldier's point of view we have lost our conscience, lost respect and self-respect.

"What would it feel like for a U.S. soldier to defend the Constitution? The soldiers in the era of World War Two probably felt their sacrifice was worth it.

"Not once since I took that oath of office, in 1966, have I supported and defended the Constitution. But by pointing out the errors of our present administration and of the past, I am supporting and defending the Constitution.

"Dissent is the greatest form of patriotism. You pay a huge price for it."

"Is it worth it?" I asked.

"I don't have a choice. Because I understand what is happening."

"It would [be] easier for you personally to be silent," I said.

"It would be like being in a building that's on fire and not pulling the fire alarm," he answered.[16]

AMERICANS DELIBERATE WITH THEIR NEIGHBORS; WE DISAGREE WITHOUT VIOLENCE

The unity of freedom has never relied on a uniformity of opinion.
—John F. Kennedy

America has believed that in differentiation, not in uniformity, lies the path of progress; it has advanced human happiness, and it has prospered.
—Louis D. Brandeis

The founders gave us a map to an America in which citizens can deliberate with one another without fear of violence.

All over the world, neighbors respond to their differences in culture, opinion, ethnicity, and religion with violence. Sunni and Shia in Iraq, Bosnian and Serb in Bosnia, ANC and Boer in apartheid South Africa: it is the norm in places not supported by the American idea. Do we disagree—on women's role, on Sharia versus secular law, on national historical narratives? Can we resolve it? All over the world, bloodshed is the resolution.

We read about these conflicts with a kind of fatalism; is this just human nature? "America" redeems human nature. Here we can disagree profoundly, even vehemently, with our neighbors without violence. The main exceptions to this rule—our shameful history of lynching and, of course, the butchery of the Civil War—erupted from the suppression of liberty and equality. And certainly riots—conscription riots, race riots, fights between laborers and conspiracy agents—have turned Americans against one another. But for the past few decades, to an extraordinary degree, people with no shared subculture, ancestry, belief system, or social mores have lived side by side in our nation without organizing in groups to murder each other. Red states these days do not engage in pitched battles with blue states; conservative Utahns do not cross over into liberal California to abduct travelers at gunpoint or bomb electrical plants and dams; gay people in San Francisco do not gather at night in militias to travel to Sacramento to torch the homes of homophobes; ranchers in Idaho do not murder the children of environmentalists in their beds. It is not that these different factions like each other; they may actually hate each other. But all our diversity doesn't—though it could—lead us to be more like sectarian Iraq or Northern Ireland during the Troubles.

This is so obvious a good that we scarcely think about it. What is the source of this incredible blessing? *Why* do Americans as a rule not find it necessary to harry and kill those with whom they disagree?

We have seen that we are able, in general, to do this because we have access to free speech; because we cherish the rule of law; and because we are protected from the state establishing religion. But one support for this blessing is that we have been asked by the founders to deliberate seriously with our neighbors.

Citizen Deliberation

We need to reclaim our history of citizen deliberation with one another, which is now in decline. Ordinary people in America are meant to be the pundits; they are meant to discuss the issues of the day with one another and reach their own conclusions to put into policy terms for their representatives' actions. We are not meant to be passive recipients of the deliberations of an elite. Ever since before the nation was founded, observers have been amazed by our expectation that the average person must deliberate the issues at hand. In New York in the 1750s, a commentator remarked on "how common it is to see a shoemaker, tailor or barber haranguing with a great deal of warmth on the public affairs."[1] With surprise, he noted that a colonial worker would "condemn a general, governor or province with as much assurance as if he were of the [king's] privy council." Workingmen throughout the colonies would meet weekly in clubs such as that formed by Benjamin Franklin, called the Junto (or the Club of the Leather Aprons), to debate and deliberate issues such as indentured servitude or civil liberties.[2] The well-known founders, most of them proud of this situation, which was unique among nations in that time, championed the need for citizens to remain informed; consequently, of course, many of them, including Jefferson and Franklin, felt strongly the importance of a rigorous public education to support such deliberation and to train future generations to sustain it in turn. "Only a politically informed citizenry could keep a people free," Gary Nash remarks of this point of view. As John Adams wrote in 1765, "The preservation of the means of knowledge among the lowest ranks, is of more importance to the public, than all the property of all the rich men in the country."[3]

The publication of Tom Paine's pamphlet *Common Sense* is a classic example of the power of the revolutionary idea that ordinary people should lead national debate and determine national outcomes. The argument for seceding from Britain grew stronger the more people discussed the pamphlet and heard one another out in relation to it.

But we have lost touch with our identity as the leaders of debate and deliberation. These days, most of us tend to watch rather than to drive our national debates. Many citizens I heard from seemed almost shy about asserting their views on major issues of the day in front of their neighbors. Even if they were able to do this comfortably, they did not feel that their discussions with their neighbors about such issues "counted." It was media debate, they often believed, that was legitimate; they told me that they felt that what happened on TV was more "real" than what might happen in their town hall meeting, let alone in their own living rooms.

But when Americans deliberate with one another, it changes everything. Studies of citizen participation—summarized in Yale professor Bruce Ackerman and Stanford's James S. Fishkin's book, *Deliberation Day*—show that this is utterly necessary if we are to be revolutionaries again. Right now, we have, in Curtis's term, "abdicated."

"The general public's political ignorance is appalling by any standard," Ackerman and Fishkin found. A researcher in the citizen engagement field noted that "the political ignorance of the American voter is one of the best-documented features of American politics." Still another concluded that "the verdict is stunningly, depressingly clear: most people know very little about politics, and the distribution behind that statement has changed very little, if at all over the survey era."[4]

A major study by the Shorenstein Center at Harvard University of the 2000 election asked respondents about six key positions held by Bush or Gore. Most Americans questioned could correctly identify only one of the candidates' positions. In the average answer, 46 percent of those surveyed said they did not know and 16 percent got it wrong.[5]

Three fourths of U.S. citizens queried in another survey about key aspects of democracy could answer only 13 percent of the questions correctly, though "many of the facts known by relatively small percentages of the public seem critical to understanding—let alone effectively acting in the political world: fundamental rules of the game; classic civil liberties . . . the names of representatives; many important policy positions of Presidential candidates or the political parties; and significant public policies."[6] Horrifyingly enough, if you take seriously the founders' belief in an informed citizenry leading the nation, "surveys show the American public does slightly worse in locating the parties' positions than it would do if it proceeded by flipping a coin."[7]

Fishkin and Ackerman offer a hopeful, concrete solution to this. They have found that Americans are not doomed to clueless exclusion from civic understanding and leadership—indeed, that given the chance to learn the issues in a clear, un-"spun" format and discuss them in a substantive way with one another, citizens' levels of being accurately informed, engaged, and active shoot up dramatically. A 2003 issues convention along these lines in Philadelphia, for instance, started out with only 19 percent able to identify rightly the amount the U.S. spends on foreign aid.[8] "But after a weekend's discussion, 64 percent knew the right answer, and 53 percent wanted to increase spending levels."[9]

The two men propose a new civic holiday—Deliberation Day. They suggest that it be "more like Thanksgiving than Washington's Birthday—something you really want to participate in." It would actually be a two-day holiday (one of the days picking up on Presidents' Day) to accommodate emergency workers such as police officers and firefighters. Deliberation Day would take place during presidential election years and a Congress Day would take place during federal midterm elections.

In their model, which they have tested with great success, citizens gather for National Issues Day (though perhaps we could, together, come up with a zingier name). Citizens join one another in a set of large- and small-group discussions at schools and community centers. The candidates respond to questions chosen by representatives of a cross-section of citizens and present a seventy-five-minute debate, divided into sections by key issues. The candidates would also distribute to everyone as he or she arrives a 1,500-word statement on each issue. You couldn't help knowing where everyone actually stood. It would be much less spinnable than our current setup.

Then the debate goes to citizens themselves. The model begins with a debate in a small-group format—then moves to a five-hundred-member Citizens' Assembly with a nonpartisan moderator.

Representatives of the two parties are onstage. The moderator takes questions that the small groups have decided on together. "The Citizens' Assembly will, in short, be a real-life continuation of the National Issues Debate that began on television," explain the authors. "Only this time, it won't be a 'representative town meeting' asking the questions"—what I would say is the current bogus format of televised debates. Rather, "local citizens will be doing the job themselves, and local party members will be trying to respond on behalf of their candidates." [10] That means you get follow-up questions and someone really present tasked to answer them. It means that you can pin them down. And it will mean substance, not trivia, since local people are unlikely to put up with one another's wasting collective time on boxers versus briefs.

Another session convenes after lunch, when citizens—who by now are acquainted with one another—can give their foremen and forewomen more questions for clarification and cross off the list the ones that they feel have been covered. By four p.m. there is a concluding session, giving citizens the chance to sum up their impressions.

There is no voting on these days. The point is "not to come to final decisions but to think about what's at stake." At five p.m. citizens receive a certificate of participation—and a $150 stipend, an amount the authors defend on several grounds. Citizens leave their discussion site to face TV cameras and press who are eager to hear how it has gone and to talk over the events of the day with their friends who are attending the second day coming up.

Is this Utopia? The authors have run events based on this model in cities around the nation, as have others in the "deliberative democracy" movement. The results are clear. This kind of event yields "large and statistically significant" differences in waking people up in civic life. In one study, deliberation changed people's opinions for two thirds of the issues. Respondents realize after the experience that they might as well toss out their previous views since they were insufficiently informed. People in such gatherings read more, absorb more information, and pay more attention—since they know they will be personally speaking about the issue.

Studies also prove that such deliberation among citizens not only raises the quality of people's informed opinions but of their skill in understanding what was at stake when they voted.[11] It does not favor any one group. The data also show that everyone has the potential to deliberate, regardless of background, and that discussion leaders emerged from every demographic. Americans from all walks of life found that they were learning a lot from their fellow citizens, also regardless of their backgrounds. One final amazing outcome backed up by the research was that this kind of event, whether on a local or national level, "leads respondents to take some responsibility for the solution of public problems." Citizens in Texas, for instance, were far more willing to pay more for renewable energy after deliberations convened to give citizens a say in how utilities should provide power for the future.

Finally, the studies find that this kind of deliberation makes people happy—probably in Jefferson's sense of the word "deliberation is satisfying," the authors found. Three out of four Americans rated such events they had participated in as being "an extremely valuable experience." Overall, such deliberation led to a strengthening of what the founders would have called "public spirit."

So let's have a national Deliberation Day—and local ones as well. Let us confer with our fellow citizens and see their faces once again, as we were asked by the revolutionary generation to do. Deliberation Day too, along with direct democracy, must be part of our renewed American revolution.

THE RISE OF PUNDIT CULTURE

How is it that we stopped taking our deliberations with one another seriously, or forgot how to deliberate altogether?

We were trained to. The past three decades have seen the rise of an institutionalized corporate pundit culture whose profits would be threatened by the people locating the source of ideas and authority in themselves and the minds and opinions of their neighbors, threatened if we were locating the most exciting debate available to us in the community center down the road rather than in our passive absorption of *Hardball* or *The O'Reilly Factor*. So to protect media profits, citizens must become acclimated to the notion that their ideas aren't good enough, aren't interesting enough, that they are not "experts" and that only "experts" can appropriately drive national debate. And corporate interests quite apart from media conglomerates are satisfied when the national debate is driven by a handful of subsidized think-tank "experts"—who will never demand real accountability—rather than by the people themselves. Is this a conscious mandate? No, of course not; but it is one unconscious reason you will almost never find ordinary citizen activists or grassroots citizen leaders in the Rolodexes of producers of national TV or radio programs.

I often go on national TV debates as part of my job. The exchange is designed to be adversarial and superficial. In a pre-interview, which screens you, you are often coached or encouraged to take a diametrical position to that of the other "expert." If you say, "Well, there's some truth to that position," you are not playing ball.

I have also been privileged to have been able to listen to citizens in various contexts discussing the same issues. There is no doubt that ordinary American citizens' discussions with one another tend to be better informed, more collegial, more judicious, more personally engaging, higher-minded, and obviously less scripted. They would certainly make more informative television. The debates on the community level have the luxury of going into greater depth—for they are not constrained by a break every six minutes for a commercial.

But even in a reality-TV era when ordinary Americans are put center stage to eat insects or engage in catfights, corporate culture will surely never reflect the powerfully interesting deliberations of American citizens without an uprising of our own. For if the people can stage exciting, informative debates for themselves, why would they need Chris Matthews or Bill O'Reilly? And if they find that what they are saying to one another in their own homes, or the videoblogged debate they stage and post, is more engaging than the "debate" on national television, that is a direct threat to the market value of the advertising space involved.

The media market has no incentive to listen to you or reflect your real concerns. So stop paying so much attention to the puppet show that now passes for debate. *You* need to be the pundit.

The most profound experience I ever had in my life along these lines—about how we can disagree with our neighbors and deliberate with them powerfully—was brought home to me by a group based in Washington, D.C., called Search for Common Ground, with their "Project for Life and Choice."

I received a surprising invitation: this group invited me to join other pro-choice writers and activists—and, remarkably, a group of pro-life writers and activists—for a weekend of discussion and deliberation under their auspices on a campus in Madison, Wisconsin. I was both horrified and intrigued; like most pro-choice activists, I had lived a whole lifetime formulating my ideas about abortion rights without ever having come in contact with a pro-lifer. My impressions about pro-life activists were based on seeing them protesting in highly emotive clips on national TV, or on watching speakers from both sides engaged in the adversarial posturing that Sunday-morning political TV shows stage-manage, or on accounts, filtered through pro-choice advocacy groups' literature with its own agenda, of pro-lifers' hostile, antiwoman, religious-fanatic attitudes. In the pro-choice rhetoric of the time, pro-lifers were seen as motivated primarily by the desire to repress women for religious reasons. Pro-choice interest groups often portrayed their opponents as wishing to ensure that women suffer through pregnancies they do not want and bear children they cannot support. Then, we were told, they just turned their backs on the babies once they were born. Horrible people. I had experienced, from this acculturation, a lifetime of demonization of absolutely anyone who held any pro-life views. And I had never had any face-to-face deliberation with any such citizen to shake or complicate these stereotypes in my head.

Needless to say, the pro-lifers I met that weekend had experienced exactly the same lifetime's worth of acculturation in demonized stereotypes of us. Most of them had never actually met a pro-choice activist either. Many had received a mirror-image set of distortions of us: pro-choice activists were all antagonistic to the nuclear family, sexually promiscuous, or anti-motherhood ideologues; that almost none of us were mothers ourselves, or if we were, we would not be good mothers; that we were personally amoral or immoral, we were callous about the suffering or death of innocents ("baby killers"); and that we were actively hostile to all religious faith. Horrible people.

I had never entertained the remotest notion that a pro-life activist might have come to her or his position through motives recognizable to me—through sincere concern for poor women, or for women's well-being, or for the sincere well-being of children as a whole. And many of the pro-life activists I met had never entertained the remotest notion that a pro-choice activist might have reached his or her position through motives recognizable to them: through a faith life, through ethical concerns, or through caring passionately about the well-being of mothers and children. Few had ever heard abortion-rights activists acknowledge, as I knew we did among ourselves, the painful ethical dilemma in choosing abortion, or the sadness with which many women terminate their unwanted pregnancies.

For that entire weekend, we were guided by the skillful, gentle group discussion leaders through exercises that compelled us to hear one another out and confront one another face-to-face. The exercises also compelled us to dredge up and look at our stereotypes. This let us go into a place that TV debate almost never gets to: not who is up or down, not what law will prevail—but rather, citizens' true confrontations about the real issue at hand: the problem of suffering women, the problem of millions of unwanted pregnancies in America.

This was a revelation to me. I was sitting at a table with "the enemy"—and yet the men and women I had been taught to disdain were decent, compassionate people. To my amazement, all of us in that bland conference room in that small town in Wisconsin that weekend, whatever our political backgrounds, had more in common with one another than we did with most people outside that room— whatever their political backgrounds. Overwhelmingly, the people gathered were there because they cared more than most people did about the suffering of women and children.

I know that "the enemy" was having the same surprising experience of "us."

Eventually, the group leaders from Search for Common Ground led us through exercises that actually let us talk about possible ideal outcomes.

Again, to my amazement, the solutions we developed together as citizens deliberating with one another were far better than the policies on offer on the national level— filtered as they are through established, even massive, non-profit organizations on both national sides, through politicians on both sides, and through media outlets determined to showcase only conflict. Both sides offer positions without nuance: the pro-choice lobby crafts policies that go further on the abortion-on-demand spectrum than most citizens wish to go; the pro-life lobby crafts policies that go further on the no-abortion-for-any-reason spectrum than most citizens wish to go. Why should the national debate not more closely reflect the ambiguities about the issue that most thinking Americans actually feel? Because the profits and the continued relevance of the institutions of both sides depend on maintaining these extreme positions— and on maintaining the other side as "the enemy." The pro-life and pro-choice professional leaderships are actually threatened when we talk to one another constructively, just as media and corporate interests are threatened. Indeed, I have come to believe that the national-level stoking of partisanship and labels—gay, straight, Republican, Democrat, left, right, pro-environment, pro-business—is a divide-and-conquer tactic, part of the push back against the citizen power of the last thirty years.

But when we deliberated with one another directly, their side agreed to make contraception much more easily accessible—which was a surprise to me. Our side agreed to give out information at abortion clinics about adoption possibilities and referrals to organizations that would help mothers support their babies if they chose not to terminate their pregnancies—a concession from our team that surprised them as well. I know that both of these examples of our loosening aspects of our original positions came from our having experienced a raised level of trust in the basic good intentions of the people who disagreed with us overall.

And when we were done? We had, together, sketched out a scenario of outcomes that would actually give real women a much greater level of help in avoiding unwanted pregnancy—and would also give them a much better range of choices and practical support in the event that they did face such a pregnancy.

I left that small, humble conference having experienced a complete dismantling of my prejudices, and I could never return to them. I understood that fine people on both sides believe in different policies to address our shared concern for women's and children's struggles. After that experience, I could never assume that those I faced on the other side of the spectrum—the pro-lifers, the evangelicals, or the staunch Republicans—weren't good, smart, caring people. From then on, I had to assume the "enemy" was likely to be someone I should approach with respect and should be ready to learn from.

That experience in Wisconsin was unusual. That tradition is almost dead.

To drive our revolution we must turn to one another once again. We will see how you can lead such moving, meaningful, and ideally cross-partisan or transpartisan deliberation—in your living room and your community as you take back your America.

LIBERTY IS UNIVERSAL: AMERICA CANNOT MAINTAIN AN OPPRESSIVE EMPIRE

*Self-government: . . . Why, these people are no more fit
for self-government than gunpowder is for hell.*
—General William Rufus Shafter in Cuba, 1898

D o Americans own "America"? Or were we rather asked to provide and offer "America" to everyone in the world who longs for it?

Thomas Paine believed that "no man or country can be really free unless all men and all countries are free."[1] Robert Kennedy wrote that our power to hold up the light of liberty overseas would protect us far more effectively than would an aggressive use of our military might: "Over the years an understanding of what America really stands for is going to count far more than missiles, aircraft carriers, and supersonic bombers."[2] He noted that John Adams believed America's freedom was part of a divine plan to support liberty worldwide: "This faith [of Adams's] did not spring from grandiose schemes of empire abroad. It grew instead from confidence that the example set by our nation—the example of individual liberty fused with common effort—would spark the spirit of liberty around the planet; and that once unleashed, no despot could suppress it, no prison could restrain it, no army could withstand it."[3]

Jefferson was categorical about the universal right to liberty: he wrote to his friend John Dickinson, "A just & solid republican government maintained here, will be a standing monument & example for the aim & imitation of the people of other countries; and I join with you in the hope and belief that they will see from our example that a free government is of all others the most energetic; that the enquiry which has been excited among the mass of mankind by our revolution & its consequences will ameliorate the condition of man over a great portion of the globe."[4] To John Priestley, Jefferson mused, "It is impossible not to be sensible that we are acting for all mankind: that circumstances denied to others, but indulged to us, have imposed on us the duty of proving what is the degree of freedom and self-government in which a society may venture to leave its individual members." Addressing the citizens of Washington, Jefferson said: "The station which we occupy among the nations of the earth is honorable, but awful [that is, "awesome"]. Trusted with the destinies of this solitary republic of the world, the only monument of human rights & the sole depository of the sacred fire of freedom & self-government from hence it is to be lighted up in other regions of the earth, if other regions of the earth shall ever become susceptible of its benign influence."[5] And to his former political rival but lifelong friend John Adams, Jefferson wrote: "The flames kindled on the 4th of July 1776 have spread over too much of the globe to be extinguished by the feeble engines of despotism. On the contrary, they will consume those engines, and all who work them."[6]

• • •

I was forced to face something categorical—yet one more overturning of fake patriotism. To be "American" is not, properly understood, to be a U.S. citizen, nor is it a designation of one's birthplace or one's parents' passports. Americans, properly understood, do indeed form a nation, but it is a nation held together by a common consciousness, not by geographical limits. "Americans" are not confined to the United States. They do not form a nation contained by the boundaries of the coast of Massachusetts and the southernmost point of Texas and the northern edges of the Great Lakes. They constitute a nation whose borders are psychological. The writing of the founders absolutely holds that the principles of universal rights upon which our own nation was founded must apply to any people anywhere in the world.

The longing for "America" is universal—and it is not a longing for the stuff we have. "That longing for freedom is so visceral, so deeply felt as an inalienable human right, that [dissident] writers like Anna Politkovskaya and Ken Saro-Wiwa valued it over life itself," writes Carole Seymour-Jones, chair of the Writers in Prison Committee of PEN. Orhan Pamuk, the Turkish novelist, writes that "modern people" long for freedom of thought and expression "as much as they long for bread and water."[7]

Today, the United States holds military bases around the globe. If these were only looking out for our strategic interests, this policy would not so violently contradict the founders' mandate for us. But since 1893, when the U.S. helped overthrow the Hawaiian monarchy, and the Spanish-American war five years later, we have often abandoned our founding mandate as a republic, as the brightest upholder of others' liberties, to commit some of the cruelest subversions of the liberties of other men and women.[8]

As historian Stephen Kinzer puts it in his history of U.S. regime change, *Overthrow,* "The invasion of Iraq in 2003 was not an isolated episode. It was the culmination of a 110-year period during which Americans overthrew fourteen governments that displeased them for various ideological, political and economic reasons."[9] Kinzer's study looks at those cases in which "the United States arranged to depose foreign leaders. No nation in modern history has done this so often, in so many places so far from its own shores." If slavery was the first dark temptation by which we lost our true soul, this kind of commercial imperialism is the second. Kinzer argues that the Spanish-American War led to "a radically new idea of America" that was far more "globally ambitious" than the original—than the founders'—idea. More alien still, this would be a different America, one that "had assumed the right to intervene anywhere in the world" not only through pressure or diplomacy but through simply overthrowing other governments—including, sometimes, democratically elected governments that shared the founders' own ideals—to replace them, often, with murderous puppet dictators.

In 1909, corporations got involved directly for the first time. President William Howard Taft wished to ensure that Nicaraguan president José Santos Zelaya would be overthrown. Taft told the American people that this was necessary "to protect American servicemen and promote democratic principles," but his real goal was to clear the way for "the right of American corporations to operate as they wished in Nicaragua. . . . This set a pattern."[10] In the ensuing century, America again and again used its military and intelligence forces to overthrow governments in order to advance the agendas of U.S. corporations who had "maneuvered friends and supporters into important positions in Washington." Many times after 1909 when corporate interests drove such an intervention—to their own benefit, not the American people's, I would add—Kinzer demonstrates that the action was sold to the U.S. public with a narrative about U.S. safety and upholding foreign freedom: "Each time, it cloaked its intervention in the rhetoric of national security and liberation. In most cases, however, it acted mainly for economic reasons—specifically, to establish, promote, and defend the right of Americans to do business around the world without interference"— including legitimate "interference" from local populations on issues such as basic taxation, workers' rights to minimal standards including the right to unionize, and environmental protections.

Throughout the twentieth century, industrialists moved beyond merely influencing U.S. foreign policy and started frankly to determine it. When President McKinley contravened Cuban independence in 1900 and Congress passed the Platt Amendment in 1901, a new set of notions—greatly deviating from the founders' ideal of the universality of liberty—entered the American self-concept. McKinley's decision, and the Platt Amendment, "gave the Cubans permission to rule themselves as long as they allowed the United States to veto any decision they made."[11] Imagine what Tom Paine would have had to say about that.

Cuban patriots, who had been fighting for independence using the very ideals of the American founders, were shocked to be treated "as a people incapable of acting for ourselves" and forced into a role of "obedience" and "submission." McKinley's goal? An island suitable for U.S.

investment at 6 percent. In that conflict too, Americans were propagandized with a narrative that they were offering Cubans unalloyed "liberation"—and they were surprised and offended that the Cubans were not grateful. Is this sounding at all familiar?

With this new, lucrative twist in the American mission, we began to betray our promise to the founders in a new way. In Nicaragua, lumber interests did not want to replace the trees they had cut down or pay a tax on the lumber concession. And President Zelaya made the mistake of borrowing money for his country from Europe, not from the U.S. In retaliation, the U.S. secretary of state began a propaganda campaign—one of what would be many in the future aimed at heads of state we wished to overthrow, whatever their personal qualities—to portray Zelaya as a bloodthirsty monster. Soon American newspapers were screaming that Zelaya had imposed " 'a reign of terror' . . . President Taft gravely announced that the United States would no longer tolerate and deal with such a medieval despot." Taft sent warships to the Nicaraguan coasts, and Zelaya resigned—"the first real American coup." [12]

President Dávila of Honduras—who was not deferential to U.S. power—was deposed in 1910 under pressure from an American banana king, Sam Zemurray. The U.S. forbade Dávila from using his own army to protect himself. After Dávila was gone, U.S. lumber interests, combined with the power of the American corporation United Fruit, "controlled a string of presidents" in Central America— propping up several of the bloodiest despots of the twentieth century.

The methods were refined in Latin America, which is why historian Greg Gandin calls that region "Empire's Workshop." [13] But they didn't stay localized there. In 1953, the CIA turned against passionate nationalist and democracy advocate Mohammad Mossadegh. Mossadegh supported civil liberties and due process. When he became prime minister of Iran in 1951, "he was determined to expel the Anglo-Iranian Oil Company, nationalize the oil industry, and use the money it generated to develop Iran." The Iranian people saw that monopoly as having caused untold poverty and wretchedness in the country. Both houses of the Iranian parliament voted in support of this plan.[14] But a U.S.-backed coup was successful, Mossadegh was arrested, and Shah Reza Pahlavi took the throne. The U.S. installed its own guy, General Zahedi, as prime minister, and the secret police, Savak, began their reign of terror. Iran's moment of opening to embrace aspects of democracy was crushed, and Iran swung to fundamentalism partly in reaction to the excesses of the Shah and his police state.

Just a year later, the CIA "crushed a democratic experiment that held great promise for Latin America" by overthrowing Jacobo Arbenz Guzmán, who had taken office during Guatemala's "democratic spring" of 1944–54. Arbenz had the temerity to challenge United Fruit.

Guatemala's National Assembly passed the Agrarian Reform Law, which sought to break up the monopoly that United Fruit held over 550,000 unused acres of land. The assembly was not anarchic: it wished to give United Fruit full compensation for the land. But United Fruit and its allies in Washington saw this as communism. A CIA-backed army invaded Guatemala; planes bombed the settled countryside. Arbenz was forced to surrender. As he bade his people farewell in a last radio message, he said, "The United Fruit Company, in collaboration with the governing circles of the United States, is responsible for what is happening to us. . . . I have not violated my faith in democratic liberties, in the independence of Guatemala and in all the good that is the future of humanity."

As Kinzer concludes: "As in Iran a year earlier, [the U.S.] deposed a regime that embraced fundamental American ideals but that had committed the sin of seeking to retake control of its own national resources. "[15] Remember the Stamp Act?

Remember Jefferson? He wished to place a column at the southernmost end of Cuba and inscribe it *"ne plus ultra"*—or "not more beyond." He hoped the U.S. would accept no territory that could not be defended without a navy: "Nothing should ever be accepted which would require a Navy to defend it," he wrote. Indeed, he envisioned America's influence as "an empire for liberty."[16] "What a germ we have planted," Jefferson wrote proudly to Benjamin Austin from Monticello. "And how faithfully should we cherish the parent tree at home!"

Cuba, the Philippines, Hawaii, Nicaragua, Guatemala, Iran. If we are to be revolutionaries again, it is worth this brief tour—so we can't pretend we don't know what is being done in our name, and so we can force our representatives to spread democracy through moral suasion, "soft power"—not cruelty, military or dictatorial "hard power"—wherever the U.S. flag appears in the world.

After so much of this, our light, which Jefferson and Adams saw as a global gift and global responsibility, is dimming worldwide. Says Karina Gerlach of the United Nations, "In most of the rest of the world our problem is that we don't have checks and balances, separation of powers. But people thought, 'At least in America there will be due process. . . .'

"This—what you are doing with subverting liberties—goes against everything America stood for. The Constitution is an amazing, amazing document. It's been so subverted. It's a message of 'Do what I say, not what I do' to the rest of the world now.

"America was always looked at as an influence for good. You should care about this. You're no longer an example. When you talk about democracy worldwide, you have no moral standing any longer.

"What is the UN legitimacy? Only its moral power. Your power used to be far greater and it too was moral power.

"Without America as a light to the nations, what else do we have?" [17]

Stephen Kinzer argues that each time corporations would benefit from a conflict, hyped war fever swayed most citizens to support the conflict. So, there has been a century in which American citizens were often manipulated to support policies that were not in their own interests—and that crushed liberties overseas. [18]

With our taxpayer money, many of these U.S.-backed puppets have used exactly the methods our founders rebelled against: funded pretty directly by us, they have stripped journalists of freedom of speech, imprisoned citizens without warrants, tortured opposition and labor leaders, rewritten constitutions to solidify their hold on power or torn them up altogether, used secret police and secret prisons, terrorized citizens—and gone most violently against those citizens who are most bravely seeking for their nation what our founders sought for us.

It is a sad truth that, because of the nature of the media bubble around us, most of us have only impressionistic knowledge of these foreign-policy crimes in our names against liberties overseas. But the rest of the world does know a great deal about it. This history of our subversion of liberties globally drives much of the hostility to the U.S. worldwide today—hostility to the very nation that was so admired by developing democracies at the higher points of our history.

But many of us do actually know something about this. And most of us have chosen to pay almost no attention. Or we rationalize the policy with some smug half-conscious assumption—yes, democracy is good for us here at home, but *we* can handle it. Surely if our government is suppressing democracy overseas it is because something scary will happen if liberty falls into the wrong hands. I must tell you, this is how slaveholders spoke about slaves when the nation was founded. This is how landed gentry in the revolutionary era talked about ordinary Americans who were not extremely wealthy: the franchise, representation, is good for us—but those working people, those black people, those women can't handle it. Or else we believe the corporate conflation of *their* interests with *our* interests: surely keeping that dictator in that place is somehow in our national interest. We believe this, even though a strong case is made by current political philosophers that global democracies keep us safe—that democracies are more stable and do not easily go to war against other democracies.

We have closed our eyes to the crimes committed worldwide by our own representatives with our own money against our own legacy to the world.

Can we live with this failure of our leadership, not only domestically but globally? And personally, can we stand this contradiction?

By the founders' definition of our mission, an "American empire"—let alone a repressive one—is a contradiction in terms. The American DNA holds that liberty is universal and transitive—that everyone in the world is equally entitled to it. As the nation discovered with anguish, in the centuries of slavery and in the Civil War, you simply cannot be a true American while subduing liberty in others. As we must painfully learn today, you cannot be a true American and train dictators to subvert freely elected governments around the globe.

OPPRESSIVE AMERICAN EMPIRE: A "CRUCIFIXION OF FEELINGS"

Abraham Lincoln said that a house divided against itself could not stand. He also said that to support slavery as a true American, you had to "crucify" your feelings. I believe he meant this to be true psychologically, not only tactically.

We too are crucifying our feelings by turning away from how corporations are driving our foreign policy to repress others. We too require a change in consciousness to be whole again today—this time in relation to our nation's perverted addiction to our empire. To reclaim ourselves, and essentially our reason for living, we have to be willing to look directly at it and be sickened by what we have become.

We have a bad conscience that we do not wish to examine. It banks the fire of felt liberty within *ourselves*. It violates what we instinctively know to be true, which is the universal and transitive nature of freedom. Psychiatrists know that a violent split within the self can lead to psychiatric problems. The same is true for us as a nation. There is a pain that is depression, certainly; there is a pain that is loneliness or overwork; but there is also, especially if you are American and thus exposed to the light of the original ideal, a muffled pain that is a corrupted conscience about how we are suppressing our brother and sister "Americans" overseas.

The notion of our occupying Iraq, holding now eight international journalists there in our own prisons, and sending our theorists surrounded by armed men to "teach" democracy abroad at the point of a gun would have horrified a Jeffersonian revolutionary. The Kissingeresque notion of realpolitik—in which you accommodate violent despots such as the monsters of the Soviet Union and turn a blind eye to dissidents locked up in their prisons—would have also horrified the original patriots. While stark geopolitical interests did, of course, inform the choices of foreign policy that the infant country made, also central to discussions of who our true allies were at the end of the eighteenth century were assessments of which country— France or England—was a more genuine friend not only of our own people's but of their own people's liberty.

Imagine if the way a foreign government treated the liberty of its subjects were not at most a side item in U.S. foreign policy, but rather formed the central consideration for which nations could boast an alliance with the great United States.

Natan Sharansky spent years in the gulag system, accused of treason, because he organized Soviet Jews who wished to emigrate. Recall that in his book *The Case for Democracy*, Sharansky argues that the distinction between what he called a "free society" and a "fear society" is one of consciousness. He asks those of us in the free world to ask of every nation we interact with the following questions:

Can people in that country speak their minds?

Can they publish their opinions?

Can they practice their faith?

Can they learn the history and culture of their people?[19]

And the actions of those in the free world have a profound effect on those fighting for liberty abroad: "We dissidents could ready ourselves psychologically for a life of risk, arrest and imprisonment. But we could never fully prepare ourselves for the disappointment that came from seeing the free world abandon its own values."[20]

Sharansky and other leaders in the fight for global democracy beg the United States to base its foreign policy on these questions. Our leaders will not do so if we do not demand it of them ourselves—driving global change with our "democracy commando teams." "The nations of the free world," Sharanksy argues, "can promote democracy by linking their foreign policies toward nondemocratic regimes to how those regimes treat their subjects. Those regimes are much more dependent on the West than the Soviets ever were."[21] The problem, Sharansky says he soon discovered after he began to make this case, was not that "the West lacked the power to spread freedom around the world, but that it lacked the will." He notes with despair that American leaders tried "to stifle democracy for the sake of 'stability.' *Stability* is perhaps the most important word in the diplomat's dictionary. In its name, autocrats are embraced, dictators are coddled, and tyrants are courted." Sharansky proposes though that our truly exporting liberty would actually make the world more stable. "Rather than attempt to thwart the democratic will of these peoples, I suggest that America focus its efforts on helping all parties manage the difficult transition to democracy." He points out that our support for human rights made us immensely safer in at least one example: support for dissidents in the Soviet empire—and the monitoring of human rights abuses there by the Helsinki Group—helped to bring down the Berlin Wall a few short years later and to ensure for our children the end of the dangerous brinksmanship of the Cold War. "By facilitating that process [of supporting democracy and human rights] America would earn the lasting appreciation of those peoples," enhancing its own security and, he adds, placing us in a better position truly to lead a volatile, post–Cold War world.[22]

If Jefferson were transported forward in time by a time machine, if he were president today, would he be planning, as our president is as I write, to attend, bringing U.S. prestige, the opening ceremony of the Olympics in a nation that sent its own military to mow down protesters for democracy?

What if our new clout—with our democracy commando teams and with our new powers of national initiative and referenda—forced our diplomats, our State Department officials, our CIA, our presidents, and our congressional leaders, in their dealings with foreign powers, to act as patriots on our behalf, in line with the original DNA of the true "American" idea? Imagine if we would be safer or less safe in such a world, even given the complexities of the international political scene. We could, in fact, be a "light to the world," a city on a hill, as John Winthrop charged us to be.

Republican candidate for president Ron Paul drew a tremendous grassroots following in 2007–8 because he had the courage to say out loud, "Let us give up our empire and become a republic again." His audiences intuitively realized the connection between our domination of others and our sense of our own diminished liberty. They understood that our often brutal empire creates global dependencies, addictions to entanglements, and henchmen. Worst of all for us, it leaves us as a nation existentially unfree.

Sharansky notes, "Even those who do hate America do not necessarily hate free societies. Rather, part of their hatred is due to the perception that by supporting the nondemocratic regimes that are oppressing them, America is betraying the democratic values it claims to uphold."[23]

"A nation torn by injustice and violence, its streets patrolled by army units—if this is to be our country," wrote Robert Kennedy, "we can doubt how long others will look to us for leadership, or seek our participation in their common ventures. America was a great force in the world, with immense prestige, long before we became a great military power. That power has come to us and we cannot renounce it, but neither can we afford to forget that the real constructive force in the world comes not from bombs but from imaginative ideas, warm sympathies, and a generous spirit. These are qualities . . . of a people pursuing decency and human dignity in its own undertakings without arrogance or hostility or delusions of superiority toward others, a people whose ideals for others are firmly rooted in the society we have built for ourselves."[24]

All over the world today people live in hope of receiving this inheritance of ours and of entering "America." Carole Seymour-Jones notes that in one year alone (2006), over one thousand "journalists and publishers in one hundred countries . . . were imprisoned and persecuted for exercising the right to write. Over the last two years, there have been over four hundred uninvestigated cases of writers and journalists murdered with impunity." (The three sections of the PEN anthology *Writers Under Siege* are divided into "Prison," "Death," and "Exile.")[25]

Who are these people? These are true "Americans" as well. Jiang Qisheng is a Chinese pro-democracy activist who was arrested in May of 1999 because he wrote and distributed an open letter marking the ten-year anniversary of the crackdown in Tiananmen Square; in his letter he asked Chinese citizens to light candles in memory of those killed standing up for liberty; he was charged with "propagating and instigating subversion" and thrown in prison for four years. Ali al-Dumaini is a Saudi writer and poet who called for reform of human rights abuses. He was charged with threatening "national unity" and spent nine years in prison. He was beaten, threatened, and tormented with cold water. In a terrifying interrogation, he saw posters on a basement wall that read CONFESS AND YOU WILL SAVE YOURSELF. In his interrogation he learned that a dear friend and colleague of his in the democracy movement, Khaled al-Nuzha, had sadistically been tortured to death. Al-Dumaini concluded, "He died an innocent man, as did many others before him such as Sa'ud al Muammar, Wasfi al-Madah and Abd al-Rahman al-Shamrani, yet they remain symbols of steadfastness and witnesses to the sacrifices made by patriots who are seeking to establish justice, freedom and democracy."

In Syria, Faraj Ahmad Bayrakdar was held for seven years and tortured, falsely accused of being a communist.[26] In a stunning elegy for liberty, he writes of his yearning for his lover—years-old memories of sexual intimacy, revisited with no hope of his ever touching a woman or feeling her love again; he writes of the fading call of his child: "Her mouth smiles / her eyes teary / she calls out / in the photograph / Daddy!" He writes of his mother folding away "fourteen skies" of his absence like a fabric. What is incredible about these patriots for liberty is that someone like Bayrakdar knows he may well lose all this personal love and pleasure, all his family life, but risks it nonetheless for universal principles.

Above all this personal loss he writes of the greater loss:

> There is no freedom
> outside this place
> but it cries
> whenever it hears keys
> laughing in their locks . . .
>
> Freedom is a homeland
> and my country an exile . . .
>
> Scientists and priests,
> historians and philosophers,
> fortune-tellers, leaders and sages,
> religions,
> parties,
> and armies
> but no truth.[27]

Asiye Guzel is a young Turkish woman, the editor of a newspaper, who was arrested in 1997, "accused of involvement in an 'illegal' organization," held for five years without trial, just as we are holding the detainees in Guantánamo; she wrote of being raped and tortured in prison.

What we did in Guantánamo between 2001 and 2008—a place where JAG lawyers were told that there must be no acquittals, a place where torture elicits false confessions—is what the Turks did to Guzel. The state used false documents to frame her.[28]

" 'What do you think these are that we found in your flat?' asked the security forces.

" 'What do you mean?' I [Guzel] asked, looking at the

various false documents that were laid out in front of me. I replied, 'There was nothing like that in our flat, they don't belong to us,' and as I said that, I was slapped heavily by someone at my side. Was my jaw broken? I wondered.

" 'I want to get in touch with my lawyer and my family.'

"They laughed."

In Uzbekistan, the state seized Mamadali Makhmudov, an opposition leader, and "ceaselessly" tortured him and dozens of other young activists—with techniques such as menacing by dogs, electrocution, and sexual threats against female family members.[29]

Like the founders, his courage is unbelievable. In the face of overwhelming authority, they just do not shut up. While still in Jaslyk death camp, being beaten by truncheons daily, starved, and forced to crawl naked, at risk of being murdered at any moment, he would *still* not stop talking about liberty: Makhmudov wrote a letter that he smuggled out to the rest of the world criticizing his captors. When you read this, he will probably be put at further risk because Makhmudov *is still there*.

" 'Stability,' 'peace,' all that is a lie," he wrote while in the hands of his captors. "When will this mob become human? . . . Science and agriculture have died out. Depravity is everywhere. Everything—riches, the press, radio and television, publishing—everything serves one person only."

Yuri Bandazhevsky is also a true "American." He is a Belarusian medical professor who wrote critically of how the state had handled the aftereffects of Chernobyl on its citizens. Specifically, he believed that the fallout had caused higher rates of birth defects among babies in the Chernobyl area. Consequently, he was arrested on false charges of "taking bribes from his students." "Armed men," he wrote, burst into his flat, terrifying his wife and daughter, and "began searching the place, destroying everything in their path." They dragged him off under Decree No. 21, declared by the president of Belarus, which permitted such arrests "under urgent measures in the struggle against terrorism and other particularly violent and dangerous crimes." Held in solitary confinement, denied care for a duodenal ulcer, he nearly died. While he was chained to a bed, the government destroyed the important collection of embryos he had assembled that demonstrated the "congenital malformations" that he believed had resulted from the contamination at Chernobyl.

The man did not know what was good for him. He did not shut up about liberty. After he was provisionally released, even as the state continued to ready its case against him, Bandazhevsky did not go home and disavow everything; rather, he raced to his lab.

Knowingly risking his life, he "worked feverishly to prove the connection between radioactive fallout and malformation in the embryo." He hurriedly carried out the experiments he had begun on laboratory animals, the results of which stunned him:

"We were able to demonstrate that relatively small doses of radio-Caesium induced congenital defects. I believe that this was one of the most successful results of my whole long life in scientific research."

The verdict in his case was to be declared in only two days when the scientist was grabbed off a city street, apparently by the KGB, and driven to the Ukrainian border, where he believed he was to be killed. The KGB gave the guards fake passports; the scientist cried, "I'm professor Yuri Bandazhevsky. Please help me!" Bandazhevsky had been known for trying to find out what was wrong with Chernobyl's babies. At great risk to themselves, the guards then refused to let the murder vehicle pass. Nonetheless the scientist was dragged back to court and charged with trying to escape the country. He was imprisoned again for three years, his health continually deteriorating. Yet in his reflections on all this, the man wrote:

"In spite of the brutal and tragic change in my circumstances, and in my social standing, I have never lost the desire to think, reflect and analyze." [30]

Bandazhevsky, a true "American," did not know what was good for him.

Guzel and Bandazhevsky are Jefferson's descendants and, therefore, our brothers and sisters. It's time to rejoin our family. With them, we are in our true home.

A NEW AMERICAN
REVOLUTION

The true ideal is not opposed to the real but lies in it.
—James Russell Lowell

So the war is upon us. These subversions of our liberties now institutionalized forever, no matter which party leads the nation, unless we say no. No candidate on either side is seriously talking about fighting the war to restore liberty. Reclaiming our rights and freedoms—our true "America"—will have to be up to us.

But our capacity is great—if we use it.

Patrick Henry, when he called his countrymen and countrywomen to rebellion, did not say that true Americans were more powerful than the enemy. He said that true Americans were brave:

> The battle, sir, is not to the strong alone; it is to the vigilant, the active, the brave. . . . The war is inevitable—and let it come! I repeat it, sir, let it come! . . . I know not what course others may take; but as for me, give me liberty or give me death![1]

Patrick Henry has a many-times great-grand-daughter, born long after he died. She is Laura Berg, a psychiatric nurse who works at a Veterans Affairs hospital in New Mexico.

Berg wrote a letter to her local newspaper in Albuquerque, the *Alibi*. She denounced the U.S. government's handling of the Katrina disaster and criticized the Iraq War—whose destruction of brave Americans she seeks to heal every single working day of her life.[2]

"I am furious," she wrote, "with the tragically misplaced priorities and criminal negligence of this government. We need to wake up and get real here, and act forcefully to remove a government administration playing games of smoke and mirrors and vicious deceit." She identified herself, in her letter, as a Veterans Affairs nurse.

She was doing exactly what the founders had demanded that she do, what they themselves had risked their lives for her to do.

But what then?

"Her superiors," reported the *New York Times*, "at the hospital soon alerted the Federal Bureau of Investigation and impounded her office computer, where she keeps the case files of war-scarred veterans she treats. Then she received an official warning in which a Veterans Affairs investigator intoned that her letter 'potentially represents sedition.'" *Sedition?* That criminalization of speech critical of the government was exactly what Thomas Jefferson had fought to overturn more than two hundred years before. It took a senator and a slew of lawyers, reminding Berg's superiors of the Constitution, to get them to back down.

After Laura Berg fought back, her sector administrators advised her that they would not in fact prosecute her for "sedition." But they insisted that she must not identify herself as a Veteran's Affairs Nurse in any future letter writing.

So, being a true descendant of Thomas Jefferson, Elizabeth Freeman, and John Hancock, Laura Berg talked to reporters and went public.

"Some of my fire," she insisted, "in writing this about Katrina and Iraq is from my experience as a VA nurse.

"And so," Laura Berg said on the radio, loud and clear, "I am saying: *'I am a VA nurse.'* "

She had made a commitment to a piece of paper put together by Thomas Jefferson but inspired by the highest possible law.

And Laura Berg was sticking to it.

If I understood one thing now that I had not before my journey, it was that "America" was a place in the heart—it lived when Laura Berg spoke out, when David Antoon gave up a scholarship, when Josh Wolf chose prison. They had shown me how we could act to reclaim what we loved.

I had the chance to sail with a friend onto the Hudson River. It was at dusk in early summer. The last time I had seen the Statue of Liberty so close up was some time before. I had felt hopeless; she seemed like a memorial.

We anchored in a cove, sheltered behind her, in sight of the massive folds of her gown and far below the flame she held high.

I felt differently about her now than when my journey had begun.

Now I felt I could almost see the faces of the patriots I had met shining in her lit window and forming part of her flame. I now understood that it was they who were her light. And that light was far from extinguished.

PART III: AMERICA: THE USER'S GUIDE

I asked patriots in various fields—a citizens' council—to offer guidelines for action, recommendations, and summaries of some aspects of our system to equip any American who wishes to defend liberty. Each citizen's recommendations follow his or her bio. In addition, I've offered some of my own recommendations, and additional resources are presented for you, too.

Some contributions will be familiar to some readers depending on their age, background, and experience, and new to others. Skim and select as you choose. The overview offers a basic set of civic tools. We compiled a wish list at the end for laws, entities, and practices that we need to brainstorm about, create, enact, or build.

I. DRIVING CHANGE

Curtis Ellis gave an insider's view on how we can maximize our power as groups of citizens organized to drive democracy's changes—his term: "democracy commando force multipliers."

"DEMOCRACY COMMANDOS" [Curtis Ellis]

Curtis Ellis was born in Passaic, N.J., a tough blue-collar town, and grew up near Newark. His father, Joseph, was a furrier and his mother, Lorraine, a businesswoman. His father had been a longtime member of the fur union and he would tell Curtis stories of the fur strike in the 1930s: "He felt that FDR was the greatest president ever," Ellis remembers his father saying: "We criticize the United States, it's not perfect, but don't you ever forget, it's the best country on earth."

"My parents encouraged us to think for ourselves, to be proud of our heritage as Jews, and to try to make the world a better place. We always discussed politics, news, and world affairs around the dinner table. I remember having a Kennedy scrapbook when Kennedy was running for president.

"We organized concerts to raise money for the Chicago Seven and antiwar groups, we challenged local police to a snowball fight to protest laws we felt discriminated against youth—and we succeeded in getting publicity for our events. Media was a tool to disseminate the message and I pursued broadcasting as a career." When Ellis felt that the country had gone too far off track and the Constitution was under threat, he moved from CNN to Capitol Hill to try to help elect to Congress people he thought could fight the good fight.

How to Increase Your Clout with Electeds

I say, first and foremost, register and vote. When you call or write your congressman or senator (and possibly, though to a lesser extent, other local elected officials) on a given issue, often they check your name against the voter file (a list of all registered voters and their voting history, which tells them which elections a voter cast ballots in). If you vote, and vote regularly—that is, in nonpresidential years, in local elections, and in primaries—you are taken very seriously. If you're not registered, or registered but don't vote, you are not regarded seriously.

Votes Trump Money

The thing to remember is that votes trump money. The only reason politicians raise money is to buy ads that will reach voters. If you can deliver votes and voters, you have as much, if not more power, than people who deliver money.

Democracy Commando Force Multipliers

With that in mind, you become a democracy commando force multiplier by making certain that your friends, family, and neighbors are registered and that they vote regularly. Gather as many of their names together (on a letter, e-mail, or whatever you're using to communicate with your representative) when you communicate with your elected officials, and let those officials know that all these people vote—and that they talk to people (word of mouth, or as they call it now, peer to peer, being the most effective form of advertising).

You want to develop this group of friends and family into an *electoral affinity group* that works on issues that matter to you. Members of the group can register their friends to vote, write letters to the local newspaper, attend meetings of local government and party organizations (such as school board meetings, where they could press for civics education in the curriculum), and volunteer on local campaigns. You can also use your group to build community: bring food, hold debates, invite spokespeople on issues of the day, keep a website to monitor your community's agenda and leaders, break local news on the site, and leak the news to local and regional press. You are very powerful if you do those things, and it's fun.

Example

You can press the city council, town board, or county board to adopt a resolution calling on the U.S. Congress to uphold the Bill of Rights. It's purely symbolic, but you can use it to get press, and to encourage higher offices to adopt similar resolutions. You can talk to council members directly and go to local and county Democratic Party officials to let them know the number of people you represent (and whose names, phone numbers, and e-mail addresses you have) who vote regularly (though they have not been active in local party politics) and talk to other voters. You want the town council to adopt this resolution and would like the local party officials to talk to the city council members about introducing the resolution. You can also ask for the name of the person in the U.S. congressman's office you should contact about setting up an appointment. Let them know that if they help you with this, you will help them in the future by volunteering in local election campaigns.

You and your friends will develop a lot of influence by volunteering and bringing volunteers to campaigns for local officials, your congressman, and state reps. Such influence increases your clout exponentially. If you have a dedicated group of even five people who can be counted on to turn out and volunteer, your reps will never forget you and always listen to what you have to say.

ADDITIONAL RESOURCES

Driving Change

- For the full list of congressmen's names and contact information, as well as information about what committees they serve upon: http://forms.house.gov/wyr/welcome.shtml
- For a list of what is currently on the House floor and to search roll call votes: http://www.house.gov/
- Contact your U.S. senator: http://www.senate.gov/general/contact_information/senators_cfm.cfm
- Contact the president or vice president: http://www.whitehouse.gov/contact.
- Search for your congressperson's recent votes at *Congressional Record* online: http://www.gpoaccess.gov/crecord

II. SPEECH

Having begun by understanding the great strength ordinary citizens have in a democracy—that is, the strength of our numbers—we need to use our voices.

HOW TO PETITION

We can drive change with the power to *petition*. The First Amendment gives us the right "to petition government for redress of grievances." Petitions help citizens to use the strength of numbers to counter the power of wealthy donors and shareholders.

A *petition* is a list of names of people who are willing to back up a statement, assertion, or complaint. People are often unaware of the effectiveness of petitions because the powers that be do not really want that knowledge to be widespread. The Care2 petition site ("Start a PETITION, change the world!") at http://www.thepetitionsite.com includes a *template for a petition* that can be printed out and used to advance any cause. MoveOn.org's "Create an Effective Online Petition," in their pamphlet "50 Ways to Love Your Country," also describes the petition process. For example, an American who posted "No New Coal Power Plants!" collected more than 33,000 names to present to Congress.

Have people sign your petition by printing out multiple pages, clipping them to a clipboard, bringing pens, and going to your town square. Bring printed material, such as a *press release*, that explains your concern and the action you want the people you are targeting to take. You can also collect names online through generic petitions,

though politicians may not consider them to be as powerfully representative of their constituency's feelings. If you
are driving legislation that targets a corporation (say you
want to protect your community from a polluting power
plant or big-box development), send your petition in hard
copy with a cover letter to that corporation's chairman of
the board, who is listed on the corporation's website. Follow up with the head of the press office or communications office, whose information may also be found online.
This is your pressure point. These people will listen to you
and not pass you from phone line to phone line. Be polite
but clear with each person you speak to. And *leak your petition* drive either "on background" or "on the record" to
the reporter at your local and regional papers' business
news sections (see "How to Leak to an Investigative Reporter"). Taken as a whole, this strategy will get the attention of your community leaders most effectively because
both political and corporate leaders seek to avoid negative
local and regional press.

ADDITIONAL RESOURCES

How to Petition

- Start a national or global petition: http://
  www.gopetition.com
- Care 2: The Petition Site: http://www.the
  petitionsite.com/

HOW TO PLAY HARDBALL ONCE YOU HAVE
PETITIONED

It is fine to say politely but firmly what the outcome could
be if your group doesn't get a proper response. For exam-

ple: "Hi. I'm Jane Richards. I represent a group of citizens here in Tuscaloosa, Alabama. We are very strongly opposed to Acme Corporation's plans to open a plant on the river that will add to the level of particulates in the air that our kids are breathing and we are giving our petition against this, with its two thousand names, to Bill Smith at the *Tuscaloosa Herald*." At the same time, contact your town or city councilmember or your state representative. If your group's issue is national or international, inform your congressperson's communications director that you will alert the press if you don't get a proper response about the issue. Leave your phone number. Then tell the local and regional press about your petition and tie it to some newsworthy event that you will create. Also let the press know how the corporation and leader in question responded.

BECOME THE MEDIA YOURSELF

Stop relying on the corporate media; you must *become* the media. Everything you want to have the media cover starts with a *press release*. This is a one-page document that you will send to your local and regional media (as well as a few national outlets). The release should describe what is happening, lead with an attention-getting paragraph to grab the interest of the editor, give two or three paragraphs explaining why the subject of this release is news, and end with the who, what, where, and when of the activity you are highlighting. It must provide your name and contact information. Fax it to every outlet on your list.

Though citizens often feel invisible to the makers of news, the truth is that every local and regional newspaper has at least one reporter on staff whose job it is to cover what you and your fellow citizens are doing when you drive change. That is actually his or her beat. The best way for that reporter to learn about what you want them to know is to send them a press release and follow it up with phone calls.

Go to your local library and get *Bacon's Directory*, which is updated annually. It lists every media outlet in your region and in the nation. The three main targets you want to saturate are your local print media—meaning newspapers—and your local radio and TV stations.

Before your group of democracy commandos goes public, you should identify and train two or three people who should serve as spokespeople. Ideally, your group should send out each spokesperson according to how well suited each is to the demographic that is being targeted: a young person for your alternative newspaper, for instance; a parent for the morning TV show; a local shopkeeper to speak to the business section reporter.

HOW TO WRITE A PRESS RELEASE [Lisa Witter]

Lisa Witter is a vibrant, dark-haired, thirtysomething new mother. She is also chief operating officer at Fenton Communications. She has been passionate for years about helping citizens compete powerfully with corporate and other media messages because she believes that raised citizens' voices constitute what she calls "the essence of democracy." She shares what she learned doing commentary for MSNBC, FOX News, the Huffington Post, *the* New York Times, Newsday *and CNN.com.*

What is a press release and why would you write one?

A press release is simply an accurate, useful, and interesting statement prepared to distribute to the media about your piece of news. So, you write a press release when you want to alert the media.

A press release is your version of the perfect article about your event or issue. Write it so the journalist could cut and paste it if need be. Newsrooms are more short-staffed than ever and are relying on press releases to short-cut their work.

What is "newsworthy"?

Just because something is important to you doesn't make it important to the media. This is often a tough pill to swallow. Don't despair though; creativity is your friend and you can figure out ways to frame your issue/event in a way that is newsworthy.

What are the main elements of a press release?

- Contact Information: Make sure your press release has accurate contact information: name; phone; cell phone; e-mail; and website address. The reporter may want to call you for more information or a quote.
- "For Immediate Release" and Date: Make sure this goes in the upper-left-hand corner of the release. It tells the media when they can report on your news.
- Dateline: This is the location of the event or where the news is coming from.
- Headline: A headline can often make or break a news release. Reporters receive tens, sometimes hundreds, of press releases a day. Your headline needs to stand out. For exam-

ple, "New Report Says Breast Milk May Be Flammable" is much better than "Report Says Toxins Are in Our Bodies."

- Lede: The lede is often the first sentence of the first paragraph of the press release. It must answer who, what, where, and when. Remember that first impressions really matter, so make sure the lede is clear, well written, and says why the reader should care and why they should care now. If you had one sound bite describing the issue, the lede would be it.
- Second Paragraph: The second paragraph should provide additional information to support the lede. This is often the most important and newsworthy data or details.
- Quotes: When writing quotes make them short, pithy, and memorable. This is where your rhetoric can come in. Remember to write them exactly how you wish to be quoted.
- About Paragraph: At the end of every press release you should include a sentence or two about your organization. This often gets mentioned in the story.
- Hash Marks (###): These go at the very end of a release. They are from the era of the telegraph and tell the reader that anything after can be ignored. They are considered part of the formal grammar of a release.

This is the typical structure of a press release:

- Contact information
- Release date

- Headline
- Dateline
- Lede
- Second paragraph (supporting data/information)
- Quote #1
- Third paragraph (supporting data/information/other flavor)
- Quote #2
- Fourth paragraph (if necessary)
- About paragraph
- Hash marks

Other tips

- Length: It's critical, if at all possible, for press releases to be one page.
- Value language: When writing a press release it is important to use non-value-laden terms outside of the quotes. Any opinion must be inside of quotes and attributed. For example, never say "groundbreaking" or "important" or "excellent."
- AP Stylebook: It's important to have an *AP Stylebook* around while you're writing. You want to make sure you're using the correct words and spelling that reporters do. For example, the *AP Stylebook* says "Web site" or "Web" vs. "website" or "Website."
- Be clever: Reporters get a lot of press releases thrown at them. Being clever is important to breaking through the clutter. This does not mean metaphors with multiple

shades of gray. Sometimes you'll want to find
a good time hook (holiday or anniversary),
explain how your efforts fit into a trend, or
use an elegant turn of phrase.

CREATE THE DEBATE YOURSELF

The most powerful place in your local newspaper for you
to reach is the *op-ed page*, where you write the essay yourself. The op-ed page is not the same as the editorial page.
The editorial page is written by the newspaper's editorial
board. You can ask to meet with these people to educate
them, but they write the editorials themselves. *Editorials*
interpret the news, offering readers the newspaper's
"voice."

The open door for you, rather, is the op-ed section.
The "op" in op-ed does not come from "opinion"—though
these are opinion pieces. Rather, it comes from the fact
that the section is opposite the editorial page.

Op-eds are traditionally written by commentators who
are *not* on the publication's staff and are not syndicated
columnists. Believe it or not, most good op-ed editors are
longing for a well-written, passionate, informed, and publishable piece by you or your neighbors to come in "over
the transom," which means unsolicited. But non-experts
almost never send such pieces. So editors are forced to depend on a steady stream of submissions from the army of
dependable hacks that they are sick of hearing from: "experts" who are trained and funded by think tanks under-
written by corporations and vested interests.

A typical op-ed is 750 words. You start with a hook—
something surprising or newsworthy.

The structure is no more complicated than the basic

outline for an essay, which you learned in middle school. Give your hook, then your thesis statement, a sentence that tells the readers your main argument. Your first paragraph illustrates it and provides examples. Then a transition. Your second paragraph makes your second point and supports that point. Transition. The third paragraph does the same for your third point. Transition. Then call for action steps and/or make a specific recommendation. Your final paragraph is your conclusion, which is where the strongest punch or emotion should be. Obviously you can play with the paragraph count.

You can weave variations on this theme. If you have more than three main points, you will certainly have more than three paragraphs. But you must never exceed the stated word count, and if you use a lively, colloquial tone—not formal, jargon-laden, or fussy—fact-check, and follow this main template, punctuate and spell correctly, your op-eds will be publishable. Use personal stories, those of other people or your own, as long as you connect them to the larger point you are making. Feel free to say who you are and why you care about the subject at hand. Speak from the heart, and be aware that your expertise as, say, a factory worker, a parent, a soldier, or a homemaker is more interesting to an op-ed editor than more predictable material.

When you have written your 750-word op-ed, fax or e-mail it to the editor. Put your phone number and e-mail address on a cover sheet along with a one- or two-sentence pitch describing your subject and why this piece is timely. Be aware, though, that editors won't acknowledge the submission personally unless he or she accepts it.

If it is accepted, you will be contacted. Drop everything; take a sick day if you have to. You need to be available to edit this piece with your editor right away, because if it has been accepted this likely means that the editor wants to run it in the next day or two.

The editing process takes place first by e-mail. A professional approach is to go along with every edit that you can. Your editor sees things you can't. It is more important to work effectively with your editor and get the piece out quickly and smoothly than it is to be territorial about changes. That smooth turnaround ensures that this editor will now put you in his or her Rolodex—you are now an "expert"—and may well commission you the next time something comes up in the news that speaks to you or your group's issues or is more likely to take your next submission.

After your op-ed comes out, you may get responses—some of them agreeing with you, some attacking you. Your phone may start to ring from bookers for other media. You cannot go into hiding now. You have to follow through because you have engaged in democracy's debate and set its terms.

HELP FRAME THE NEWS COVERAGE

You can also get coverage for you or your group's concerns in the news section of the newspaper (also referred to as "hard news"), which is usually the front or main section. This section is where you want to *leak information* that you or your group may have about scandals, controversies, malfeasance, or corruption in your community, which an investigative reporter can pursue.

Most newspapers have investigative reporters on staff whose job it is to follow up on the information you leak, decide if it is newsworthy, document it themselves, and then turn it into a story. The powers that be are probably not scared of you as an individual, but congresspeople, business owners, and corporate interests are scared to death of this kind of investigation and disclosure in a newspaper's news section. An investigative report based on information you provide can affect the behavior of shareholders, the actions of federal investigators, and the decisions of voters.

HOW TO LEAK TO AN INVESTIGATIVE REPORTER

Look at the byline of the reporter who covers this kind of news in the front section. Call the main switchboard and ask for him or her by name. You will usually be put right through. Most reporters, even prominent national reporters, try to answer their own phones when they can. (Some well-known reporters have assistants who take calls, but if it is a strong pitch, a good story will get through.)

It doesn't matter to the reporter that you may not be famous or powerful. The quality of your information is what matters. Reporters are curious people and they know that a big story can come from anywhere. They will give you a minute and a half to hear you out. You need to decide how you will speak to the reporter in the time you have before he or she decides either to listen further or to thank you and hang up.

Speaking to a reporter *"on the record"* is the most personally risky way to pass on information, but it also has the most impact. If you are calling or speaking in person on the record it means your full name is attached to what you have said. You should assume that absolutely everything you are saying, even an aside or a joke, can be reproduced as a direct quote. In the rules of this particular game, everything is assumed to be *on the record* unless you specifically say you are speaking *on background* or *off the record*. You have to say "I am now going off the record" or "This entire conversation is off the record" to actually speak off the record. You can also go off the record, say what you want to say that the reporters can't write about, and then go back on the record by saying "I am now going back on the record."

If you say something you regret without having used those magic words, and then after the fact say "Please don't publish what I just said," your reporter is acting perfectly within the ethics of the game to publish *exactly* what you said as well as to publish your plea to him or her not to publish what you said.

It is not always necessary to go on the record, though a good reporter will always push you to do so (you can always resist if it is not the right thing for you to do). Another powerful tool for leaking information to a reporter when you do not want your name attached is to speak *"on background."* This means that he or she can reproduce your quotes but may not identify you by name as a source. You even have the power to help craft an identification that you both agree upon—one that backs up your basis of authority, which the reporter will wish to do, but does not actually name you. You could be described as "a source who is familiar with Earth First! practices."

The least effective way to leak to a reporter, but one you should not rule out, is to go *"off the record."* This means you talk, but the reporter can't quote you or identify you at all. However, the story is now in the reporter's mind if he or she wishes to source or investigate it and try to confirm it from a different direction. Whichever way you bracket your conversations with reporters, you have raised your voice, given your fellow citizens a powerful ally, and helped enable the operation of a free press.

HOW TO PITCH A FEATURE PIECE

Also try the feature section, which is "soft news," or lifestyle- and community-oriented news. This is an easier sell than the hard news section. Send the reporter you identify on this section a press release and follow up with a call that pitches an angle that would make the story interesting or timely for the readers.

What is a "pitch"? The people who run the country—news, politics, and entertainment elites—pitch to one another continually: in the elevator, at cocktail parties, at their kids' softball games. When you pitch to a reporter, you want to set it up so that you have already done most of the work to make the piece a reality. This makes it much more likely the reporter will be able to hear what is truly newsworthy about your story. The journalist has to think, with every call or press release: Is there a good individual I can find to tell this story? Where will I dig that person up? Will he or she be able to speak well about it or will it be a difficult interview? Is there a visual? Do I have to ferret out all the documents? Try to provide answers to as much of this as you can. The reporter can follow up or not but it makes your piece easier to produce.

A common mistake that groups or individuals make when pitching is to insist on telling the reporter what *they* think is important about their own project or event. I don't know how to put this more politely: It is not an editor's or a reporter's job to care what *you* think is important. Their responsibility is to their readers. Rather, look at your message from the reporter's (and their editor's) point of view and identify what angle would make it interesting or news-worthy for the reader.

When you contact a reporter, do not waste any time. Identify yourself and get to the point without using an extra syllable or engaging in chitchat. "Childhood asthma here in Tuscaloosa, Alabama, is up this year by twenty percent. We have school nurses on standby to talk to you who are saying it is a crisis. We know that the concrete plant by the river has exceeded the legal limit for emissions and the Acme Corporation is making it harder for our kids to breathe. We expect two hundred parents and kids to rally for cleaner air at a Breathe-In next Sunday at ten a.m. at the plant, which is located at 311 Center Street. We have asked a hundred Tuscaloosa citizens to show up wearing gas and surgical masks, so it should be a great visual. I can get you the very eloquent mother of a seven-year-old girl who has been hospitalized for asthma twice. We are also delivering a hundred of our kids' drawings about their wish for clean air to John Reese, the CEO of Acme Corporation, on Monday morning at ten. I can fax you three of the drawings—they look great. We have called the mayor twenty-three times for a meeting and he has not gotten back to us—I can fax the call record. I hope you can cover this. Can we expect you there on Sunday?"

So your story comes out. Your cause is on the radar. You are now a spokesperson.

This too may mean the local or national media will start to call you to expand on or defend what you have said.

RADIO

Once you or your group has been identified as a leader on your issue, you may be asked to speak on the radio. A producer will arrange to call you at a given time for a live or taped interview or will bring you into the studio. If you are interviewed by phone, stick to three main points and expand them to suit the format. You will go in and out of commercial time, which can be as long as three minutes; each segment for commercial radio is about eight to twelve minutes. Your host will indicate the cue to go on and off the air. You may be asked to take calls. Be polite to all callers, including those who may want to argue with you. It is all a chance to get your message across. Enjoy the exchange, tell stories, chat with the host, be warm and human, and speak from the heart about your issue. You have more time on radio than you do on TV.

TV

If TV producers wish to have you on a show, you will get a call from a "booker." The booker will say something like: "We are doing a piece on the controversy over the Acme Corporation plant tonight at six. Are you free?" There is often almost no lead time and the time they offer you is not usually negotiable—it is what they have an opening for. Say yes if you possibly can. The booker or a producer may then have a conversation with you to figure out what you are likely to say. This is called the "pre-interview." Be clear and concise, and stick to your three key points. The booker is making notes that will be given to the person who will interview you on the air. If it is a debate format, the booker or producer may give you a taste of the other side's position: "Some business leaders say that if we do things your way the community will lose good-paying jobs. What would you say to that?" Don't get defensive, either in the pre-interview or on screen. Being defensive never works well on TV. You should view any challenge or disagreement as simply one more opportunity to get your point across.

If the show is live, you will be cued and then the cameras will roll. The set is very hot, the lights are intense, and the time goes fast. The typical news segment is only three or four minutes. *Keep your comments short.* If the segment is taped, it will be a bit calmer since errors can be edited out, but your job is the same. If you are interviewed by satellite, you will be seated alone in a room with a monitor in front of you and an earpiece clipped to your ear, and you must imagine you are face-to-face with your host.

In a debate format, good-advice media coach Barbara Browning gave her clients what she called the "hit, bridge, and sparkle" technique: when confronted, you hit the criticism directly by acknowledging it and not defending yourself; bridge to what you really want to talk about; and sparkle in sharing with the TV audience the content of your chosen message.

When your opponent snarls, "You people are driving good-paying jobs out of Tuscaloosa!" you can reply, "I know many people are wondering if cleaning up your emissions will cost our citizens jobs. It's a fair question. I am glad to share the news, reported in May's *Tuscaloosa Register,* that in nearby towns, when citizens forced the plants there to clean up the air, it actually boosted the economy. Four major employers decided to move in. And I am sure eventually your own leadership will want to make the right investment in new technology to clean up your emissions, so we can boost growth while protecting the health of our kids."

The host will thank you both, and the segment wraps. Do not get up till you are told to by the tech people or camera crew; you may still be on camera. Don't stay and chat; your host is still about to go on live and has to focus on the next segment. Say good-bye to the host and your opposite number and leave the set quietly.

ADDITIONAL RESOURCES

Become the Media Yourself

- For issues and calls to action by groups and organizations that span the political spectrum in the U.S.: http://www.congress.org/congressorg/issuesaction/orgs
- The Center for Citizen Media enables and encourages grassroots media, especially citizen journalism, at every level: http://citmedia.org/about
- The First Amendment Center's website covers key issues and topics concerning the First Amendment: http://www.firstamendmentcenter.org
- The First Amendment Project is a nonprofit organization dedicated to protecting and promoting freedom of information, expression, and petition: http://www.thefirstamendment.org/

PRODUCE NEW MEDIA

New media technologies are allowing individuals who would not be able to have a voice in mainstream, traditional media venues to share their thoughts and opinions with a larger public. Web logs, or blogs, are one example of DIY Internet publishing that has created an alternate sphere of reporting and social commentary—and they are becoming increasingly accepted and popular as primary news venues. Elizabeth Curtis offers us her thoughts on creating a blog that will effectively get the word out:

HOW TO CREATE A BLOG [Elizabeth Curtis]

Elizabeth M. Curtis was born in Houston, Texas. Currently, she lives in Harlem. Her father, who is from Madison, Wisconsin, is a port engineer. Her mother, who is from Rockland, Massachusetts, works in an elementary school library. She feels as if many regions of America are part of her heritage. "Although I can't pinpoint an exact moment of my political awakening, I have been socially and civically active since I delivered a surprisingly liberal speech in first grade about what made me proud to be an American," says Elizabeth. Today, she uses her skills in electronic communications and her commitment to citizen education and organizing as a program director at the Woodhull Institute for Ethical Leadership.

1-2-3 Blog

Blogs have been proven to be effective tools for social activists to spread information and organize initiatives. To be heard in the blogosphere, all you need is an Internet connection and a little know-how.

By following these three easy steps, you can take your activism online via the blogosphere.

1. Become a "blog connoisseur" before you start your own blog.

Before you start you own blog, you need to get to know the "rules of the road" of the blogosphere. But succeeding as a blogger will take more than learning the do's and don'ts of Web log etiquette. Spending a little time acquainting yourself with blog activism will allow you to create a better blog product for more effective activism.

First, find blogs on topics that you find interesting and that report news that is relevant to your pursuits (later, you can link to this material to create your own blog content). For finding progressive blogs, AlterNet (http://www.alter net.org) is a good place to start. A great resource for finding blogs in your area of activism is BlogCarnival.com (http://www.blogcarnival.com), a website that lists blog posts that contain roundups of the best blog writing on the Web on specific topics. Blog carnivals are helpful if you do not have a lot of time to read blog articles daily but would like to read a current summary of what is being written on a specific topic in the blogging world. Plus, once you get blogging on your own, you can submit your blog posts for inclusion and spread your message to larger audiences.

Once you have found a few favorite blogs, you can automate information delivery by signing up for e-mail alerts and RSS feeds from the websites and blogs you most frequently visit. I recommend using Bloglines (http://www. bloglines.com) or Google Reader (http://www.google.com/ reader/). Analyze your favorite blog authors—how do they reach their audiences and keep them interested? What features do you most love about these blogs—do the bloggers use podcasts, video blogs, viral videos, or other Web 2.0 tools? And what content and features can you add to your blog that will innovate on the material that is already out there?

Once you're a blog connoisseur, you can start to build your blogging persona by sharing your opinion on others' blogs, by commenting on blog posts. Commenting on blogs is a great way to start dialogue, to network with other activists, and to share your opinions and ideas. Once you feel comfortable with the blog genre, you should submit your own blog articles to blogs for publication as a guest poster or columnist. You can build an audience in advance of your own blog launch by being a frequent guest on well-established blogs.

2. If you can send an e-mail, you can create a blog post.

I like to tell people who are feeling intimidated by building their own blog that they should feel confident—if you can send an e-mail, you can create a blog post. Many websites offer free publishing software that the average Internet user will feel comfortable using. Blogger (http://www.blogger.com) and WordPress (https://wordpress.com) offer great tools (and help discussion boards!) to novice users.

The most critical period in your blog's life will be its launch. Like any publicity campaign, you only want to make your blog public after you know that your product is tried and true. The best way to accomplish this is to spend one month blogging privately without making your blog "live" (i.e., available to the general public on the Internet). This strategy will allow you to develop a posting routine and voice that you feel comfortable with, work out any growing pains, and robustly populate your blog with content that will keep new readers coming back for more when you do launch.

Once your blog is live, spread the word. Comment on other blogs and provide links to your posts. Offer to guest-post on a blog with high traffic or invite a more established blogger to post on your blog to build your blogosphere street credibility. Submit articles to blog carnivals and, when appropriate, journalists or members of the press.

Go multimodal—incorporate social networking tools like Facebook (http://www.facebook.com) or Twitter (http://twitter.com) into your efforts to raise awareness about your work. Keep your content strong, spread the "link love" (remember, give more than you take and you will see a greater return in building community in the blogosphere), and experiment with different formats and technologies. Track what content or formats bring the most readers to your blog using website metrics like those offered by Google Analytics (http://www.google.com/analytics) or Site Meter (http://www.sitemeter.com). Soon you will be the staple of other RSS feed readers!

Also remember that consistency is key. Nothing will turn off a potential reader or viewer more than visiting your site and finding that your last post is two weeks old. Even two days is too long. If you want your effort to have any credibility, you have to make it a part of your daily routine. You don't need to reinvent the wheel five days a week, but you do need to offer some daily evidence of your commitment to stay on top of your particular issue or subject.

Finally, find blog mentors. The blogosphere is a very supportive place. You may be surprised by the support—technological and ideological—that you will find in other bloggers. Plus, you entered the blogosphere to build community around your cause—start with your fellow bloggers.

3. Don't forget about the digital divide.

While the world may be becoming increasingly wired, conscientious activists should keep the digital divide in mind. There are many individuals whose Internet access is limited—by geography, literacy, availability, and other issues. Before you start a blog campaign, first assess whether or not you will be able to effectively reach that audience online. And beware the bells and whistles (podcasting, video blogging, etc.) that require high-speed Internet connections or specific software to view if the individuals you hope to reach have limited technological capabilities. While viral videos might be effective for some activism campaigns, going door-to-door and passing out fliers might be a better way to reach certain communities. Blogging offers much promise in terms of enhancing your ability to spread information about the issues you care about, but the digital divide does create some barriers to its potential. As with many things, covering both print and electronic bases is probably the best strategy.

ADDITIONAL RESOURCES

How to Create a Blog

- Blogger: http://www.blogger.com
- Wordpress: http://wordpress.com
- Live Journal: http://www.livejournal.com
- Twitter: http://www.twitter.com
- Moveable Type: http://www.movabletype.org
- Site Meter: http://www.sitemeter.com
- Google Analytics: http://www.google.com/analytics
- AlterNet: http://www.alternet/org
- Blog Carnival: http://blogcarnival.com
- Bloglines: http://www.bloglines.com
- Google Reader: http://www.google.com/reader

Another effective way of spreading the word electronically is via video. We asked Will Coghlan for some tips on making a Web video that stands out.

HOW TO CREATE A WEB VIDEO [WILL COGHLAN]

Will Coghlan is a senior producer and founding partner at Hudson Street Media, a Manhattan-based Web video, film, and music production company. He is also the host of Political Lunch, *http://www.politicallunch.com, a daily commentary program on political affairs. Before joining Hudson Street Media, Will worked as the communications director for a national nonprofit organization, a communications adviser for a successful gubernatorial campaign, and a reporter covering presidential campaigns for a daily newspaper in New Hampshire.*

1] What made your Web video successful?

It became clear early on that our viewers appreciate the quick, engaging, no-nonsense style of our program. So in many ways, we found a void and filled it. You should apply that principle to most online content: if you don't have a clear mission or objective, something your viewers or readers know they can count on, then your content will just get lost in the millions of blog posts and videos posted online every day.

2] What tips would you offer other producers of online video?

In producing online video, keep it clean and professional. Resist the urge to use all those fancy transitions and effects that come with your editing software. Learn the basics well, and stick to them.

You don't need to spend thousands of dollars on your equipment. A decent, consumer-grade digital video camera and basic editing software will do the trick. Much more important than the money you spend on equipment is the time you spend learning to use it. Figure out how to compress your video files so they look good but don't take forever to download. Usually that's a trial-and-error process—frustrating, but worth it.

As much as we're using the Internet to *improve* on what the mainstream media fails at, we can also learn a lot from traditional media sources. We're talking about basic stuff: have you ever seen a shaky camera shot on CNN? Probably not. So copy the pros: get a tripod, and use it. You don't need a full studio set, but don't film with your laundry in the background. Find a neutral background that won't distract your viewers. Listen to your audio: if the in-camera microphone won't offer clean sound, pick up an inexpensive lapel microphone. These are the basic things that make a big difference but are often overlooked.

Once you've written a post or produced a video, ask a friend or colleague to give it a look. Listen to the feedback, and make the changes that you're comfortable with. It doesn't mean you're giving up control. If you listen to your audience and you find out what they want, eventually you'll figure out how to get your message across while growing your audience.

3] How should a new Web video producer make content?

Keep your online presentation clean. Resist the urge to clutter your blog with a dozen different widgets about your horoscope and the weather and all the places you've traveled. Again, it's about knowing your mission and sticking to it. Don't let your valuable content get lost behind superfluous clutter.

Most importantly, you have to be your own best advocate. If you think you have a particularly good post or content that no one else has published, send a link to other blog authors, reporters, publicists, politicians, professors, and experts. Don't be shy about promoting yourself and your content: if you don't believe in the value of what you're producing, no one else will.

ADDITIONAL RESOURCES

How to Create a Web Video

- Current TV is a popular website that supports citizen journalism through video: http://current.com
- Video editing software resources: http://desktopvideo.about.com/od/editingsoftware/a/freevidedit.htm
- Websites to help you create a video and share it on the Internet:
  - YouTube: http://www.youtube.com
  - blip.tv: http://blip.tv
  - Yahoo! Video: http://video.yahoo.com
  - Google Video: http://video.google.com
- Websites to help you upload a video to multiple sites simultaneously:
  - TubeMogul: http://www.tubemogul.com
  - Hey!Spread: http://heyspread.com
  - VidMirror: http://www.vidmirror.com
  - Vidmetrix: http://www.vidmetrix.com

- Photo-sharing websites:
  - Flickr: http://www.flickr.com
  - SnapFish: http://www.snapfish.com
  - Shutterfly: http://www.shutterfly.com
  - Picasa: http://picasa.google.com
  - Photobucket: http://photobucket.com

III. PROTEST

HOW TO DRIVE A BOYCOTT

Your group of "democracy commandos" can also drive powerful change by organizing a *boycott*.

The American Revolution began with a boycott. After the Stamp Act imposed extra taxes on goods in the colonies—infuriating colonists who were affronted by "taxation without representation"—the colonists reacted by refusing to buy and consume tea, fabric, and other goods imported from England.

Capitalism responds quickly and inexorably to market pressure. In America, the boycott is a legal and potent weapon to tweak the bottom line, where vested interests and corporations can feel the pressure. Boycotts by ordinary Americans, such as the campus-led push during the 1980s to divest—withdraw investments from—racist South Africa, helped lead to the more racially just democratic South Africa we are privileged to see today. In 1998, U.S. citizens organized more than 750 chefs nationwide to stop serving swordfish in their restaurants because of concerns that the populations of the species were being seriously depleted by market demands. Two years later, to protect swordfish from being fished out, the U.S. government passed laws that prohibited fishing in the areas where they reproduced. Citizens, accordingly, ended the chefs' boycott.

Co-op America can teach your commando group how to boycott. This organization (http://www.coopamerica

.org/about/) has a fourfold strategy: "buy, invest, boycott, demand change." According to the leaders of Co-op America:

"Any concerned group can call a boycott and any consumer is a potential boycotter. If you buy things, you have the power not to buy. If your friends and neighbors are among the target customers for a specific product or industry, you are in a very powerful position indeed.

"Investments you have bought can also be used to drive change. A majority of Americans own stock, and you can use the stock you own—even if it is only a small amount—to drive a shareholder resolution. A shareholder resolution happens when shareholders get together to demand a course correction by a corporation by putting it out for a shareholder vote. Shareholder resolutions have helped bring about such immense changes as divestment in apartheid-era South Africa; because of such actions, companies such as Nike have had to face their exploitive use of sweatshops and been forced by ordinary people to ensure that conditions in Nike's factories are not abusive.

"According to boycott movement leader Todd Putnam, 'Boycotts used to take between five and ten years to get results, but now they take about two. That's because they're better organized and get more media attention: corporations recognize the damage potential much earlier.' "

ADDITIONAL RESOURCES

How to Drive a Boycott

- Co-op America: http://www.coopamerica .org/about
- Online NewsHour website that lists all discussions and protests nationwide that emerged from a boycott: http://www.pbs.org/

newshour/bb/law/jan-june06/immigration2_
05-01.html
- National Black Boycott Information Bureau
  (NBBIB): http://www.nbbib.org/
- Boycotts.org: http://www.boycotts.org

Once you have run your successful boycott and beaten Goliath, you will want to register your success at http://www.boycotts.org to inspire others. Your democracy commando group must take to the streets.

Go to the Los Angeles chapter of the National Lawyers Guild's website to consult the section entitled "Your Right to Demonstrate and Protest" (http://nlg-la.org/). Marjorie Cohn, who runs the National Lawyers Guild, offers the following guidelines for how you can protest. These apply to California, but your own community's guidelines are also available from the National Lawyers Guild.

HOW TO TAKE TO THE STREETS [MARJORIE COHN]

Marjorie Cohn is the president of the National Lawyers Guild, a criminal defense attorney, and a professor at Thomas Jefferson School of Law. She publishes extensively in the academic and popular press about criminal justice, U.S. foreign policy, and human rights and provides commentary for local, regional, national, and international media. Her articles are archived at http://www.marjoriecohn.com.

Can your right to speak out be restricted because what you want to say could be considered controversial?

No. The First Amendment prohibits restrictions based on the content of speech. But your local police and government officials are allowed to place certain non-discrimina-tory and narrowly drawn restrictions on when, where, and how you can exercise your First Amendment rights.

Is there a specific location in town where you are entitled to use your First Amendment rights to speak and protest?

Generally, all types of expression are constitutionally pro-tected in traditional "public forums" such as public side-walks and parks. In other words, you are free to say anything you want in public spaces. Usually, you do not need a permit to picket or protest on the sidewalk, in a park, or in front of a government building so long as you allow pedestrians to pass on the sidewalk and you obey all traffic rules. You can march in public streets "subject to reasonable permit conditions," which means that you need a permit if you want the street closed to vehicular traffic for your parade or protest. That is, like the pro–Korean refugee and pro-Tibet groups, you will need to get a per-mit from the mayor's office, and they can't unreasonably deny it to you. You can also use your right to free speech in public locations such as the plazas in front of govern-ment buildings which the government has opened up to similar speech activities.

Is there anything else you need to know to keep your rally on track?

Generally "free speech activity," meaning your rally, can't take place on someone's private property if the owner of that property does not consent to it.

The National Lawyers Guild notes that some kinds of events require permits: if your march or parade is not going to stay on the sidewalk, or if you plan to block traffic or streets, or if your city requires sound permits for a rally that will need a "sound amplifying device" such as a bullhorn or sound system. Many permit ordinances let officials constrain the route of a march or the level of amplification your sound equipment makes. You may need to file for those permits some weeks or months in advance of your rally. However, the good news is that the First Amendment prohibits such advance-notice requirements from being used to prevent "spontaneous" rallies or demonstrations that are rapid responses to unforeseeable and recent events, such as a police shooting or bombing another country.

Can you pass out leaflets and other written material on public sidewalks?

Yes. You can approach pedestrians on public sidewalks and give them leaflets, newspapers, or petitions. You are also free to ask them for money donations, but some cities limit face-to-face solicitations for money on the spot. Check your local ordinances. You can set up tables to help you do this as long as you don't block people's way or block building entrances.

Can you be silenced if you provoke the crowd?

Generally, no. Even the most inflammatory speaker cannot be punished for merely inciting the audience. A speaker can be arrested and convicted for incitement only if he or she specifically advocates violence or illegal actions and only if those illegalities are imminently likely to occur. You could run a rally with signs that say SAN BERNARDINO SCHOOLS

SUCK as long as you don't tell your listeners to attack the school board members.

Do counterdemonstrators have free speech rights?

Yes. Although counterdemonstrators should not be allowed to physically disrupt the event they are protesting, they do have the right to be present and to voice their views. If another group runs a countermarch with signs saying SAN BERNARDINO SCHOOLS DON'T SUCK, they are perfectly free to do so. The police may keep two antagonistic groups separated but should allow them to be within the general vicinity of each other.

Is heckling protected?

In general, heckling is protected, unless hecklers are attempting to physically disrupt an event, or unless they are drowning out the other speakers.

What other types of free speech actions are constitutionally protected?

The First Amendment covers all forms of communication including music, theater, film, and dance. The Constitution also protects actions that symbolically express a viewpoint.

You can, say, wear masks and costumes—you can wear anything you want—or hold a candlelight vigil. It may be rude but the Constitution does not say you have to be polite. You can burn an American flag or the president in effigy. It is protected by the First Amendment but could be prohibited by local laws that prevent burning objects without certain protections against fire. Again, this is going to be a local law, so check with your local Guild lawyers. The rules for protesting on federal property may be significantly different from your local city and state laws, so be sure to check.

STAGING A PROTEST

Choose a significant venue. Think about a location that will be most effective. It should be symbolic, the way Boston Harbor was symbolic of the fight against taxed imports.

Look interesting. Almost every protest I have attended as an adult in the U.S. was uncoverable visually because there was nothing interesting happening for cameras to capture. People were dressed in boring ways, holding boring signs, and saying boring things. The great protests had color, a mass of uniformity, or a mass of spectacle, and used theater, music, and humor.

You want to have color so that you will be on the front page of your newspaper or so that footage of your protest will make good TV news clips. If you are protesting for the Constitution, for instance, have everyone dress in red, white, and blue; that will guarantee a front-page image rather than one on a black-and-white inside page.

Use theater. Ron Paul supporters tend to have at least one attendee dressed as an eighteenth-century patriot, in waistcoat, wig, and breeches.

Bring music. Today's protest leaders tend to talk and talk. Sing instead. The great protest marches used the singing of the marchers to uplifting effect and included protest songs, folk songs, national ballads, or spirituals.

Hold hands. Civil rights marchers often held hands.

The Estonians actually entwined their hands, creating lines of people that could not be broken. It is harder for agents provocateurs to claim that a crowd has instigated violence if they are peacefully holding hands.

ADDITIONAL RESOURCES

Staging a Protest

Protest against war: http://pax.protest.net/
* National Lawyers Guild: http://nlg-la.org
* Protest.Net: http://protest.net/

HOW TO BE SAFE AS YOU PROTEST

To protect yourself at the protest, you can:

* Wear a bulletproof vest, which will protect you from body blows and, to some extent, from Tasers. These are available at sporting-goods stores.
* Wear a bike helmet or a hard hat to protect your head from blows and Taser shocks.
* Wear work gloves and strong hiking or work boots for the same reasons.
* Carry a camera to document any police violence you see at the event. Try to learn the name of the officer involved and write it down on a small pad you can keep in your pocket. Also, write down a description of the violence and get the names of any witnesses as soon as you can.

ARREST

Most police officers are devout patriots and do not wish to beat or terrorize citizens or force them into narrow non-spaces for protest activity, but local regulations have compelled them to do so. As a result, if you break restrictive permit requirements, which I argue you must, they may need to arrest you.

Now what? It is illegal for you to do anything that can be construed as "resisting arrest." If a police officer takes you out of the crowd and says "You are under arrest," go quietly. This is not the moment to fight. You may be placed in handcuffs in front of your body or cuffed with your hands behind your back. You may be put in a police car—the officer will probably push you in with a hand on the top of your head; this is to protect your skull—or in a paddy wagon with other protesters.

Judges want the argument about whether an arrest was warranted to take place after the altercation, between lawyers, and not in the street, between police and protesters.

When the police seize you, "Try to stay calm. If you struggle at all, even if you lie on the street and refuse to move, it can be considered resisting arrest."

When you are arrested, *stay silent*, but do give your name and address. The police have the right to pat you down to see if you are carrying a weapon, but they may not search you until they have formally placed you under arrest. If you think you might be arrested, you should, of course, not be carrying illegal drugs. Don't carry sharp objects of any kind, as these can be classified as weapons, and don't carry on you names or phone numbers of your friends. However, keep your lawyer's number memorized.

Once you have been put in a police car or van, don't try to escape or try to persuade the police to release you. When you arrive at the police station, you must ask to call your lawyer. You can't count on someone else giving you coins or access to a free phone; have a cell phone, calling card, or pocket change on you. Ask a friend to bring as much money as possible down to the courthouse where you will be taken. If you are not told which courthouse it is, tell your friend the name of the precinct station where you are being held. Your friend should also call your lawyer or the defense committee that is overseeing your protest and arrest. The lawyer will meet you either at the precinct station or in court, depending on how serious the charge is you are facing.

You will not be permitted to take notes, so try to remember the name of the officer who arrested you, the time and place where the arrest took place, and any possible witnesses that your lawyer will want to speak to. If you can't find or afford an attorney, a Legal Aid lawyer will be provided for you for free.

At the arraignment you will hear the charges that will be pressed against you. You will be told your court date and what bail you will need to post. Your friend should arrive with a few hundred dollars toward your bail; if the bail is higher, there are bail bondsmen close to the courthouse who will lend you the balance for a fee if other responsible people cosign the loan. Once you are bailed out you should be in contact with a private attorney for the duration of your case.

You will be read your Miranda rights. This means that you must be told by the police officer arresting you that you have the right to remain silent and to consult with your counsel. If the police question you without having read you your Miranda rights, it means that nothing you say can be used against you at your trial. There are some exceptions to this, and it is also not true that your case will be thrown out of court if the police do not read you your Miranda rights.

The following is from the audiobook *Criminal Law Handbook: Know Your Rights, Survive the System*:

After I'm arrested, is it ever a good idea to talk to the police?

Not without talking to a lawyer first. Talking to the police is almost always hazardous to the health of a defense case, and defense attorneys almost universally advise their clients to remain silent until the attorney has assessed the charges and counseled the client about case strategy (that is, figured out how to defend the client and let the client know).

How do I assert my right to remain silent if I am being questioned by the police?

Suspects do not need to use any magic words to indicate that they want to remain silent. Indeed, they don't have to use any words at all. Arrestees may invoke their Miranda rights by saying things like the following:

- "I want to talk to an attorney."
- "I refuse to speak with you."
- "Please leave me alone."
- "I don't have anything to say."
- "I claim my Miranda rights."

If you make a statement voluntarily before you are read your Miranda rights, it can be admitted into evidence at your trial. Many people who are arrested "ignore the Miranda warning" and talk to officers when they shouldn't; they feel psychologically vulnerable, "intimidated by jail conditions," and wish to please those now seemingly "in control of their lives." Be aware of all these tactics, and *just don't talk* without your lawyer present.

When you have been released on bail, you may need to keep talking to the media. Your arrest and the issues you have raised can become a cause célèbre in your community. If your concerns are meaningful to your neighbors, both support and criticism may come pouring in. Perhaps others are organizing a countermovement. They may even start saying and writing negative things about you and your group. This is all great, it is fair game, and it is how democracy is supposed to work.

THE PERMIT SYSTEM [HEIDI BOGHOSIAN]

Heidi Boghosian is the executive director of the National Lawyers Guild. She is cohost of the weekly civil liberties radio show Law and Disorder *on Pacifica-WBAI in New York and several national affiliates. She has published articles and law reviews on the topics of policing, protest, dissent, and capital punishment. Her book reviews have appeared in* The Federal Lawyer *and the* New York Law Journal. *She received her law degree from Temple Law School, where she was editor in chief of the* Temple Political & Civil Rights Law Review. *She has a master's degree in mass communication from Boston University College of Communication, and an undergraduate degree from Brown University. She is admitted to practice in New York and Connecticut.*

What is a reasonable permit system that supports free speech?

A reasonable permit system must be content-neutral and based on "time, place, and manner" factors such as traffic-control considerations (i.e., no demonstrations in front of the public school from 3 to 4 p.m., Monday through Friday, when school lets out, for safety reasons). There should be written ordinances or regulations by which the local police departments issue permits and they should contain specific and narrowly defined standards. They should also contain a clearly explained process by which permits are granted. Permitting schemes should be narrowly tailored to meet the government's interest in keeping the streets open for movement and leaving alternatives for expression. They should provide guidelines limiting police discretion in granting or denying permits within specific time periods and contain a mechanism for appeal of denied permits. Unwritten policies directing officials to deny permits based on applicants' dress, for example, are not constitutional.

Is it a million lawsuits or can we vote to abolish permits?

In most cities and towns we cannot vote to abolish permits. We need lawsuits because we need legal remedies to hold public officials and police accountable for violating our constitutional protections. Lawsuits are generally the best forum for exposing unfair permitting schemes to the judicial system and the public at large. And when such permit schemes are unfair, a judgment by the court is the best way to reform unconstitutional permitting policies and to broadcast, through the media, that such reforms will take place.

What can we *do* as citizens to roll back this proliferation of permit barriers?

Concerned citizens can fight the proliferation of barriers to obtaining permits by following their local application guidelines and applying early. Don't take no for an answer if permits are not granted and you suspect it is because of the message that will be conveyed at the rally or demonstration, or because of the organization or people applying. Demand a written reason why the permit was denied.

Then take your story to the local press; show how non-political groups are granted permits for the same location, such as corporations or police athletic leagues. Seek legal assistance from progressive attorneys like the National Lawyers Guild [or, Zach Heiden adds, your local or national ACLU] to challenge permit denials in court. In other words, raise your voice in the streets, in the press, and in the courts. Some groups may decide to go ahead with their event without a permit and risk arrest in order to propel their message into the public eye. [Lawyers can't ask citizens to break the law but other citizens can. Knowing what I know now about effective protest, I say we have to be ready to mass even without permits and be ready to be arrested.]

What is your wish list for what a mass citizens' movement could do?

Unfair laws continue to exist because the citizenry doesn't challenge them, even if the injustice is from the local town hall or police station. In the case of parade and protest permits, a mass movement needs to start with going through the proper application process and pointing out its defects. If a town hall continually denies permits to certain groups, but gives them to others, get together and fight. Share each story widely with friends, colleagues, and strangers. Do not be afraid to challenge those in charge of permits. Go to the local body in charge of making decisions and start a petition or a letter-writing campaign to draw attention to flawed policies. Grassroots modes of communication work especially well on the local level— word of mouth, local flyering in stores and public places.

Identify the injustice and give it a human face—the local families of killed soldiers are denied a permit to protest the war. Find support from other like-minded group or individuals and expose how their voices were stifled. With each victory—small or large—a people's movement is born.

Are permit barriers part of a backlash against citizen speech?

It may appear that there is a backlash simply because more groups and individuals are moved to take to the streets to broadcast their discontent with governmental policies, and the government is fighting back with more sophisticated strategies than decades ago. Making the process of obtaining permits more difficult is one of those strategies designed to discourage public dissent. Another is treating protesters as criminals. The police have upped their arsenal of weaponry used to accompany large mass demonstrations, and the mass media is complicit in depicting protesters as disrupters or deviants. It portrays protesters as violent and shows striking images of weapon-bearing police officers in riot gear well in advance of given events. [Marjorie Cohn adds: "The National Lawyers Guild has monitored governmental interference with First

Amendment activities in the street for over four decades. They have documented an orchestrated pattern by which local governments around the country engage in tactics that make it daunting or difficult to engage in political speech. Such tactics include imposing exorbitant permit fees or asking for deposits in the amount of a city's estimated cost of police protection and cleanup. Or local authorities may cause undue delays in the granting of permits so that organizers cannot make plans and publicize the events. Municipalities may deny permits altogether, or pass ordinances placing unreasonable or undue restrictions on marches and public demonstrations.

"The requirement that liability insurance be taken out by demonstrators before a permit is granted is another way that authorities make it costly or difficult to secure permits for constitutionally protected events. Often sponsoring groups cannot afford the thousands of dollars such insurance costs.

"When challenged in court, many of these tactics are found to be unconstitutional and an unlawful interference with free speech. Such unlawful practices are dangerous to a democracy because they may intimidate or discourage Americans from taking to the streets to voice their viewpoints. The uniformity of such strategies around the country, and the relentless application of tactics suggest a highly organized threat to civil liberties."]

HOW TO SPEAK IN ANY PUBLIC CONTEXT

Practice at home. Stand straight and tall. When you stand up straight, it opens out your throat and rib cage and expands your lungs, allowing your true voice to emerge from deep in your chest. Place a hand on your diaphragm. This is an area about three inches below your heart, right between where your ribs start to bend away from the breastbone. You want this area to vibrate when you speak. Feel how, when you drop your voice so that it emerges from your diaphragm rather than higher in your chest or throat, you can project naturally much farther.

Keep your speech simple. And speak from the heart. The biggest mistakes speakers make include couching their remarks in generalizations, using jargon, getting too complicated, and going on too long.

You want your speech to be as short as possible. Giving a specific example is always better than a generalization, and a human story is always better than an abstraction. Rather than announcing "Particulates in the air have a negative effect on our children's respiratory systems," tell your audience about a single child you know of—Alex, who is seven and is in first grade, and who really wants to be well enough to play softball this spring with his friends, but who was hospitalized twice this winter for breathing problems. You can move from a human story to a general point—"Asthma in our community is up twenty percent and we now know why"—but for heaven's sake, don't neglect the individual story.

If you are a nurse, don't use medical jargon— "Children are compelled to raise the level of preventive treatment to manage their reactivity to particulates." Instead say, "Our kids have to take steroids to keep them from getting sick just from breathing the air." If you are an activist, don't use activist jargon—"By being inclusive and proactive as a diverse community consisting of various interest groups in coalition, we can prevail." Say, "We can win this fight together." If you are a businessperson, don't use business jargon—and so on.

Use Anglo-Saxon rather than Latinate words wherever possible. Anglo-Saxon words tend to be punchier, shorter, more colloquial, and more vivid: "push," "win," "run," "fight," "hope." Latinate words are fancier, more abstract, and more intellectual: "problematize," "advocate," "conceptualize." Government websites are death to follow because they tend to be written in Latinate language: "select" rather than "choose"; "assist" rather than "help."

Choose in advance the three things you want to say. These three things should be phrased in *sound bites*. A sound bite is ideally memorable, quotable, and punchy. You will give these in your speech. But as your movement gathers momentum, you may be called upon by local and national media to be a spokesperson. You can contract your three sound bites for a three-minute TV interview or expand them with details and examples for a twenty-minute public-affairs radio interview, but your job is to know them and get them across each time. "Message discipline" means sticking to your message no matter the venue and sending it out fresh each time as if for the first time, so that you are sure, no matter what your interviewer throws at you, you have gotten it across.

As is true of your op-ed, you want to open a speech with a hook, something that grabs the audience's attention. This can be a relevant joke, some startling information, an account of a recent news event, or, one of my favorites, a contrarian statement. The hook lets your listener know that he or she needs to pay attention.

Then you make your first assertion; expand it by explaining it further or giving examples. Then conclude it. Let your audience hear the punctuation. Pause when there is a comma. Let your voice get stronger when there is a period. Pause longer between paragraphs. It makes audiences uneasy if you rush or speak in run-on sentences, because it's hard to follow them. Powerful speakers have a strong internal logic in their speeches and always let the listener know where they are. Again, as in an op-ed piece, use transitions to link thoughts logically. Transitions can include such phrases as "Not only that . . ." or "Even more seriously . . ." or "If that doesn't make you mad enough . . ."

Transitions can be as basic as "I am going to tell you three things that need to change if our kids are going to breathe easier. The first thing is . . . The second thing . . ." and so on. Your transitions are like the string on which you assemble the beads of your argument, or the stairs by which the listener ascends the different stories of your argument. Then you offer your listeners action steps—what the audience must do to take action. And, finally, you give them your conclusion. Here is where you can use various rhetorical devices that always work. You can use a technique from Greek rhetoric called anapraxis, which means repeating the opening phrases as you build up the excitement: "Will we let our air get dirtier and dirtier? Will we sit by as our kids get sicker and sicker? Or will we do something about it?"

You can use "call and response" technique:

"Are you with me?"

"Yes!"

"Are we going to close this plant down?"

"Yes!"

End with your strongest sentence. By strengthening your voice to its fullest at the very end of your speech, your audience understands that this is the climax of your remarks. It will trigger their applause. In classical rhetoric, this is called the crescendo.

But if this technique is not natural to you and you are a more quiet personality, don't pretend to be something you're not. You can also use a more meditative conclusion—asking the audience, for instance, to imagine a community in which the air is always clean and a child never misses a day of play because of asthma. You can conclude with a quieter hope or wish. This is also effective and it is called a diminuendo.

IV. DELIBERATE, COMMUNITY-BUILD, AND ORGANIZE

HOW TO START A POLITICAL MOVEMENT

Do not imagine you don't have power to start a national political movement. Many Americans have. The child labor, suffrage, antinuclear, pro-choice, pro-life, gun rights, and gun control movements were all started by individuals or small groups of citizens.

The Ron Paul movement was driven by ordinary citizens who worked entirely at a grassroots level, raising a great deal of money from citizens, each giving a small amount, and uniting hundreds of thousands of Americans in defense of liberty.

We asked Trevor "Oyate," who is a citizen leader of the Ron Paul grassroots movement, for advice.

DIRECT-ACTION ACTIVISM [Trevor "Oyate"]

Trevor Oyate likes to keep his head low and out of the spotlight. His recent activist experience includes working with Aaron Russo and his survivor organization, Restore the Republic, as national director of technology. Oyate has been keeping busy with several meetup groups. He is still the nominal coordinator of one Restore the Republic state group. Oyate brings large-scale mobilization techniques to http://RevolutionMarch.com and currently serves as march logistical officer. In addition to being heavily involved with the permitting and planning process, Oyate will conduct their marshal and medical volunteer training and will supervise them during marches. Being a marshal or medical volunteer is one of the most exciting and fun volunteer positions in these actions, so Oyate encourages all revolutionaries to volunteer.

What form of activism do you do?

I specialize in direct-action activism. It is a form of political activism where I and my partners use nonviolent civil disobedience to advocate for a cause. We have taken to the streets and done demonstrations, protest marches, and so on. We want to solve problems that our government is not addressing.

What are your goals when you organize an action?

First is to get media attention. That is the most difficult and costly. We have to gather hundreds or thousands of people to demonstrate, perhaps hold a protest march in order to get, maybe, thirty seconds of news coverage. Second is to infuse and invigorate your base. They need to know what you are planning to do and have clear direction as to how you will achieve it. Third is to have a positive interaction with the community, both the community where you are protesting and the community you are fighting for.

When we are protesting our goals are to effectively plan the entire action.

My best advice for a major protest? Become familiar with the location and find out how people can get there. Find out about all the resources at your disposal at the location. Knowing where the nearest hospital is, the security details, water sources, and so forth helps you respond to emergencies and problems efficiently. Also, the organizers and the leadership should have clear communication channels open at all times. Having walkie-talkies or mobile phone devices helps.

Remember, you want to have a positive community interaction. Always smile. Have a loud, protesting voice but be gentle with the people around you.

What is your personal advice for a new citizen activist?

Be humble and know that you are here to serve others. In my work I have relied on scholars whose philosophies guide our movement; then I take those ideas and apply them at street level. You should read history and works of eminent scholars.

Activism is not glamorous. We sacrifice a lot. I live in a twenty-year-old camper on very little money. I am under surveillance all the time.

My only security is that I am doing this for the people. I work under an alias: "Oyate," which means "the People." When someone says, "Trevor did this," I say "Oyate, or the People, did this."

You need to train fellow citizens if you are starting your own political movement. We also spoke to Raymond D. Powell, the cohost of *The North Virginia Patriots,* a local Ron Paul democracy movement radio show.

STARTING YOUR OWN POLITICAL MOVEMENT
[RAYMOND D. POWELL]

Raymond Powell learned to program computers at the age of seven in the early days of home computing. Even with his disinterest in schooling and other social "norms," Ray managed to get hired as a programmer right out of high school. After a few years working in "the cubicle," Ray realized that a nine to five job was not the life for him.

While he always recognized that he had a different view of the world than most, he didn't realize that he was probably a libertarian until around 2001. He was one of the early members of the Free State Project and even got to vote in the state selection process. It was at the FSP PorcFest in 2004 when Ray first heard the name Ron Paul being mentioned. When he saw Ron Paul was running for president around July 2007, Powell was one of the first to show interest in creating a meet-up group in Albuquerque. Once he got involved in the "Ron Paul Revolution," he found that he was having trouble focusing on anything but *using this opportunity to cause real change. In November, 2007, he started an Internet radio show,* The North Viginia Patriots. *You can learn more about Ray Powell at his website: http://www.Raymond Powell.com.*

Why did you choose to participate in the Ron Paul movement?

I am a libertarian and I was attending a meeting in another state where Ron Paul was mentioned. I went home and logged on to his site and read about him and the issues he stands for. I believed in what he stood for and I wanted to help spread the word about him.

How did you start your movement?

I am a computer geek, so I started looking at various networking sites on the Internet. I found out that a few members had already joined forces with him at http://www .meetup.com—a networking site that I am part of. I became one the first people who started the movement in

Albuquerque. I discovered that such organically grown movements were starting up all over the country. There were 1,400 such groups emerging all over.

We were all roughly connected via the Internet and we all had the same focus. We started sharing resources and expertise with each other. We gathered information from Ron Paul's campaign and decided to raise funds. One person started a website called http://www.this november5th.com, where people would pledge to donate money to his campaign. We chose November 5 because is it also Guy Fawkes Day. Guy Fawkes was a famous conspirator who intended to blow up the Parliament in England, hoping it would trigger a great uprising among English Catholics who were distressed by the increased severity of laws against the practice of their religion.

We made history on November 5, 2007. We broke all records. We raised more than $4.3 million on one single day, the highest ever for a political cause over the Internet.

Inspired by this, we started another website and called it http://www.teaparty07.com. We wanted to re-create the success we had in November and this time we hosted another fund-raiser on December 16. It was also to commemorate the Boston Tea Party. We were surprised to see that we broke our own record and got pledges totaling $6.04 million on a single day.

Two days later the news media caught on to our efforts and Ron Paul was interviewed by all news channels. Ron Paul was finally on TV and we felt we were getting somewhere.

Why did you choose the Internet to start this movement?

If we were to organize a meeting, rent a room to host the meeting, and then gather everyone there to talk about everyone's talents and intentions, we would just be creating red tape. This does work but on a local level. We wanted a nationwide contribution and the Internet is the only platform available to us to do so.

What tools or techniques did the movement use?

The websites we created were simple. We put up a very inspirational video on the main page. We were very clear about our objectives and about Ron Paul. The video delivered a powerful message. It brought tears to the eyes. We wanted people to pledge their support. We put up a real-time ticker to show how many people had pledged. And when you would see it going up and up, it inspired a lot more people to pledge.

One of us went on to create another, related website that was linked to the official website called http://www.ronpaulgraphs.com. It listed all donations coming in real time through graphs.

When you are cheering with your fellow activists in the same room, you feed off of each other's energy. It is not the same on the Internet. Creating the real-time counter and the graphs helps us feel that we are part of a powerful group of people who are there to create change. We also mentioned the names of people who had donated money. Every time you went on the site, you saw how much money was donated, you watched the participation, and that was invigorating.

The websites were connected to the official Ron Paul

website. We never collected any money. All donations were made directly to that website. Every campaign has lawyers and legal arrangements to monitor donations. That also helped us gain the confidence of our supporters.

What other Internet-based technology would you recommend for activism?

Create videos and upload them on the Internet. Create inspirational messages through them and share them with members of your network and ask them to forward them to their networks. YouTube is still giving out free bandwidth, so you don't have to worry about your server space or how much it will cost you to post a video. The technology to create and distribute videos is available to you for free.

You can ask the Web programmer in your group to create some open source codes for you to create applications on. You can create forums, message boards, and so forth by using this application software for free. It builds a central communication system.

ORGANIZE A TOWN HALL MEETING

Many cities and towns hold town hall meetings at which you and your team of democracy commandos can drive change at the local level. The guidelines at the state of Massachusetts website (http://www.sec.state.ma.us/cis/cistwn/twnidx.htm) apply only to towns in that state; check your state guidelines online for the rules about town meetings where you live.

At a town meeting, the salaries of the town's elected officials are decided. Votes to appropriate—which means to direct or apportion—money to run a municipality are taken, which might interest you a good deal if you are worried about how your community balances its budget and what its spending priorities are. Finally, there are also votes on the town's local statutes, which are called bylaws. In your town meeting, if it is an open rather than a representative town meeting, you and your democracy commandos can influence whether your town will, say, protect zoning that keeps green spaces in which your family can ride bikes, or whether your community will get a new hospital or lower taxes or more affordable housing.

Any member of the public may attend a town meeting. All registered voters may speak in an open or representative town meeting. In a representative town meeting, a registered voter who is not a town meeting member has a right to speak subject to conditions prescribed by the meeting.

It is very important for you and your democracy team to attend town meetings from time to time or at least to send a member to do so and report back. The agenda for town meetings as well as for local and state legislative sessions is usually very hard to identify and is not reported transparently online—a gaping hole in our republic's matrix of citizen engagement. You and your team need to address this.

Your democracy-commando team should, as noted, create a community website where citizens can check on the proceedings as reported by fellow citizens, leak and report news about the community that is being ignored or distorted by the corporate or local-news media, blog about issues and concerns locally, send e-mails to town leaders, register signatures on petitions, and help drive the agenda for future town meetings.

HOW TO RUN A MEETING [Wende Jager-Hyman]

Wende Jager-Hyman is the executive director of the Woodhull Institute for Ethical Leadership. Wende has an extensive background in the worlds of both education and business. She was for many years the executive director of a major private independent school on Long Island with an enrollment of over seven hundred students. Prior to serving in a not-for-profit educational environment, Wende's entrepreneurial spirit led her to be the founder and owner of a personnel recruiting firm. A daughter and daughter-in-law of Holocaust survivors, Wende's love of freedom and appreciation for how America allowed her family to rise from the ashes has made her a passionate defender of the American ideal.

Running a meeting puts you in the position of assuring that the meeting is held utilizing the "rules of order." You are acting as the moderator and it is your responsibility to guarantee that all parties are heard and that the organizational mandates and directives for the meeting are upheld. If you want to express your opinion passionately and in public you may decide that you don't want to run the meeting. However, assuming a leadership position may force you to chair a meeting. Should that be the case, make sure that you are well prepared.

You must understand the meeting rules of the group. The most common rule book used is *Robert's Rules of Order.* First compiled in 1876 by Henry Martyn Robert under the name *Pocket Manual of Rules of Order for Deliberative Assemblies,* the tenth edition was published in 2000 under the title *Robert's Rules of Order: Newly Revised.* When this army engineer was embarrassed by not knowing how to manage a meeting that he was called upon to run, he investigated parliamentary procedures and codified them into one document that established a widely accepted standard for maintaining decorum and treating participants fairly. *Robert's Rules* covers everything from how to make a motion to how to call for a vote. For more historical information and details on the rules see http://www.robertsrules.com/. Note that not all organizations use Robert's rules; you must also understand the bylaws and procedures of the organization whose meeting you will be heading.

Some simple rules to follow are:

1. Always have an agenda. The agenda should clearly state the topics that will be discussed. The agenda should be distributed to participants well before the meeting. This allows them to think through their opinions and encourages structured participation. Consider whether your agenda is too ambitious for the time that has been allotted for the meeting. It is far better to call several meetings and achieve resolution to a few items at a time then to try to tackle too much and leave participants frustrated because the items that they cared about were never discussed or resolved.

2. Always have a minute taker—someone who can track the discussions and record any decisions for perpetuity.

3. Begin the meeting by accepting the minutes from the last meeting. This approach seals decisions and avoids any possible misunderstandings about what has already been resolved.

4. Set a time limit for your meeting. This will get people to want to participate—everyone is on the same page about their time commitment. It will also allow you to monitor the progression of the agenda and help you make sure that the discussion is kept brief and focused.

5. If you are running a board or committee meeting, make sure that the participants have all the information that they need to have an intelligent discussion. Pre-meeting conversations are also the time where you can state your case to the voting members and try to convince them of the validity of your opinion.

6. If you are offering a presentation at the meeting such as a PowerPoint display, make sure that the technology is running smoothly. Do a run-through prior to the meeting. There is nothing that is more aggravating to attendees than having to wait and wait for computers to sync or plugs to be secured.

7. Always be respectful of participants. Even if you do not agree with their opinion remember that they too have freedom of speech.

8. Never allow the discussions to become personal—always bring them back to the focus of the topic at hand. When countering an argument, never say things like "That is the stupidest thing I ever heard" (even if it is), and formulate your counterargument with clear points that address why your position is the correct one.

9. If participants' discussions become heated it is your job to bring them back to point. Do

not let the meeting degenerate into a mud-slinging fest. You will not be able to accomplish your goals.

10. Always look for common ground in differences of opinion.

11. Become an active listener. People tend to believe that the more they talk about their position the easier it is to convince the opposition. That is not always the case—it is your job to try to bring the group to consensus, and in doing so you have to understand what the *needs* of your constituents are. Yes, what they need rather than what they *want*. What do they need to feel heard? What do they need to feel that their position has been recognized and validated? You cannot determine this by speaking—only by listening. Even if the opposition does not get what they want, if they feel respected chances are they will not walk away angry, and you may need them as an ally for a future decision.

12. If one item's discussion is running overtime and you feel that it cannot be resolved quickly, you can table the discussion for the next meeting and move on to the next item on your agenda. This tactic serves several purposes. You can work on a resolution when you are not in the public eye. You can take time to rethink the situation and study other options. You can take time for extended conversations and necessary research. You will have the time to understand the opposition's *needs* and strategize to bring them into the

consensus. It also allows you to move to a topic that may be resolved during the allotted time period, making participants feel that their time was well spent and that something was accomplished.

13. If you cannot get to the end of the agenda before time runs out, formally table the open items and put them at the top of the agenda for your next meeting.

14. Remember to thank everyone for coming—a constituency that feels respected is one that will work with you diligently to create positive change.

15. Being able to run a good meeting is a skill like all others; the more you do it, the better you will become at it. Do not shy away from taking on the responsibility. Meetings allow people to be heard and can be very effective vehicles in helping to create positive change. Take the challenge.

DELIBERATE WITH YOUR NEIGHBORS
[MARY JACKSTEIT]

Mary Jacksteit is the "deliberative democracy" leader and patriot who opened my eyes at the Search for Common Ground Conference for Life and Choice in Madison, Wisconsin. A skilled mediator and large-group facilitator, she was appointed in 1995 by President Clinton to the Federal Service Impasse Panel, on which she served for seven years; she has also developed and directed projects for Search for Common Ground, Collaboration D.C., and the Public Conversation Project, as well as worked in private practice. Mary also volunteers in large-group facilitations, assist-

ing neighborhoods and neighborhood associations in disputes with local governments and in conflicts between private developers and residents, and in the district courts of Montgomery County, Maryland, in day-of-trial mediation, resolving conflicts between neighbors and within families. Here is what she wants us to know about talking to one another again.

What's deliberation and why do it?

Public deliberation is simply people coming together to talk about a community problem that is important to them. Participants deliberate with one another eye-to-eye, face-to-face, exploring options, weighing others' views, considering the costs and consequences of public policy decisions.

It sounds straightforward, but the idea of deliberating *productively* can be challenging because of differences (like different viewpoints or personal attributes—for example, race, economic level, region, religion, etc.). Or it's challenging because people have no previous experience with what they want to do, or are being asked to do, in terms of discussing a public issue. The goal of deliberative talk is for the people doing it to express what they both think and feel, connecting the topic to their own experience; to believe that others have considered what they've said; and for them to consider all the experiences, information, and opinions that they hear from others. The aim is to create learning, better understanding between people, and often, new, good ideas. Sometimes deliberation has a very specific intention, that is, to produce input or policy recommendations for government decision-makers, problem-solving strategies, community priorities, a plan of action.

In every situation the goal is *impact*—the conversation makes a difference. People feel differently about themselves ("I'm capable of wrestling with this issue and being part of the public discussion"); about others ("They have a point," "I can see where they're coming from—even though I don't agree with them," "He's a real human being," "She's a good ally/someone I'd like to work with"); and about what might happen next ("We're going to be listened to"; "We can work together"; "We can debate this without it getting ugly"; "We've got some new ways to work on this problem"; "We've got a great new network of people"; "We're going to learn more about this"; "I'm going to think about this differently from now on").

Here are tips for bringing people together for deliberation:

- Actively recruit people who should be part of the conversation—aim to be inclusive. If the goal is to learn a variety of viewpoints, then make sure you're reaching wide enough.
- When you invite people be clear about the reason for the meeting and what's going to happen. Say that the goal is for people to hear from each other. It's not a lecture or presentation.
- If there is another goal (or hope)—for instance, to make a plan or give input to someone (the mayor, your member of Congress)—be clear about that, too.
- Make a time frame and plan for the meeting that you announce, post, or hand out.
- Start by asking people to offer their experiences and ideas on the issue. Then invite people to compare the experiences and

views they've heard. Ask people to listen for any common ideas/themes.

- Remember that deliberation is different from advocacy: *you're inviting people to grapple with an issue, not to try to persuade them to adopt one view.* So encourage people to consider and weigh of a range of ideas and options. If differences are making it hard to take some action step, a useful principle borrowed from the group Search for Common Ground is "Understand the differences; act on the commonalities."

- If the group is too big (usually over ten), divide up into smaller groups for some of the time so everyone really can talk. Then bring people back together to share highlights.

- Have "guidelines" (or whatever name you like) about listening, not interrupting, and other rules of common courtesy that people think are important.

- If you think people would like to know more about the issue before discussing it, Everyday Democracy and National Issues Forums have study guides on a variety of topics that provide a range of views and background information (see below). If you're talking about a local issue, there may be some basic information it would be helpful to have on hand (e.g., demographics, unemployment rates, school graduation rates, etc., etc.). Fact-finding can always be an action step that *follows* a first meeting.

- Assign some roles:
  - Someone who looks after time, participation, and the agenda. This "facilitator" needs to be fair and committed to not taking advantage of the role by dominating or talking too much. He or she watches the clock, the group, and the meeting plan to see if you're getting where you want to go.
  - A note taker or someone writing on a flipchart so people can keep track of the ideas coming forward.
- Have a wrap-up that summarizes any next steps, any results. Remember that people want to leave thinking this made a difference. If the group is small enough, you can even ask people—what are you taking away? It's also good to get feedback on what people thought of the meeting and ideas for how to do it better.

ADDITIONAL RESOURCES

Deliberate with Your Neighbors

- The Community Organizing Toolbox: http://www.nfg.org/cotb
- Internet networking sites where people and organizations can exchange resources and ideas and locate opportunities and supporters:
  - Meetup, Inc.: http://www.meetup.com
  - Personal Democracy Forum: http://www.personaldemocracy.com

- MoveOn: http://moveon.org
- Action Without Borders: http://www.idealist.org
- Volunteer Match: http://www.volunteermatch.org
- Do Something: http://www.dosomething.org
- Urban Survival Project: http://urbansurvivalproject.blogspot.com
- The People Speak: http://www.thepeoplespeak.org
- Student Public Interest Research Groups: http://www.studentpirgs.org
- Facebook.com: http://www.facebook.com
- Meetup Alliance: http://www.meetupalliance.com
- The Point: http://www.thepoint.com
- Social Actions: http://www.socialactions.com
- The National Coalition for Dialogue and Deliberation's website features a lot of online resources: http://www.thataway.org
- The League of Women Voters' Building Communities: The ABCs of Public Dialogue is a great how-to handbook by leaders in the field: http://www.thataway.org/exchange/files/docs/abcs.pdf
- Everyday Democracy supports community organizing and dialogue-to-action, and it offers good study and how-to guides: http://www.everyday-democracy.org
- The Deliberative Democracy Consortium (DDC) website provides helpful online re-

sources: http://www.deliberative-democracy
.net

- America Speaks serves as a neutral convener of large-scale public participation forums, using twenty-first-century town hall meeting technology: http://www.americaspeaks.org
- National Issues Forums has produced dozens of issue guides covering important issues ranging from day care to affirmative action: http://www.nifi.org/discussion_guides/index
.aspx
- The Public Conversations Project offers guides on and assistance for initiating dialogue on divisive issues that involve differing values: http://www.publicconversations.org

BECOME THE LEADERS OF AMERICA

HOW TO START A NONPROFIT ORGANIZATION

Your group of like-minded citizens can also start a nonprofit organization to drive continued, institutionalized change.

It is important for you to daydream—to think about your mission—and listen to the internal call that you certainly hear if you are reading this section with any interest at all. Take time out of your day to attend to this inner prompting—while on walks, in the shower, or on your commute to work. What is it that is drawing you? What does it feel like? Just as important as listening to this inward call is to believe in your own agency so that self-doubt does not interfere with your sense of mission. Of course you can do this if you are meant to. It is pretty straightforward—actually it's kind of easy—to start a non-profit, though I won't pretend that raising money is not sometimes hard work.

Once you have identified your mission, there are ten steps you need to take:

1. You need to file a certificate of incorporation.
2. Choose the people you wish to serve on your board. It is best to have an odd number of people on the board so you do not have to worry about a tie vote. Typically, from nine to thirty people serve on a board.
3. Sit down and write your "vision statement" (meaning the big picture of what you want to do) and the "mission statement" (meaning the explanation of what is motivating you and what you feel is important for your organization to do and why).
4. Establish bylaws and board policies. These are the rules by which you all will agree to operate.
5. Get an employer identification number (EIN) so you can hire people.
6. Open a bank account and establish check-signing procedures so that you can pay your staff and your expenses.
7. You also need to file for a federal tax exemption so that the IRS knows you are a real non-profit and does not charge you taxes, and also so your donors can give you money that they can claim on their own tax returns as charitable contributions. Learn about your state and local nonprofit regulations to ensure that you

are complying with the rules in your area. You can also obtain a fiscal sponsor, which is an organization that is already recognized as a nonprofit organization. This allows you to accept tax deductible donations immediately while you are awaiting your determination.

8. Hire your staff. Recruit interviewees for the positions you need to fill in order to get started; hire the applicants you want; and write a personnel manual that explains how the jobs work in relation to one another, what is expected of each staffer, and what is expected of the organization in relation to its employees.

9. Establish a payroll system—many professional service providers can arrange one for you—and obtain the necessary insurance coverage for your employees.

10. Last, figure out your overall fund-raising plan so you can move ahead and grow.

ADDITIONAL RESOURCES

How to Start a Nonprofit Organization

- Guidelines on starting a nonprofit organization: http://foundationcenter.org/getstarted/tutorials/establish
- This website offers a nonprofit organization good practice guide: http://www.npgoodpractice.org
- Legal guidelines on starting nonprofits:

- Tax Information for Charities & Other Non-Profits: http://www.irs.gov/charities/index.html
- Citizen Media Law Project: http://www.citmedialaw.org/legal-guide/nonprofit organization
- BoardSource provides resources on how to develop a nonprofit board: http://www.boardsource.org
- TechSoup provides technical training and sometimes free technology to nonprofits: http://www.techsoup.org
- The Communications Consortium Media Center offers tips on how to use media and new technologies as tools for policy change: http://www.ccmc.org

HOW TO FUND-RAISE [STEPHANIE BERGER]

Stephanie Berger is the president of Berger Hirschberg Strategies, Inc., a political fund-raisng and nonprofit development company headquartered in Washington, D.C. She is an extraordinarily competent, get-it-done mover. She started her own business in Washington, D.C., to help citizens raise money to fund the change they wish to see. She believes it is powerfully effective to teach citizens to raise money so they can fight for what they believe in on their own terms.

Today the media reports that federal, state, and local elections—most specifically presidential elections—will cost close to a billion dollars, most of which is raised from individuals. Because this amount of money is astronomical and almost impossible to grasp, those who are unfamiliar with fund-raising believe that they lack the appropriate skills or confidence to raise money. This sentiment is not true; everyday citizens can raise money for their favorite charity, school events, citywide races, or any other group—successfully!

Fund-raising is about getting other people—your friends or business colleagues—to invest in your ideas and goals. If you have ever waited a table or worked in retail you have the skills to be a great fund-raiser. Giving back to your community by raising money is selfless and a great way to improve the world around you. Finding the common linkage between your cause and the donor's ideals is what creates successful fund-raising. By using tested tools of the trade such as call sheets, call time, and events, anyone can be a great fund-raiser. It is also important that you have the confidence to raise money and to remember that the worst that can happen from asking someone to contribute to your cause is that they will say no, which is not that bad!

Fund-raising allows anyone to transform their cause from a simple idea to a successful reality. Fund-raising gives people the opportunity to give back to their community. The key to fund-raising is getting people excited enough about your cause to act with their most important asset, their wallet.

Creating a Fund-raising Plan

- **The Cause**—You must be able to state your cause in a way that it is not only universal in appeal, but specific enough to reach a target group. It's important to find a group of people who are going to be passionate about your cause. Describe the cause and explain how it will help other people.

- **Targeting Prospective Givers**—Create a list of people you would like to contact to ask for money. This list is the base from which you will try to grow your givers.
- **Research Tools**—The Internet is an incredibly easy and important tool to find your next donor. These websites are a great way to research potential donors in the political world and nonprofit world:
  1. OpenSecrets.org: Searches for political contributions
  2. Foundations.org: Directory of charitable grantmakers.
  3. Foundationcenter.org: Search donors to nonprofits.
  4. Google.com: Get to know your donors; do research so you can better convince them of the worthiness of your cause.

Starting your fund-raising plan and making it successful!

- **Create a Fund-raising Plan and Set a Goal For How Much Money to Raise**
  1. Set a goal that is realistic and stick to it.
  2. List how you will use each fund-raising tool (call time, direct mail, etc. . . .) and which of your target donors would fit into each category.
  3. Make sure to keep accurate records of who you've contacted when and their re-

sulting contributions/pledges; it will save you time and money.

4. Use Excel spreadsheets to track your money in and out as well as to record who attends your meetings and events.

- **Work from the Inside Out (Work from Your Closest Friends Outward and Build a Network)**
  1. Make a list of your closest friends.
  2. Make a list of your work colleagues.
  3. Make a list of people who would be interested in your cause—businesses, non-profits, and local groups.
  4. Look at groups and organizations with the same mission and see who is sponsoring them for ideas about who to ask.
- **Sell Your Cause**
  - **Marketing Materials**
    1. Explain the importance of your cause/candidate.
    2. Specify why giving to your organization will help others.
    3. Should be attractive, easy to read, and brief—try to keep it to two pages or less.
- **Fund-raising Tools**
  - **Making the Ask**—You will need to ask your friends and potential targets to get involved by writing a check for a specific amount of money.
    - A call is wasted if specific details for meetings, the event, or contributions are not given.

- **Call Time**—Set aside a specific amount of time every week to make calls.
  - Stick to the plan, because the more calls that are made the more money will come in.
- **Finance Committee, Host Committee, or Party Committee**
  - Ask ten of your friends to send your invitation to ten of their friends.
  - Turn these friends into a fund-raising "tree" that will grow every year.
  - Tell them if they raise $XXX they will have their names listed on an invitation.
  - This list will be useful for years to come and give you a large network to reach out to.
- **Events**—Use these to not only raise awareness about your cause but also to raise money. Try to find local businesses to host these events to bring in extra attendees and support.
  - Always have a price and dates for your event ahead of time.
- **Online Outreach**—E-mail and e-vites are a great way to keep everyone up to date and to spread information quickly and solicit donations.
  - Today most people communicate online.
- **Follow Up**—Make sure that your donors are up to date on your cause and know about any events or opportunities.

- **Getting the Confidence to Ask**
  - Practicing with friends and family is a great way to get ready for the real thing.
  - Know that the worst thing anyone can say to you is no.
  - It gets easier over time, so start with people you know and work your way up.
- **Know the Rules/Laws**
  - When raising money for political candidates, nonprofits, and organizations, you will need to know the federal and state laws that apply to reporting money and types of money you can solicit (individual, corporate, LLP, LLC).
  - Consult Fec.gov.
  - Consult the secretary of state for your state for state rules.
  - Consult Irs.gov.

Most importantly, know that you have the skills to raise money and that every friend, colleague, and person on the street is a potential donor. Good luck and go make your dream happen!

ADDITIONAL RESOURCES

How to Fund-raise

- The Grassroots Institute for Fundraising Training website provides info on how to fund-raise at a grassroots level: http://www.grassrootsfundraising.org

- Idealist.org fund-raising: http://www.idealist
  .org/tools/fundraising.html
- Foundation Center: http://www.foundation
  center.org/
- Management Help: http://www.management
  help.org/fndrsng/np_raise/np_raise.htm
- Complete Campaigns: http://www.complete
  campaigns.com/article.asp?articleid=42
- Fund-raising Rules/Laws:
  - Federal Election Commission: http://www
    .fec.gov
  - Internal Revenue Service: http://www.irs
    .gov

V. RULE OF LAW: CREATE OR CHANGE LAWS YOURSELF

INITIATIVES AND REFERENDA

Depending on where we live, many of us have a powerful tool to affect the laws that affect our community: the *initiative* and *referendum* processes.

Twenty-four states have systems that let you start and even complete the process of making state law with the support of neighbors. In the initiative process, citizens have the ability to adopt laws or amend the state Constitution. In the referendum process, citizens have the ability to reject laws or amendments proposed by the state legislature.

If you do not live in a state that gives you this power, you can start a movement to force your state leaders to change the system. If you do live in such a state, you can start your own initiative by going to http://www.iandr institute.org.

Say you want to create green zones around all the cities in your state to limit sprawl and encourage smart development, as Oregon has successfully done. This approach aims to ensure that your own property values rise, desirable companies that care about their employees' quality of life will want to move in, new development will better use water and electrical resources, your commute will be shorter, your mass transit will be cheaper and easier to use, and your kids will get to see some trees. Studies show that

70 percent of such initiatives tend to pass on local ballots and that people love the outcome.

But you will be up against powerful forces who contribute a lot of money to the people who are running the show in your community. Once you and your democracy commandos know how to start an initiative, you have become their enemy.

First, you should reach out to other groups that share your concerns. You don't have to agree with everything they believe in order to work well as a *coalition*. Meet with them—your house, community center, or a coffee shop is fine, and many libraries have meeting rooms—and suggest that you work together.

Name your coalition. It should be a catchy, memorable name.

Go to your secretary of state's website for the rules relevant to your state. Start circulating your petition.

Send all your neighbors, kids, and friends to malls, sports games, movie theaters—anywhere people congregate—to get signatures for your issue. Call or write your town council or board of selectmen to schedule a meeting to present your petition and ask for legislation to put the greenbelt around your town. And call or write your state assembly member to arrange a meeting at which you can present your petition.

Meanwhile, have your friends and coalition partners (as well as yourself) do press outreach, as you have seen earlier. Write *op-eds* explaining your efforts and ask other citizens to bombard their own town councils and the state assembly with calls and e-mails in support of the greenbelt. If time goes on and there is no action, write op-eds shaming your representatives for inaction.

When you have your issue on the ballot, powerful in-

terests may mobilize money, ads, and "talkers"—pundits—
to defeat it. Don't be intimidated: keep your base informed,
keep your own team out there framing the issue back in
your terms, and keep informing your contacts in the local
and regional press about newsworthy details of the fight.

ADDITIONAL RESOURCES

Initiatives and Referenda

- Initiative & Referendum Institute: http://
  www.iandrinstitute.org/
- What initiatives and referenda are and how
  many states have this process: http://www
  .iandrinstitute.org/New%20IRI%20Website
  %20Info/Drop%20Down%20Boxes/Quick%
  20Facts/Handout%20-%20What%20are%20
  the%20I&R%20states.pdf
- Learn more about the history and process of
  initiatives and referenda in each state: http://
  www.iandrinstitute.org/statewide_i%26r.htm
- A recent study on the impact of initiatives on
  the California budget process: http://www
  .iandrinstitute.org/New%20IRI%20Website
  %20Info/I&R%20Research%20and%20His
  tory/I&R%20Studies/Matsusaka%20-%20CA
  %20Budget%20and%20Initiatives%20-%20
  IRI.pdf
- To learn about the impact money has in the
  initiative process, go to: http://www.iandrin
  stitute.org/Quick%20Fact%20-%20Money.htm
- An account of efforts in Texas to start the initiative and referendum process: http://www
  .initiativefortexas.org/texas11.htm

- A report comparing state constitutional amendment processes: http://www.iandrin stitute.org/REPORT%202006-3%20Amend ments.pdf
- Referenda in Europe and Asia:
  - Short overview of direct democracy in Switzerland: http://www.iniref.org/swiss-dd .html
  - Irish referendum voices: http://news.bbc .co.uk/2/hi/europe/7378421.stm
  - The Citizens' Right of Initiative in the European constitution: http://www.eumap .org/journal/features/2005/demodef/wallis
  - IRI-Asia: http://www.iri-asia.net

MAKE EVERY VOTE COUNT
[MARK CRISPIN MILLER]

Mark Crispin Miller was born in Chicago; his father ran a press clipping service and organized festivals to bring poetry and the arts to Chicagoans. He and Miller's mother eventually started up a small publishing house that brings important documents—such as the Conyers report, about voting fraud in 2004—to the general public. When Miller went to graduate school and began to follow the consolidation of the corporate media, he started to feel that neither his education in U.S. history nor the mainstream press was adequately enabling him or others to engage fully in the "revolutionary spirit" of America or to be informed as citizens. Because of the founders' ideals, Miller is passionate about alerting his fellow Americans to voting fraud, which he has tracked in his book Fooled Again *and which he sees as systemic and a great, transpartisan danger to the republic.*

The citizens of a democracy have quite a range of instruments for making change whenever they see fit. This is an important fact, and yet Americans are often unaware of it, because we've all been raised to think that there is only *one* legitimate political activity: casting votes in our biennial elections. This very narrow view of democratic action leaves us largely paralyzed by delegitimizing all those other methods that the Constitution guarantees to us, explicitly or indirectly: protest of all kinds, including strikes and boycotts; organizing face-to-face or through the press; petitioning and/or lobbying our representatives; litigation; running for office *ourselves;* and so on. Those citizens who *only* vote are doing too little to protect their rights and liberties—including, paradoxically, their right to vote.

Indeed, our right to *vote* is now in jeopardy, because America's election system is a shambles, and this is a disastrous situation. For while voting certainly is not the only civic action we can take, it is the most important one available. Without the right to vote, we can't be free—as Tom Paine clearly understood, for it was he who noted that the right to vote is the foundation on which all our other rights depend. We therefore *must* take action to reclaim our voting rights and to make America's elections honest, fair, inclusive, and transparent. For voting *in itself* is not a hallmark of democracy: Saddam Hussein's Ba'ath party held elections, and even Hitler's Reich held plebiscites (a very simple form of yes/no referendum).

As bad as our elections are—and, as Jimmy Carter once observed, they are among the worst in the developed world—the fact is that our system *can* be rectified. To do so, however, requires that we use all the civic instruments at our disposal. First of all, we have to educate ourselves about the true condition of U.S. electoral democracy—a daunting job, because the media has largely shrouded the unpleasant facts in a gigantic fog of comfortable myth. And yet it is a job that *can* and *must* be done, by reading up on how the Bush regime *seized power* back in 2000, then *stole* its "reelection" four years later—and also how the regime variously fixed elections for the House and Senate, in order to enhance its power still more.

While learning all about the theft of our last few elections, we must, of course, also prepare for the election this November:

1) If you are eligible to vote, make sure to register before the deadline. This is not enough, however. *Even if you've registered,* contact your Board of Elections *before* the deadline and make sure that your name is still on the rolls. (If possible, get written proof of your registration from the board.)

2) Tell your Board of Elections where you live, and ask where your polling place will be.

3) On Election Day, bring all required documentation to the polling place (including your written proof of registration, if you were able to get it from the Board of Elections).

4) If there are long lines at your polling place, be patient.

5) If you have *any* problem with the voting machine, ask a poll worker for help. If the machine isn't working, ask to use another one.

6) If your machine has a "paper trail," check yours to make sure that it recorded your vote accurately.

7) If paper ballots are available, use one of those instead of voting by machine.

8) If you have *any* problem that is not resolved, call an election hotline, the presidential campaign that you support (and which will probably have poll monitors on hand), and—most important—local election officials. (This last step provides a record that will strengthen a court case, if one should prove necessary.)

9) Be prepared to *monitor* the process. Bring a cell phone or video recorder to make a visual record of irregularities or improprieties, and consider interviewing people as they leave the polls and jotting down their firsthand accounts of their experiences, making sure to have their names and contact information.

ADDITIONAL RESOURCES

Make Every Vote Count

- Mark Crispin Miller's News from Underground: http://www.markcrispinmiller.com
- The Brad Blog: http://www.bradblog.com
- Election Defense Alliance: http://www.election defensealliance.org
- Why Tuesday?: http://www.whytuesday.org
- Rock the Vote: http://www.rockthevote.org
- The League of Young Voters: http://the league.com

ORGANIZE A NATIONAL HEARING
[ANNETTE WARREN DICKERSON]

Annette Warren Dickerson is the Director of Education and Out-reach at the Center for Constitutional Rights (CCR). She is re-sponsible for helping to develop the Center's non-litigation and advocacy strategies as a companion to CCR's legal work. She most recently coordinated a national hearing on the disparate impact of law enforcement in the reconstruction of New Orleans on commu-nities of color and immigrants in partnership with Safe Streets, Strong Communities, a leading New Orleans community based or-ganization.

One of the most effective strategies for bringing national attention to an issue—particularly one that has a signifi-cant impact on a particular city or community—is to orga-nize a national hearing. Often, issues like police abuse and shootings, inadequate housing, underperforming public schools, lack of public health care, environmentally unsafe conditions, and unfair labor practices are allowed to con-tinue unchallenged and unabated because there is little public scrutiny or accountability to a larger constituency. National hearings provide the members of a community the opportunity to bring their issues before a panel of aca-demics, policy experts, researchers, advocates, and elected officials with access to the means not only to illuminate the problem but to develop policy and legislative recommen-dations for reform based on direct testimonials from com-munity members. These hearings—and the reports that emanate from them—are extremely effective most often because the panelists are recognized experts in their fields and lend an enormous amount of credibility and gravitas to the discourse around the issue. Additionally, city and state officials—and local media—are much more likely to sit up and take notice upon learning that a group of ten or more renowned national leaders are arriving to examine any number of issues that have been ignored or allowed to worsen under the watch of local officials.

Meaningful and substantial leadership by community members is a critical element in putting together any successful national hearing. Virtually without variation, the issues that necessitate national attention have existed for years, if not decades, and there are always strong, committed community leaders who have been engaged in challenging, advocating, and struggling to address these problems with few, if any, victories. Know that the real expertise rests with those whose lives are directly affected and that they are to be front and center of any efforts to elevate the issues to a higher level of awareness. If you are a community leader, insist that you and other active members of the community have a highly visible, decision-making role in organizing any hearings, and that spokespeople come from the ranks of the directly affected.

Key elements include:

- Strategically selected national panel members with demonstrated expertise, and, if at all possible, a history of previous attention to the issues they are being asked to address.
- Development of a testimonial panel that includes at least one, but ideally two or three, members of the community who can address the issue based on personal experience.
- Inclusion of at least one advocate, policy expert, or if they are so inclined, a local or city

official who can provide their perspective on the issue at hand.

- Submission, whenever possible, of written testimony to panel members in advance of the hearing to provide adequate opportunity for review and the preparation of informed questions and analysis of the materials.

- Establishment of strong relationships with local community-based leaders and members of the local press who have extensively covered the issue(s) in their respective media. Allow adequate time for advance notice for press representatives. Do not underestimate local progressive radio outlets.

- Encourage those providing testimony to include their input on possible solutions and also on strategies that have been tried in the past with little or no progress. Panelists may be able to bring a fresh perspective to problem-solving in these areas.

- Have a clear follow-up plan. Know to whom the recommendations will be addressed and if there are fiscal impacts and other so-called impediments to executing reform that you can preemptively consider and offer solutions for.

- Partner with an organization or a number of organizations with ample resources to issue a report and play a major role in seeing that the recommendations are carried out. Extract commitments from panelists—via their organizational affiliations—as criteria for involvement before appointing them to the panel.

- Most importantly, claim victory on even the smallest progress. This will energize the community and create a momentum to move forward with resolve.

For more information on how to organize a national hearing, contact the Center for Constitutional Rights at adickerson@ccrjustice.org.

EXPOSE GOVERNMENT SECRECY: A GUIDE TO GETTING GOVERNMENT FILES
[LAUREN MELODIA]

Lauren Melodia works at the Center for Constitutional Rights, where she organizes several coalitions and campaigns, including the New York Campaign for Telephone Justice, and collaborates on popular education and advocacy work with her co-workers and grassroots allies.

The U.S. government has a long, established history of withholding information from its citizenry. Our right to access government files, however, is codified in the 1966 Freedom of Information Act (FOIA) and the Privacy Act of 1974. Though these laws have been expanded and limited over time, the basic tenets are the same: the government must make information accessible to the people, but only if the people ask for it.

Whenever you feel that the U.S. government is either outright lying or not telling you the whole truth, take the initiative to demand all of the facts. The information you glean from a FOIA request may provide significant leverage for news media, a grassroots campaign, a lawsuit, or a legislative initiative. FOIA requests have successfully prompted the CIA to release documents detailing mind-control experiments it conducted on U.S. citizens in the 1950s; the Air Force to release a history of its use of Agent Orange and other herbicides during the Vietnam War; and the FBI to release papers from its 1950s–60s COINTELPRO program, which infiltrated leftists and civil rights groups.

Be warned: the federal government makes it incredibly difficult to use the FOIA and Privacy Act to get the information you need. We hope this quick guide will make the process easier for you and more likely that you will get the information you've requested.

What is FOIA?

The Freedom of Information Act is a federal law based on the presumption that individuals have a right to know what their government is up to and that government agencies have a duty to provide full disclosure of all records that are not specifically and reasonably exempt. All departments and federal agencies under the Executive Branch are subject to FOIA and required to comply with your requests. However, FOIA does not apply to the president, Congress, the courts, or state governments (though each of the fifty states have their own freedom of information laws).

FOIA requires that agencies publish some information outright, both in print and online.It also grants individuals the right to request copies of records not normally prepared for public distribution. Under FOIA, some records may be withheld from disclosure by agency discretion based on the law's exemption and exclusion rules. FOIA outlines the procedures individuals should follow for requesting records and for appealing the decision if information is denied. It also establishes the right to judicial remedies if an agency does not comply with the law.

What is the Privacy Act?

The Privacy Act of 1974 works in tandem with FOIA to regulate federal agency records about individuals, restricting the disclosure of personal information that might violate privacy while allowing individuals access to records about themselves. FOIA and the Privacy Act overlap but have different exemptions; therefore, information may be released under one while being exempt from disclosure under the other. When seeking information about oneself, an individual should file a request citing both acts in order to get the fullest possible disclosure. A requester seeking information that is not exclusively about him or herself should cite FOIA only.

Eligibility & Costs to Use FOIA

Anyone, anywhere, for any reason can request information from the government under FOIA. That includes individuals (including non–U.S. citizens), corporations, associations, and domestic or foreign governments (with some new exceptions). Fees will vary by status of the person or organization making the request; each agency also sets its own fee schedule.

STEP-BY-STEP GUIDE TO FILING A FOIA REQUEST

1. **Determine which department or agency has the information you need.** Each federal agency has its own FOIA website that includes a guide to filing requests with that agency as well as other FOIA-related information and its annual compliance report. The Department of Justice (DOJ) keeps updated links to all other federal agencies' FOIA websites and an updated list of FOIA contacts at all federal agencies. You can also call the DOJ's Office of Information and Privacy at (202) 514-3642 or the Federal Citizen Information Center at (800) 333-4636 for help finding the right agency.

2. **Locate two separate offices within the agency to contact with your FOIA request.** Each agency and department has its own FOIA office, where you will send your letter. It is critical that you do some research to find out which office within the agency likely maintains the records you are looking for. When you send your request to the [agency's] FOIA office, you may save a lot of time by identifying the office that maintains the records.

3. **Is the information already on the agency's website?** All agencies publish a certain amount of information prescribed by FOIA and make it available online, so check the agency's website first. FOIA also specifies that agencies must publish copies of records re-

leased in response to FOIA requests that have been or will likely be the subject of additional requests.

4. **Will you be able to get the files through a FOIA request?** As mentioned above, there are several exemptions that allow government agencies to refuse to release information to the public. To figure out whether one of the exemption rules applies to the information, review the agency's FOIA website. Most sites have both an index of the information already published and detail what additional information can be requested through FOIA. Some of the common types of files that are exempt include personal records whose release would be a clearly unwarranted invasion of personal privacy (FOIA Exemption 6); records compiled for law enforcement purposes whose release could reasonably be expected to invade personal privacy (FOIA Exemption 7C); inter-agency or intra-agency memoranda or letters (FOIA Exemption 5). PLEASE NOTE: While FOIA *allows* agencies nine exemptions to withhold certain information, it does not require that they do so. So even if information—including classified documents—qualifies under an exemption, the agency may use its discretion to release it if disclosure would not cause any foreseeable harm.

5. **Write a letter.** The procedure for filing a request for information is as simple as writing a letter. Review the agency's FOIA website sug-

gestions first as each agency seems to have a particular way in which they like their letters formatted.

The Reporters Committee for Freedom of the Press has a user-friendly letter generator on its website that prompts you for all relevant information, drafts the letter for you, and allows you to edit it before saving or printing. See: http://www.rcfp.org/foi_letter/generate.php. The Committee on Government Reform's "Citizen's Guide on Using the Freedom of Information Act and the Privacy Act of 1974 to Request Government Records" includes this sample FOIA request letter:

Agency Head [or Freedom of Information Act Officer]
Name of Agency
Address of Agency
City, State, Zip Code

Re: Freedom of Information Act Request

Dear ———— :

This is a request under the Freedom of Information Act. I request that a copy of the following documents [or documents containing the following information] be provided to me: [identify the documents or information as specifically as possible].

In order to help to determine my status for purposes of determining the applicability of any fees, you should know that I am [insert a suitable description of the requester and the purpose of the request. Sample requester descriptions: I am a representative of the news media affiliated with the (———— newspaper, magazine, television station, etc.), and this request is made as part of news gathering and not for commercial use; I am affiliated with an educational or noncommercial scientific institution, and this request is made for a scholarly or scientific purpose and not for a commercial use; I am an individual seeking information for personal use and not for a commercial use; I am affiliated with a private corporation and am seeking information for use in the company's business.]

[Optional] I am willing to pay fees for this request up to a maximum of $————. If you estimate that the fees will exceed this limit, please inform me first.

[Optional] I request a waiver of all fees for this request. Disclosure of the requested information to me is in the public interest because it is likely to contribute significantly to public understanding of the operations or activities of the government and is not primarily in my commercial interest. [Include specific details, including how the requested information will be disseminated by the requester for public benefit.]

[Optional] I request that the information I seek be provided in electronic format, and I would like to receive it on a personal computer disk [or a CD-ROM].

[Optional] I ask that my request receive expedited processing because ————. [Include specific details concerning your "compelling need," such as being someone "primarily engaged in disseminating information," and specifics concerning your "urgency to inform the public concerning actual or alleged Federal Government activity."]

[Optional] I also include a telephone number at which I can be contacted during the hours of ———, if necessary, to discuss any aspect of my request.

Thank you for your consideration of this request.

Sincerely,
Name
Address
City, State, Zip Code
Telephone number [Optional]

6. **Avoid common pitfalls.** According the Department of Justice, the reasons that FOIA requests are most often denied are: (1) No records; (2) referrals; (3) request withdrawn; (4) Records not reasonably described; (5) Not a proper FOIA/Privacy Act request for some other reason; (6) Not an agency record; (7) Duplicate request; (8) Fee-related reason; (9) Other, which may include: Administratively closed after no response to "Still interested?" letter (written by agency to requester), Available from other source, Failure to perfect request, Unable to locate requester, Litigation.

Determine the most likely agency to house the information, know how they organize their records, and clearly describe what you are looking for. If you do not have a good sense of how to describe the records in your letter, contact the agency and try to speak with someone before you send your FOIA request.

7. **Wait.** The agency technically has twenty working days to respond to your letter with its determination of whether to grant the request. If information is denied in full or in part, the agency must give the reasons for the denial by this deadline. If granted, it does not have to deliver the applicable documents within the timeframe, but must do so promptly thereafter. Many times the agencies cannot meet these time limits. They are required to notify you within the twenty-day time limit if they need an extension to process your request.

8. **Make good use of the information you've received.** If you succeeded in getting the records you requested, share them with other groups that may find them helpful: grassroots groups, reporters, campaign organizers, and public interest lawyers.

9. **Denied? File an administrative appeal.** You may file an administrative appeal if: you disagree with the agency's withholding of the information, you believe that there are additional records responsive to your request that the agency failed to locate, or the agency did not grant your request for expedited processing or fee waiver. Appeals must be filed to the head of the agency within thirty to sixty days. Sample appeal letters are available on the FOIAdvocates website: http://www.foi advocates.com/samples/3.html

10. **Still denied? File a judicial appeal.** If your administrative appeal was denied, you have the right to appeal the decision in federal court. This will probably require the assistance of an attorney. The good news is that the burden is on the government to justify the withholding of information. The bad news is that historically most court decisions have been in favor of the government agency.

ADDITIONAL RESOURCES

- "A Citizen's Guide on Using the Freedom of Information Act and the Privacy Act of 1974 to Request Government Records": http://www.fas.org/sgp/foia/citizen.pdf
- "How to Use the Federal FOI Act" by the Reporters Committee for Freedom of the Press: http://www.rcfp.org/foiact/index.html
- For a discussion of current case-law interpretations of the exemptions, see the May 2004 "Justice Department Guide to the Freedom of Information Act": http://www.usdoj.gov/oip/foi-act.htm
- State Government Resources:
  - The texts of all freedom-of-information laws enacted in each of the fifty states are at: http://www.citizenaccess.org
  - The "Open Government Guide" is a complete guide to open-government law in the fifty states and District of Columbia. See: http://www.rcfp.org/ogg/index.php

VI. DISMANTLE AN OPPRESSIVE EMPIRE: REMAKE U.S. FOREIGN POLICY

Scholars of democracy movements have found that tying foreign aid and investment to human rights works. Recent "shareholder resolutions" driven by Amnesty International have effectively driven Morgan Stanley, JP Morgan-Chase, Citigroup, and Wells Fargo to use their investment relationship with oil companies in China, India, and Malaysia to put presure on Darfur to end its genocide. Pressure your representative to tie foreign aid to democracy through your commandos. Inform your community via your website about abuses we condone or instigate. And invest in global liberty. Even if you have only a small amout of money to save and invest, you and your commandos can also become shareholder activists and pressure multinational investment to push for global change in the direction of rights and democracy.

HOW TO PROMOTE DEMOCRACY OVERSEAS THROUGH INVESTMENT [Diane Keefe]

Diane Keefe, CFA, a tall, energetic mother of two with a down-to-earth manner, is also a consultant for Robert Brooke Zevin Associates, a socially responsible registered investment adviser. Diane founded Pax World High Yield Fund, the first global high-yield bond fund established with comprehensive "social screens," meaning ethical guidelines for investments. She is a member of the board of directors of Opportunity Finance Network, which lends *prudently and productively in low-income communities in the U.S. and in Native American reservation–based markets. She was a member of the board of directors of Business Leaders for Sensible Priorities from 2005 to 2007, a national nonprofit that seeks to shift $60 billion from the federal military budget to peace-building and national-security-enhancing priorities.*

Here are some approaches an individual can take to affect global change with his or her money:

He or she can participate in shareholder activism on human rights issues by investing in *socially responsible mutual funds* and using firms or advisers dedicated to *socially responsible investment management.* Minimum investments range from as little as $250 for some mutual funds to $100,000 to $2 million for a dedicated financial adviser. Many of these mutual funds and financial advisers will pursue shareholder actions (make recommendations or introduce proposals that encourage corporate responsibility and discourage company practices that are unethical or unsustainable) by submitting resolutions for shareholder votes at annual meetings of stockholders. Individuals can, and do, do this as well, with the simple requirement of owning $2,000 worth of stock for at least one year before a resolution is filed.

Once established, the shareholder activist groups use the shareholder proxy process to push monitoring and reporting on established human rights policies and ensure that employees may exercise their rights to freedom of expression, peaceful assembly, and association.

The last way that an individual can use her dollars to support democracies overseas is by investing and asking her team members to ask their employers or alma maters to provide socially responsible investment choices in retirement funds and endowment funds, or by participating in explicit campaigns to support democracy overseas. Investing in international microfinance institutions like ACCION (http://www.accion.org) or Women's World Banking (http://www.womensworldbanking.org) fosters the development of small businesses and economic self-reliance. Economic stability at the family level plants the seeds of democracy. Where women have economic power and independence, dictators are less likely to rule.

Also, as a consumer you can purchase fair-trade-certified coffee, bananas, chocolate, and apparel. Fair trade certification guarantees that producers of commodities get higher than market prices for their products, giving increased incomes to farmers in poor countries. Fair trade certification also requires that there is democracy and worker participation in decision-making within the company that creates the products.

It's time to let your savings be part of the solution, not part of the problem. Let your money speak your values. Writing op-eds, letters to the alumni magazine, or letters to the CEO or internal fund administrator at one's place of employment can also support democracy-based investment.

ADDITIONAL RESOURCES

How to Promote Democracy Overseas through Investment

- World Movement for Democracy, a global network of democrats, including activists, practitioners, academics, policymakers, and funders, who have come together to cooperate in the promotion of democracy: http://www.wmd.org

- Business Leaders for Sensible Priorities: http://www.sensiblepriorities.org/
- Co-op America: http://www.coopamerica.org
- ACCION: http://www.accion.org
- Women's World Banking: http://www.womensworldbanking.org
- Human Rights Watch: http://www.hrw.org
- Amnesty International: http://www.amnesty.org
- Opportunity Finance Network: http://www.opportunityfinancenetwork.org
- Further information on shareholder action and social investing:
  - Interfaith Center on Corporate Responsibility: http://www.iccr.org
  - Responsible Endowments Coalition: http://www.endowmentethics.org
  - Social Investment Forum: http://www.socialinvest.org
  - The Studies of Socially Responsible Investing website summarizes academic research on comparative returns between ESG investing and mainstream investing: http://www.sristudies.org

VII. UNDERSTAND HOW
YOUR SYSTEM WORKS

If you know this already, skip over it. But if you know of or can relate to the 40 to 50 percent of Americans—especially younger Americans—who aren't sure of the way the pieces fit together, or need a reminder or an overview of the American system, here you are.

OVERVIEW [Curtis Ellis]

The federal government is made up of three branches: the executive, legislative, and judiciary. The president and the various departments (Justice, State, Defense, etc.) make up the executive branch; the Senate and House of Representatives make up the legislative branch; and the Supreme Court and federal district courts constitute the federal judiciary.

The Constitution lays out the duties as well as the organization of the branches, though like any good contract, it is open to interpretation.

Basically, the legislative branch writes and adopts laws; the president signs (or vetoes) them and the executive branch implements them; and the judicial branch enforces them. The executive branch has broad authority over foreign policy and defense. The executive appoints judges (and other officers) who must be approved by the legislative branch. The Supreme Court determines if laws or the regulations and practices implementing them conform to the Constitution.

Members of the House of Representatives serve two-year terms and the entire House stands for election every two years. Senators serve six-year terms; roughly one third of the Senate stands for election in any given election cycle. The president, of course, is elected to a four-year term and is limited to two terms, the only federal official who is term-limited.

Power is also divided between the federal government and states. Many, if not most, functions of government are the responsibility of states, though the federal government often sets legal and regulatory standards that states are required to meet as a precondition for receiving funding from the federal government. (For example, a state can be required to set a certain blood alcohol limit for drunken driving or it will not be eligible to receive federal highway funds, and the No Child Left Behind law sets testing requirements for schools to receive federal funds.)

State Government

State governments roughly parallel the federal structures, though particulars vary from state to state. All states elect governors, but some states have one legislative house while others have two. The division of powers between the governor and legislature varies from state to state.

The executive branch of state government can include a secretary of state, which often oversees elections; an attorney general; a transportation secretary (highways and motor vehicles); a finance secretary (taxes); and others. State courts try state laws, which can include the familiar offenses of murder, robbery, etc., as well as statutes unique to a particular state, such as sanctions against sodomy or "blue laws" prohibiting the sale of clothing on Sundays.

Local [City, Town, and County]

The tripartite structure, with an executive (a county executive, mayor, or city manager), a legislature (county, town, or city council), and municipal courts, is generally reflected at the local level. However, duties and responsibilities vary. Some cities have a strong mayoral system, where the city council has few responsibilities beyond approving a budget written by the executive. Other cities give more legislative powers to the city council. Some jurisdictions have most of the power centered in a county legislature.

How the city council or county legislature is elected also varies. Some seats may represent geographical districts; others may be at large, that is, elected by all the voters of the jurisdiction. Some cities have proportional representation, where voters cast ballots for a number of candidates in order of preference, and the top vote getters win seats. And in some cities, the executive is elected by the town or city council.

Likewise, judges may be appointed or elected.

Government and Politics

Unlike the former Soviet Union, where the instruments of government and the Communist Party were indistinguishable, the U.S. government is established to advance the interests of the nation, not a particular party. We elect people to government offices to serve everyone, regardless of party affiliation. It is in many cases illegal to use government positions to advance partisan political interests. The president (like governors and mayors) is entitled, even required, to appoint political loyalists to various positions in his administration. Once in those government posts, however, they are required to enforce laws equally and without prejudice to party. In the case of the Justice Department, while U.S. attorneys serve at the pleasure of the president, their job is to pursue criminals, not the president's political enemies.

At more local levels of government, the lines between government and political offices become more blurred. In towns and counties, party affiliation and personal friendships overlap, and officeholders, being human, use their positions to advance the interests of their friends. Rewarding political supporters with government jobs or contracts is a time-honored tradition, if not a legitimate function of representative government. Party officials who are instrumental in orchestrating an official's election can have enormous influence with that office.

Law and Politics

Laws are written and interpreted by people, and people are open to influence and emotion. What may seem to be a straightforward question with only one right answer is not always so cut-and-dried.

Nowhere is this more apparent than in the case laws governing local elections and ballot access. These laws are open to widely different interpretations, and decisions often require the unanimous consent of representatives from local Democratic and Republican parties.

Even at the highest level of the federal bench, Supreme Court decisions are informed by popular emotions and the mood of the country. Justices are cognizant of the fact that our government rules only with the consent of the governed. They are aware that handing down a ruling too far at variance with popular opinion risks undermining the authority of the bench and the perception that the government is an impartial instrument of popular will.

WHAT IS THE ELECTORAL COLLEGE?
[WENDE JAGER-HYMAN]

For full biographical information, please see p. 273.

While we have all heard about red states and blue states and how many electors are needed to win the presidency, many of us have no idea of what the Electoral College really is, why it exists, or whether it helps or hurts us.

The second article of the Constitution states:

> Each State shall appoint, in such Manner as the Legislature thereof may direct, a Number of Electors, equal to the whole Number of Senators and Representatives to which the State may be entitled in the Congress: but no Senator or Representative, or Person holding an Office of Trust or Profit under the United States, shall be appointed an Elector.
>
> The Electors shall meet in their respective States, and vote by Ballot for two Persons, of whom one at least shall not be an Inhabitant of the same State with themselves. And they shall make a List of all the Persons voted for, and of the Number of Votes for each; which List they shall sign and certify, and transmit sealed to the Seat of the Government of the United States, directed to the President of the Senate. The President of the Senate shall, in the Presence of the Senate and House of Representatives, open all the Certificates, and the Votes shall then be counted. The Person having the greatest Number of Votes shall be the President, if such Number be a Majority of the whole Number of Electors appointed; and if there be more than one who have such Majority, and have an equal Number of Votes, then the House of Representatives shall immediately chuse by Ballot one of them for President; and if no Person have a Majority, then from the five highest on the List the said House shall in like Manner chuse the President. But in

chusing the President, the Votes shall be taken by States, the Representation from each State having one Vote; a quorum for this Purpose shall consist of a Member or Members from two thirds of the States, and a Majority of all the States shall be necessary to a Choice. In every Case, after the Choice of the President, the Person having the greatest Number of Votes of the Electors shall be the Vice President. But if there should remain two or more who have equal Votes, the Senate shall chuse from them by Ballot the Vice President.

This was later modified by Twelfth Amendment to the Constitution as follows:

[ARTICLE XII]
[*Proposed* 1803; *Ratified* 1804]

The Electors shall meet in their respective states, and vote by ballot for President and Vice-President, one of whom, at least, shall not be an inhabitant of the same state with themselves; they shall name in their ballots the person voted for as President, and in distinct ballots the person voted for as Vice-President, and they shall make distinct lists of all persons voted for as President, and of all persons voted for as Vice-President, and of the number of votes for each, which lists they shall sign and certify, and transmit sealed to the seat of the government of the United States, directed to the President of the Senate; The President of the Senate shall, in the presence of the Senate and House of Representatives, open all the certificates and the votes shall then be counted; The person having the greatest number of votes for President, shall be the President, if such number be a majority of the whole number of Electors appointed; and if no person have such majority, then from the persons having the highest numbers not exceeding three on the list of those voted for as President, the House of Representatives shall choose immediately, by ballot, the President. But in choosing the President, the votes shall be taken by states, the representation from each state having one vote; a quorum for this purpose shall consist of a member or members from two-thirds of the states and a majority of all the states shall be necessary to a choice. And if the House of Representatives shall not choose a President whenever the right of choice shall devolve upon them, before the fourth day of March next following, then the Vice-President shall act as President, as in the case of the death or other constitutional disability of the President. The person having the greatest number of votes as Vice-President, shall be the Vice-President, if such number be a majority of the whole number of Electors appointed, and if no person have a majority, then from the two highest numbers on the list, the Senate shall choose the Vice-President; a quorum for the purpose shall consist of two-thirds of the whole number of Senators, and a majority of the whole number shall be necessary to a choice. But no person constitutionally ineligible to the office of President shall be eligible to that of Vice-President of the United States.

What does this really mean? The president of the United States and the vice president of the United States are *not* elected directly by the people. Remember that the founding fathers took a handful of independent states and tried to create one nation out of them. To recognize both the needs of the less populated states and the power of the larger states, the Constitutional Convention adapted the "Connecticut Compromise," which established the current formula of the Congress. The Senate was established by giving equal representation to all states regardless of population (two senators per state). This form of representation gave smaller states power equal to that of the larger ones. At the same time, the House of Representatives was established by "allocated representation," which means the number of representatives is based on the population of each state. This house favors the larger states. The census form that you fill out every ten years determines the number of seats your state will get in the House of Representatives.

The system of the Electoral College was created to address the concern of the smaller states; electors (or members) were assigned to each state based on the number of its representatives in Congress. In other words, each state gets to elect the same number of representatives to the Electoral College that they have in the House—plus two more that represent their senators. Supporters of the Electoral College still feel strongly that this system helps give voice to the smaller states. According to this point of view, if we went to a direct election system, the most populous states, like California, Texas, and New York, would determine the election, and the needs of the smaller states would never be taken into consideration.

So when you vote for president you are really voting for the electors that have pledged to vote for the candidate that you have chosen (note: even though they pledge to vote for a particular candidate, their pledge is not binding). The vast majority of states allocate their electors on a winner-take-all basis: whoever wins the popular vote gets all of the electors. Some states, such as Maine and Nebraska, allocate their electors proportionately. On the plus side, the Electoral College system ensures that every state feels that it has an important role in determining who the president is. On the negative side, it can seem maddening that a majority of citizens can't actually elect the president. What happens normally in a very close election? If no candidate obtains a majority of electoral votes, then the president is elected by the House of Representatives from the three candidates who received the most votes. Believe it or not, the House of Representatives did elect our president two times—in 1800 and 1824.

Especially if you reside in a sparsely populated state, you may support upholding the system of the Electoral

College. But if you feel that the only thing that makes sense is to honor the vote of the majority, then you may want to support an amendment to the Constitution to do away with the Electoral College.

How to Amend the Constitution

The founders gave you the right to amend the Constitution. Americans have successfully done this twenty-seven times. Article V states, "The Congress, whenever two thirds of both Houses shall deem it necessary, shall propose Amendments to this Constitution, or, on the Application of the Legislatures of two thirds of the several States, shall call a Convention for proposing Amendments, which, in either Case, shall be valid to all Intents and Purposes, as part of this Constitution, when ratified by the Legislatures of three fourths of the several States, or by Conventions in three fourths thereof, as the one or the other Mode of Ratification may be proposed by the Congress; Provided that no Amendment which may be made prior to the Year One thousand eight hundred and eight shall in any Manner affect the first and fourth Clauses in the Ninth Section of the first Article; and that no State, without its Consent, shall be deprived of its equal Suffrage in the Senate."

In clearer language, the easiest way to pass an amendment is to get two thirds of both houses to support the change. This is a major undertaking, but it can be done and it has been done. How would you do this? You can petition your own representatives; start a website soliciting support from other voters; formulate a petition to be presented to each and every federal legislator; collect as many signatures as possible for each petition; write an op-ed on the subject; mobilize a group of supporters to grow your group; utilize the power of the Internet to garner voter support; and start a Facebook or MySpace group.

If your passion is to preserve the electoral system, organize to do so. If your passion is to ensure majority representation, then you have to take the first step.

USER'S GUIDE TO THE CONSTITUTION AND BILL OF RIGHTS [STEVEN C. BENNETT]

Steven C. Bennett is a partner and commercial litigator in the New York City office of Jones Day. He has experience in a variety of areas, including construction, bankruptcy, and domestic and international arbitration. He is chair of the firm's e-Discovery Committee and a founding member of the Sedona Conference Working Group on International E-Discovery. He co-teaches a course on advanced civil procedure (e-discovery) at Rutgers Law School and previously taught a course in domestic and international commercial arbitration at Brooklyn Law School and a course on privacy law at Hunter College. Suzanne L. Telsey, an intellectual property attorney in New York, assisted in the preparation and editing of this User's Guide. The views expressed are solely those of the author, and should not be attributed to the author's firm, or its clients.

THE CONSTITUTION

The United States Constitution is often hailed as a marvel of brevity and of clarity. It was, however, written in the 18th century, and many of the concepts, words and phrases used seem quite odd to us today.

The following summary of the Constitution aims at an overview of the major provisions of the document. It also provides a brief history of the drafting of the Constitution and its amendments. In general, the first three Sections of the Constitution talk about the three arms of the government—the Legislature (the Houses of Congress), the Executive (the president and vice president) and the Judiciary (federal judges).

TEXT OF THE CONSTITUTION

Preamble

The Preamble to the Constitution is an introduction to the document. The government leaders who wrote the Constitution (referred to as the framers) wrote the Preamble to explain what they were trying to do. They wanted to improve on the government they had at the time (to make it "more perfect" than the prior system), to ensure that the new government would be fair, and to protect American citizens from internal conflict as well as from outside attack Perhaps as importantly, the Constitution was intended to do the same for future generations of Americans.

Article I

Article I of the Constitution establishes the first of the three branches of the government, the Legislature. Section 1 of that Article says that the name of the Legislature will be the Congress, which is to be made of two parts (referred to as "bicameral").

Section 2 of Article 1 says that there will be a House of Representatives, as the lower house of the two parts of Congress. It says that a person has to be at least twenty-five years old to serve in the House of Representatives, that the people of the United States will decide who will serve in the House of Representatives, and that representatives will serve two-year terms. The members of the House are divided among the states proportionally, according to the number of people living in each state, so more populous states get more representatives in the House. The leader of the House is the Speaker of the House, chosen by the members of the House of Representatives.

Section 3 establishes the upper house of Congress, the Senate. Again, it sets minimum requirements to be a senator, such as a thirty years of age. Senators were originally appointed by the legislatures of the individual States; but this method later changed to popular elections for the Senate. Senators serve six-year terms. Each state has the same number of senators, two each, regardless of how many people live in the state. Section 3 also provides that the vice president of the United States will be the leader of the Senate (called the "President of the Senate"); and that the vice president does not vote on proposed laws unless there is a tie among the senators, and then the vice president can break the tie, giving him or her potentially a great deal of power to approve or reject laws.

Section 4 provides that each state can choose how to elect its members of the Congress (which is why we now have different procedures in each state at each election day for electing national politicians) and requires that Congress meet at least once per year. (This was intended as the minimum number of times Congress must meet. In reality, it meets much more often.)

Section 5 sets the minimum number of members of Congress that must be present for Congress to meet, and gives Congress the power to set fines for members who do not appear. It also says that members may be expelled, that each house must keep a written record of what goes on at the meetings and the votes cast, and that neither house may adjourn without the consent of the other.

Section 6 requires that members of Congress be paid, that they cannot be detained while traveling to and from Congress, and that they cannot hold any other government position while serving in the Congress.

Section 7 details how laws are created, describing how a law starts as a "bill," which is essentially a proposed law before it is approved by both houses of Congress. To become a law, a both the House of Representatives and the Senate must accept by at least a majority of votes the same bill with the same language. Bills that pass both houses are then sent to the president. The president can either sign the bill, in which case it becomes law, or "veto" it, meaning that he or she rejects it and refuses to sign it into law. In the case of a veto by the president, the bill is sent back to Congress, and if both houses pass it by a two-thirds majority, the bill becomes law despite the president's veto of the bill.

If the president neither vetoes a bill nor signs it, it becomes a law (without signature) after ten days. If Congress sends a bill to the president and then adjourns, and the president does not sign the bill within ten days, the bill does not become law (this is called a "pocket" veto).

Section 8 lists specific powers of Congress, including the power to establish and maintain an army and navy, to establish post offices, to create courts, to regulate commerce between the states, to declare war, and to raise money. It also includes a clause, known as the "Elastic Clause," which allows Congress to pass any law necessary to carry out the various powers that Congress was given in the Constitution.

Section 9 places certain limits on Congress. Certain ex-

treme measures, such as passing laws after the fact to punish people for behavior that was not illegal when the
person acted originally (called "ex post facto laws") are
prohibited. No law can give preference to one state over
another; no money can be taken from the treasury except
by duly passed law; and no title of nobility, such as King,
Queen, or Marquis, can ever be established by the government.

Section 10, finally, prohibits the individual states from
doing several things. They cannot make their own money,
or declare war, or do most of the other things that Congress is not allowed to do under Section 9. The states also
cannot tax goods from other states; nor can they have
navies.

Article II

Article II establishes the second of the three branches of
government, the Executive—i.e., the president, vice president and other Executive departments. Section 1 establishes the office of the president and the vice president,
and says that they serve in office for four-year terms (which
is why we have presidential elections every four years).
Presidents are elected by an Electoral College, wherein
each state has one vote for each member that represents
the state in Congress. Originally, the president was the
person with the most votes and the vice president was
the person with the second most votes in an election by the
Electoral College. This method later changed, so that candidates run on a joint "ticket" and are elected together.
This Article also sets certain minimum requirements for
acting as president or vice president, such as a require-

ment that the president and vice president must both be at least thirty-five years old, and that the president must also have been born in the United States. For the vice president, the same citizenship requirement was added to the to the Constitution by the 12th Amendment (discussed below), requiring that the vice president meet the same eligibility requirements as the President (This is why foreign-born politicians can never become president or vice president, although they can hold other offices. The president is to be paid a salary determined by Congress, but this salary cannot be increased or decreased while the president is in office, so that Congress could not use the president's salary as either a punishment or reward for the president taking certain actions while in office.

Section 2 gives the President some important powers. The president is commander in chief of the armed forces and of the militia (National Guard) of all the states; the president has a Cabinet to advise him or her in making decisions, and the president can pardon criminals, meaning that the president can decide that a person convicted of a crime will not be punished for the crime. The president makes treaties with other nations, and picks federal judges and other senior members of the government (all with the approval of the Senate).

Section 3 establishes the duties of the president: to give a state of the union speech, to make suggestions for laws that Congress should consider, to act as head of the country by receiving ambassadors and other foreign governmental representatives, and to carry out the laws of the United States.

Section 4 briefly discusses removal of the president, called "impeachment."

Article III

Article III establishes the last of the three branches of government, the Judiciary—the federal judges. Section 1 establishes the Supreme Court, which is the highest court in the United States. It also says that judges of the Supreme Court and lower federal courts serve as long as they are on "good behavior," which usually means for life. So once appointed, federal judges can stay in their job for the rest of their lives, if they choose, except for certain very unusual circumstances. Article III also requires that judges must be paid, and that their pay cannot be reduced. The intent of having federal judges appointed for life, and not having to run for reelection or be reappointed was to give them independence so they could decide cases fairly and impartially, without worrying about pleasing the public or politicians.

Section 2 describes the kind of cases that may be heard by federal judges, and identifies the few specific cases the Supreme Court may decide first (called "original jurisdiction"), rather than having the case go to the lower courts before getting to the Supreme Court, which is much more common. The Section states that except for those very few "original jurisdiction" cases, all other court cases heard by the Supreme Court are by appeal from lower courts. This Section also guarantees a trial by jury in federal criminal cases.

Section 3 defines the crime of treason—acts against the United States. This was a matter of great importance to a new country that had just declared itself independent from England. During the Revolutionary War, some favored England over an independent United States, and took actions to prevent America from winning the War and becoming independent of England.

Article IV

Article IV concerns the states. Section 1 says that all states must honor (give "full faith and credit" to) the laws of other states.

Section 2 says that states must treats citizens of other states the same as they treat their own citizens. It also states that if a person accused of a crime in one state flees to another, they will be returned to the state from which they fled. This section has a clause dealing with fugitive slaves, which no longer has legal effect.

Section 3 concerns the admission of new states as part of the United States and also says that Congress decides what happens with property belonging to the United States.

Section 4 ensures a "Republican" form of government (as opposed to a monarchical government, where a country is controlled by the king) and guarantees that the federal government will protect states against invasion.

Article V

Article V details the method of amending, or changing, the Constitution. It takes a vote of at least two-thirds of the both houses of Congress or two-thirds of the states to propose an amendment to the Constitution. To become effective, the proposed Constitutional amendment must then be approved by at least three-quarters of the states. The writers of the Constitution intentionally required a higher level of public approval to amend the Constitution, to ensure than any amendment was one that a meaningful number of the citizens wanted.

Article VI

Article VI guarantees that the United States government would assume all debts and contracts entered into by the United States before the Constitution was approved. It also says that the Constitution and all federal laws are the "supreme law" of the country, meaning that if there is a conflict between the Constitution or a federal law passed by Congress and a state-passed law, the Constitution and the federal laws will prevail over state law. Finally, it requires all officers of the United States and of the states to swear an oath of allegiance to the United States and the Constitution when taking office, and also prohibits a person's religion from being part of the qualifications of being allowed to serve as a public official.

Article VII

Article VII details the method for ratification, or approval, of the Constitution. Of the original thirteen states in the United States, nine had to approve the Constitution before it could officially come into effect.

The Bill Of Rights

The first ten amendments to the Constitution were all adopted at the same time in 1791 and are collectively known as the "Bill of Rights."

The 1st Amendment protects the peoples' right to practice religion, to speak freely, to assemble (meet), and to address the government. It prohibits Congress from passing any laws that create a religion or restrict a person's right to practice any religion, that limit free speech or a free press, that restrict the peoples' right to meet peaceably or to seek change from the Government.

The 2nd Amendment protects the right to own guns, at least in certain circumstances.

The 3rd Amendment guarantees that the military cannot force homeowners to let them into their homes and give them room and board, which the British soldiers had done before the Revolutionary War.

The 4th Amendment says that the government cannot seize or search a person's property or detain a person without a valid warrant (in other words approval of a judge) based on good reason (i.e., probable cause) with proper support.

The 5th Amendment protects people from being prosecuted for a serious crime unless charged by a grand jury (i.e., a group of citizens who hear the grounds for the charge and approve or reject it), except in certain very limited situations, such as for the military during wartime. It also prohibits trying a person twice for the same crime (referred to as "double jeopardy"), and provides that a person cannot be forced to testify against himself in a criminal matter. In the popular phrase, "pleading the Fifth" the "Fifth" refers to the 5th Amendment. It prohibits the government from taking people's property without proper compensation. It also guarantees that a person cannot be "deprived of life, liberty, or property, without due process of law," meaning that a people cannot be locked up or have their property taken away by the federal government without a chance to contest the action and have their side heard.

The 6th Amendment guarantees people accused of crimes the right to a prompt and public (not a secretive) trial of the charges and the right to have their case decided by an impartial jury, and to question the witnesses who are testifying against them. The 6th Amendment also guarantees that persons accused of crimes have the right to a lawyer to assist in their defense.

The 7th Amendment guarantees people a jury trial (rather than a case decided only by a judge) in federal civil cases.

The 8th Amendment requires that criminal punishments be fair, not "cruel and unusual," and that extraordinarily large fines will not be imposed.

The 9th Amendment states that other rights in addition to those specifically stated in other parts of the Constitution may exist, and will be protected. It is this Amendment that the courts have often relied on in finding certain other rights guaranteed to the people, such as certain rights of privacy, even though they are not specifically set out in the Constitution.

The 10th Amendment essentially states that any power not granted to the federal government belongs to states or to the people. For this reason certain matters, such as education, marriage among citizens, and local community matters, among others, have been left for the states to regulate, and each state can pass different laws on matters controlled by the states.

Additional Amendments

The 11th Amendment says that the federal courts cannot hear lawsuits against a State, meaning that if a state itself (or the state government) is sued, the case cannot be brought in the federal court, protecting the state from being governed by the federal courts.

The 12th Amendment redefines how the president and vice president are chosen by the Electoral College, making the two positions cooperative, rather than first and second highest vote-getters. It also says that anyone who becomes vice president must be eligible to become president, so the same age and nationality requirements for president apply for the vice president.

The 13th Amendment abolishes slavery in the United States.

The 14th Amendment ensures that all citizens of all States enjoy not only rights on the federal level, but on the state level as well. It gives people protection from improper action by the state government, without due process of law, similar to how the Fifth Amendment protects citizens from having their property or liberty taken by the federal government without having an opportunity to contest the action and have their side heard. The 14th Amendment also requires that, for the purpose of determining how many representatives a state is entitled to in the House of Representatives, all citizens shall be counted (doing away with the pre-Civil War practice of counting slaves as three-fifths of a person for the purposes of the census). Since the 14th Amendment was passed in the wake of the Civil War, it also voided any debts or claims in furtherance of any rebellion against the United States government (thereby invaliding any debts of the Confederate government) and also any voided claims by slave owners for losses due to the abolition of slavery.

The 15th Amendment ensures that the right to vote cannot be restricted because of a person's race.

The 16th Amendment authorizes the United States to collect income tax without regard to the population of the states.

The 17th Amendment changes the method of choosing Senators from selection by the state legislatures to election by the people.

The 18th Amendment prohibited the sale or manufacture of alcohol in the United States. This restriction was referred to as "Prohibition." This amendment was later repealed (withdrawn).

The 19th Amendment ensures that the right to vote cannot be restricted based on a person's sex, giving women the right to vote.

The 20th Amendment sets new beginning dates for the terms of the Congress and the president, and clarifies how the death of a president before swearing-in would be handled.

The 21st Amendment repeals the 18th Amendment (on alcohol prohibition), and therefore the sale and manufacture of liquor is no longer prohibited.

The 22nd Amendment sets a limit on the number of times a president may be elected—two four-year terms. It provides one exception for a vice president who assumes the presidency after the death or removal of the president, establishing the maximum term of any such president as ten years.

The 23rd Amendment grants the District of Columbia (Washington, D.C.) the right to three electors in presidential elections.

The 24th Amendment ensures that people are not required to pay a fee in order to vote for a candidate.

The 25th Amendment clarifies even further the line of succession to the presidency, and establishes rules for a president who becomes unable to perform the duties of office.

The 26th Amendment ensures that any person eighteen years of age or older may vote. (The previous minimum age requirement was twenty-one years.)

The 27th Amendment requires that any law that increases the pay of legislators may not take effect until after an election is completed.

A BRIEF HISTORY OF THE CONSTITUTION

Many people believe that the United States of America, as we know it today, was "born" on July 4, 1776 with the signing of the Declaration of Independence. Yet, the Declaration of Independence, while an important statement of the rights that Americans claimed, did not establish any actual government or country, as the Constitution did.

In the summer of 1787, citizens of the different States ("framers") met in Philadelphia to begin drafting what would become the Constitution. Many important historical figures, active during the Revolutionary War (for example, George Washington, Benjamin Franklin, James Madison, Alexander Hamilton and others) attended these meetings, referred to as the Constitutional Convention. The Convention spent a great deal of time on the problem of the fair representation of large and small states, and built in to the Constitution were compromises to appease the differing interests of the various states. Ultimately, the framers agreed on a compromise, in which each state would have two senators, regardless of how many people lived in each state, while members of the other legislative branch, the House or Representatives, would be apportioned based on how many people lived in the state, so that states with more people would get more representatives (and therefore more votes in the House) than those with smaller populations. The Convention also compromised over the issue of slavery, providing that no ban on slave trade could be imposed for twenty years, and establishing that slaves would be counted as "three-fifths" persons, for purposes of determining the size of a state's population and therefore how many representatives in the House the state would receive. Finally, the Convention compromised on election of the president, choosing neither direct election by the people, nor indirect choice by members in Congress, and instead providing for an "Electoral College," to be selected by the States.

The Convention completed the text of the Constitution in September 1787. The individual state legislatures ratified it over the next two years. In September 1789, after enough states had approved (ratified) the Constitution to permit the government to begin action, Congress proposed ten amendments to the Constitution (known as the "Bill of Rights"). These amendments to the Constitution assured the people and the states within the United States certain essential rights, which in turn influenced various additional states to ultimately approve the Constitution.

The Constitution has been revised (amended) twenty-seven times since 1787. In addition to the Bill of Rights, the most significant of the amendments followed the Civil War (1861–1856). These post-war amendments (the 13th,

14th and 15th Amendments), abolished slavery, ensured that all citizens would receive the same protections of their property and freedoms, and guaranteed that race would not be used as a criterion for being allowed to vote. Later, in 1919–1920, the Constitution was amended to guarantee women the right to vote.

Many other amendments of the Constitution have been proposed over the years. Perhaps most famously, in 1971–1972, Congress proposed an "Equal Rights Amendment" (referred to as the "ERA"), which would have provided that equality of rights could not be abridged "on account of sex," in other words, men and women would be treated the same in terms of their rights under the Constitution. The states ultimately did not approve the amendment.

New amendments to the Constitution are proposed in virtually every term of Congress. The process of proposing and passing amendments, however, was deliberately made difficult, so that this essential document would be changed only after careful deliberation and only with the support of a very large percentage of the citizens.

ESSENTIAL POLITICAL CONCEPTS EMBODIED IN THE CONSTITUTION

The Framers intended to set up a government that would fix the problems the colonists had with the system that existed before the Revolutionary War, under which England dictated to the American colonies how they had to act and what they had to do, while at the same time refusing to give colonists any vote or say in what those English rules would be. As a result, the Constitution's goal was to create a government where power was shared among different branches that represent the interests of all the citizens, and no one person or select group would have total control over the rights and freedoms of citizens.

"Separation of Powers"—Power Is Shared Among the Three Branches of Government and "Popular Sovereignty"—the Will of the People

The Constitution flatly rejected a one-sided system like a monarchy (a modified form of which existed in Great Britain at the time of the Revolution), where one person, such as the King, holds all the power. Instead, the Constitution spread the power among three branches—the Executive (president and his advisors), Legislative (Congress), and the Judiciary (federal judges), and required that the three branches cooperate in order to act. As a result, no one person or small group controls all the government power. And because the people select the Executive and Legislative branch representatives, who in turn appoint the Judiciary, it is the people's will that is represented in the government (referred to as "popular sovereignty").

"Federalism"—One Nation of Many Different Parts

Although the Constitution establishes a strong central government, it also recognizes the important role of the states, so that while the federal government has power over certain areas, the states have power over other areas.

ADDITIONAL RESOURCES

Understand How Your System Works

- Electoral College
  - For detailed information on and the history of the Electoral College: http://www.archives.gov/federal-register/electoral-college
- Declaration of Independence:
  - http://www.ushistory.org/declaration/document/scan.htm
  - http://www.archives.gov/exhibits/charters/declaration.html
- U.S. Constitution:
  - National Archives, www.archives.gov (full text of Constitution and other important documents).
  - National Constitution Center, www.constitutioncenter.org (history of the Constitution and American Government).
  - http://www.law.cornell.edu/constitution/constitution.overview.html
  - http://www.constitution.org/constit_.htm
- Bill of Rights:
  - http://www.constitution.org/billofr_.htm
  - http://www.law.cornell.edu/constitution/constitution.billofrights.html

VIII. WISH LIST FOR
THE FUTURE

DIRECT DEMOCRACY

Drive a movement to make possible national direct democracy.

In order to bypass a dysfunctional Congress altogether and clean out the system, we must drive a movement to allow for nationwide direct democracy. We should not rule out a simple, powerful idea that works in twenty-four states. If a grassroots movement existed in all fifty states to drive such a law, then representatives, lobbyists, and special interests would be placed in the position of having to defend the posture that the people cannot be trusted to use power directly.

VOTING [Curtis Ellis]

Make voting mandatory, with fines for not voting. When you renew your auto registration or file your taxes, you should have to show that you voted in elections.

Barack Obama talks about changing politics and getting people involved—what better way than this? Even if people disagree with our proposal, by introducing such legislation we will begin a discussion we need to have, a discussion about changing our culture to make voting into something we're proud to do—or at least ashamed to admit we do not do.

Increase access to voting with same-day registration, early voting, and weekend voting, and make Election Day a holiday.

Set uniform standards for elections with a national election law. Right now, elections are funded at the county level. The problem is that poorer counties run worse elections (fewer machines, worse machines, fewer workers, longer lines, etc.). Some clever lawyer might find this a violation of an equal protection clause, but a straightforward solution would be national election laws with funding for election equipment and personnel furnished by the federal government (and paid for by fines collected from those not voting).

Require civics education in all schools, in as many grades as possible. Press for this at every level of government, from the local school board to the U.S. Congress, which should require civics education for schools to qualify for the school lunch program. Get local businesses to endow a scholarship to be awarded to the winner of a civics competition, such as a voter registration/turnout drive or essay contest.

A TWELVE-STEP PROGRAM TO SAVE U.S. DEMOCRACY [Mark Crispin Miller]

1. **Repeal the Help America Vote Act (HAVA).**
   This step will inevitably follow an in-depth investigation of how HAVA came to be.
2. **Replace *all* electronic voting with hand-counted paper ballots.**
   Although politicians and the press dismiss this idea as utopian, the people would support it just as overwhelmingly as national health care, strong en-

vironmental measures, U.S. withdrawal from Iraq, and other sane ideas.

3. **Get rid of computerized voter rolls.**

   It isn't just the e-voting machines that are obstructing our self-government. According to *USA Today*, thousands of Americans have had their names mysteriously purged from the electronic databases now used nationwide as records of our registration.

4. **Keep all private vendors out of our elections.**

   With their commercial interests, trade secrets, and unaccountable proceedings, private companies should have no role in the essential process of republican self-government.

5. **Make it illegal for the TV networks to declare who won before the vote count is complete.**

   Certainly the corporate press will scream about its First Amendment rights, but they don't have the right to interfere with our elections. When they declare a winner before we even know if the election was legitimate, they predefine all audits, recounts, and even first counts of the vote as the mere desperate measures of "sore losers."

6. **Set up an exit polling system, publicly supported, to keep the vote counts honest.**

   Only in America are exit poll results not meant to help us gauge the accuracy of the official count. Here they are meant only to allow the media to make its calls.

7. **Get rid of voter registration rules by allowing every citizen to register, at any post office, on his/ her eighteenth birthday.**

   Either we believe in universal suffrage or we don't.

8. **Ban all state requirements for state-issued IDs at the polls.**
   As the Supreme Court smiles on such Jim Crow devices, we need a law or constitutional amendment to forbid them.

9. **Put all polling places under video surveillance to spot voter fraud, monitor election personnel, and track the turnout.**
   We're under surveillance everywhere else, so why not?

10. **Have Election Day declared a federal holiday, requiring all employers to allow their workers time to vote.**
    No citizen of the United States should ever lose the right to vote because they have to go to work.

11. **Make it illegal for secretaries of state to cochair political campaigns (or otherwise assist or favor them).**
    Katherine Harris wore both those hats in Florida in 2000, and, four years later, so did Ken Blackwell in Ohio and Jan Brewer in Arizona. These Republicans should not have been allowed to do it, nor should any Democrats.

12. **Make election fraud a major felony, with prison time and whopping fines for all repeat offenders.**
    "Three strikes and you're out" would certainly befit so serious a crime against democracy.

ADDITIONAL WISH LIST ITEMS:

- Dedicate a national Deliberation Day period going into each election.

- Drive a movement at local, state, and national levels to offer all government websites and information on government processes in two formats: the current legalese and a translation into generally accessible, conventional English.
- Establish an easy-to-use congressional interactive website that presents in real time upcoming legislation in user-friendly English, lets you send a message about it directly, and shows how many other (voluntarily disclosed) messages for or against the legislation were sent by your fellow citizens. Make sure similar transparent sites operate covering local and state activity in every community.
- Give every graduating senior an easy-to-understand guide to running for local, state, and national office.
- Reinstate the practice of giving a handbook of American patriotic writings and values to citizens—perhaps upon graduation from high school, upon securing a driver's license, or upon registering to vote.
- Pass federal legislation to ensure that citizens have certain basic rights to assemble and protest without having to face preemptive detention, rubber bullets, microwave weapons, or Tasers.
- Abolish "free-speech plazas" on campuses and drive a movement to remind campus administrators that the founders intended the whole nation as a "free-speech plaza."

- Create a national nonpartisan clearinghouse with full-time phone and Internet advisors to help citizens run for office.
- Create a nationwide version of the 311 line— a local-level service that diverts callers to the right government department—that is gaining popularity. This national 311 hotline will advise any caller if his or her issue is a local, state, or federal issue and how to pursue it appropriately.
- Drive a pressure campaign against local and regional newspapers to ask that they post the day's, or next few days', upcoming business in Congress and at the local and state level—with contact numbers—written in accessible, conventional English.
- Establish a national, free system of American *ulpans* (the Hebrew term for a fast-track language/values immersion course) so that any new or current citizen can become not only proficient in the common language, and thus engage in debate and deliberation, but can also gain or refresh an understanding of American processes and ideals.

NOTES

Introduction

1. Jane Preston, "More Illegal Crossings Are Criminal Cases," *New York Times,* June 18, 2008. See also Jane Preston, "270 Illegal Immigrants Sent to Prison in Federal Push," *New York Times,* May 24, 2008, and Kathy Kiely, "Immigrant's Family Detained After Daughter Speaks Out," *USA Today,* October 16, 2007.

2. Thomas H. Keen and Lee H. Hamilton, "Stonewalled by the C.I.A.," *New York Times,* January 2, 2008.

3. Associated Press, http://abcnews.go.com/Politics/wireStory?id=4631535;See also Jane Mayer, *The Dark Side: The Inside Story of How the War on Terror Turned into a War on American Ideals* (New York: Doubleday, 2008), 311, and Phillipe Sands, *Torture Team: Rumsfeld's Memo and the Betrayal of American Values* (New York: Palgrave MacMillan, 2008), 14–24.

4. Mimi Hall, "Terror Watch List Swells to More Than 755,000," *USA Today,* October 24, 2007.

5. Andy Sullivan, "Bush Didn't Know About CIA Leak: McClellan," Reuters, June 21, 2008, http://www.reuters.com/article/topNews/idUSN2032779420080621.

6. Library of Congress, "H.R. 1955," http://thomas.loc.gov/home/gpoxmlc110/h1955_rfs.xml.

7. Jeremy Scahill, "Blackwater's Private Spies," *The Nation,* June 5, 2008, http://www.thenation.com/doc/20080623/scahill. See also Jeremy Scahill, "Blackwater's Bright Future," *Los Angeles Times,* June 16, 2008, http://www.latimes.com/news/opinion/la-oe-scahill16-2008jun16,0,5769512.story; Eilene Zimmerman, "Blackwater's Run for the Border," Salon.com, October 23, 2007, http://www.salon.com/news/feature/2007/

10/23/blackwater_border/; and "Blackwater USA Unveils New Subsidiary," press release, http://www.blackwaterusa. com/press/airship.asp. See also Bill Sizemore, "Blackwater USA Says It Can Supply Forces for Conflicts," *Virginian Pilot*, March 30 2006.

8. James Risen, "Bush Signs Law to Widen Reach for Wiretapping," *New York Times*, August 6, 2007. See also Eric Lichtblau and David Stout, "House Passes Bill on Federal Wiretapping Powers," *New York Times*, June 21, 2008.

9. Natan Sharansky with Ron Dermer, *The Case for Democracy: The Power of Freedom to Overcome Tyranny and Terror* (New York: PublicAffairs, 2004), xxx–xxxiv.

10. Merrill D. Peterson, *Thomas Jefferson and the New Nation: A Biography* (London: Oxford University Press, 1970), 46–47.

11. John P. Kaminski, ed., *The Quotable Jefferson* (Princeton, NJ: Princeton University Press, 2006), 83.

12. Ibid., 94. Also, Sizemore, "Blackwater USA Says It Can Supply Forces for Conflicts."

13. Lucy Popescu and Carole Seymour-Jones, eds., *Writers Under Siege: Voices of Freedom from Around the World* (New York: New York University Press, 2007), xiv.

14. Gary B. Nash, *The Unknown American Revolution: The Unruly Birth of Democracy and the Struggle to Create America* (New York: Viking, 2005), 65, 99, 122.

15. Ibid., 331–39.

16. Ibid., 124–27.

17. The Gettysburg Address, in Garry Wills, *Lincoln at Gettysburg: The Words that Remade America* (New York: Touchstone Books, 1992), 261.

18. Nash, op. cit., 202.

19. Ibid., 434.

20. Ibid., 123.

21. Ibid., 408.

22. Missouri's Dred Scott Case, 1846–1857. http://www.sos.mo .gov/archives/resources/africanamerican/scott/scott.asp.

23. "Seneca Falls Convention, July 19–20, 1848," http://www .npg.si.edu/col/seneca/senfalls1.htm. See also Pauline Maier,

American Scripture: Making the Declaration of Independence (New York: Vintage Books), 197–99, on the many groups that would in the future lay claim to the wording and argument of the Declaration of Independence.

24. Wills, op. cit., 261.
25. Thomas Paine, *Common Sense*, (Ed.) Isaac Kramnick, (New York: Penguin Books, 1986).
26. Sharansky, op. cit., 57.
27. Henry David Thoreau, *Walden: Or, Life in the Woods and On the Duty of Civil Disobedience* (New York: Collier Books, 1962), 248.

FREEDOM IS INTENDED AS A CHALLENGE

1. Maier, op. cit., 134–35. On the Declaration's "duty to rebel," see p. 137. On its use of "happiness," see p. 167.
2. Ibid., 214, on how "memories tend to fade after 'life, liberty and the pursuit of happiness.' "
3. Maxwell Taylor Kennedy, *Make Gentle the Life of This World: The Vision of Robert F. Kennedy* (New York: Broadway Books, 1998), 14.
4. Kaminski, op. cit., 50, 133, 138, 302.
5. Ibid., 121.
6. Ibid., 302.
7. Maier, op. cit., 215.
8. Joseph J. Ellis, *Founding Brothers: The Revolutionary Generation* (New York: Vintage Books, 2000), 206–48.

FAKE PATRIOTISM

1. Gustav Niebuhr, "The 2000 Campaign: The Religious Issue; Lieberman Is Asked to Stop Invoking Faith in Campaign," *New York Times*, August 9, 2000.
2. "McCain to Move On: Get Out: Senator Blasts Anti-War Group in New Hampshire," CBS News, September 14, 2007, http://www.cbsnews.com/stories/2007/09/14/politics/main 3262322.shtml.

3. Donald Scott, "Evangelicalism, Revivalism, and the Second Great Awakening," Queens College/City University of New York, National Humanities Center, http://nationalhumanities center.org/tserve/nineteen/nkeyinfo/nevanrev.htm.

4. "McCain Disavows Ad, But Calls Obama Comments 'Elitist,'" FOX News, April 23, 2008, http://elections.foxnews. com/2008/04/23/mccain-disavows-ad-but-calls-obama-bitter-comments-elitist/.

5. "Colonial Origins of American Constitutionalism," in Michael Les Benedict, *The Blessings of Liberty: A Concise History of the Constitution of the United States* (Lexington, MA: D. C. Heath and Co, 1996), 29–49.

6. Lord Charnwood, *Abraham Lincoln* (New York: Henry Holt, 1917) 122–36, 399.

7. Frederick Douglass, speech delivered on July 5, 1852, "The Meaning of the Fourth of July to the Negro," http://www.pbs .org/wgbh/aia/part4/4h2927.html.

What, to the American slave, is your 4th of July? I answer; a day that reveals to him, more than all other days in the year, the gross injustice and cruelty to which he is the constant victim. To him, your celebration is a sham; your boasted liberty, an unholy license; your national greatness, swelling vanity; your sound of rejoicing are empty and heartless; your denunciation of tyrants brass fronted impudence; your shout of liberty and equality, hollow mockery; your prayers and hymns, your sermons and thanks-givings, with all your religious parade and solemnity, are to him, mere bombast, fraud, deception, impiety, and hypocrisy—a thin veil to cover up crimes which would disgrace a nation of savages. There is not a nation on the earth guilty of practices more shocking and bloody than are the people of the United States, at this very hour.

8. Reverend Martin Luther King Jr., "Beyond Vietnam: A Time to Break Silence," sermon delivered at Riverside Church,

New York City, April 4, 1967, http://www.ssc.msu.edu/~sw/mlk/brkslnc.htm. Maxwell Taylor Kennedy, op. cit., 48. "Violence breeds violence, repression brings retaliation, and only a cleansing of our whole society can remove the sickness from our soul," wrote RFK.

9. John Winthrop, cited in George Grant, *The Patriot's Handbook: A Citizenship Primer for a New Generation of Americans* (Nashville: Cumberland House Publishing, 2004), 15.

10. Governor Ronald Reagan, "We Will Be A City Upon A Hill" (speech given at Conservative Political Action Conference, Washington, D.C., January 25, 1974).

11. Grant, op. cit., 15.

12. Reagan, "We Will Be A City Upon A Hill."

13. Grant, op. cit., 15.

14. Yale's Avalon project, http://www.yale.edu./lawweb/avalon/presiden/inaug/lincoln2.htm.

15. Charnwood, op. cit., 443.

16. Ibid., 116–18.

17. Ibid.

FAKE DEMOCRACY

1. Kaminsky, op. cit., 37.

2. Grant, op. cit., xiii.

3. Ibid.

4. Naomi Wolf, "Hey, Young Americans, Here's a Text for You," *Washington Post,* November 25, 2007.

5. Mark Kurlansky, *1968: The Year That Rocked the World* (New York: Random House, 2005), xvii-3.

6. For Civics see, http://nces.ed.gov/nationsreportcard/pubs/main2006/2007476.asp. For History, see p. 9 of http://nces.ed.gov/nationsreportcard/pdf/main2006/2007474_1.pdf. See also "College Seniors Failed a Basic Test on America's History and Institutions," report on colleges by Intercollegiate Studies Institute, http://www.americancivicliteracy.org/report/major_findings_finding1.html, and "Greater Learning about America Goes Hand-in-Hand with More Active

Citizenship," report by Intercollegiate Studies Institute, http://www.americancivicliteracy.org/report/major_findings_finding5.html, and Wolf, "Hey, Young Americans, Here's a Text for You."

7. "Teens Learning—and Challenging—First Amendment Values," Knight's Foundation Study, http://www.firstamendmentfuture.org/report91806_release.php.

8. Author interview, November 2007.

9. http://www.atlantaga.gov/.

10. "How Our Laws Are Made," Library of Congress, http://thomas.loc.gov/home/lawsmade.toc.html.

11. Illinois State Legislature website. See also, for example, http://jerseycityonline.com/jerseycityour_new_council.htm. This site lists where city council meetings are held and contact information for city and state officials but nothing about how to become a council member or other city or state official oneself. Wisconsin's site, overseen by WashLaw, a free service of Washburn University School of Law, does guide citizens clearly through Wisconsin's system and offers links to information for all states; http://www.washlaw.edu/uslaw/states/wisconsin/, even showing links to Wisconsin cities and counties. It has a window onto the current legislative session. But such clear, transparent sites are the exception and there is no category listed on the home page with guidelines for running oneself or serving on boards or commissions oneself. The Kansas Legislative Research Department offers links to national legislative organizations, federal sites, state sites, and Kansas sites, but no guidelines for citizens becoming legislators noted (http://skyways.lib.ks.us/ksleg/KLRD/GovLinks.htm). We are so unused to thinking of ourselves as citizen leaders that this omission may seem unexceptional, but it is like a course catalog for a major public university offered online but with no application form, process or deadlines listed or readily available, and no real application process systematized except for an insider elite.

12. http://www.co.shasta.ca.us/; see http://www.sec.state.ma.us/index.htm. This site does list some election information

clearly for citizens and is in some other ways a good model of transparency.

13. www.monticello.org/reports/quotes/liberty.html, June 24, 1826, to Roger Weightman, Writings 1517), Ann M. Lucas, Monticello Research Department, February 1996.

14. See Congress website, www.house.gov. See also http://democraticleader.house.gov.

15. Caroline J. Tolbert, Ramona S. McNeal, and Daniel A. Smith, "Enhancing Civic Engagement: The Effect of Direct Democracy on Political Participation and Knowledge," *State Politics and Policy Quarterly* 3, no. 1 (Spring 2003), 23–41.

16. "In a Busy Day at the Polls, Swiss Decide Nine Issues," *New York Times,* May 20, 2003. See also "Put Out More Flags," editorial, *The Guardian*, March 26, 2008, and Patrick Wintour, "Constitutional Reform," *The Guardian*, March 26, 2008.

17. For more on citizen engagement in the UK, see Michael James Macpherson, "Citizens' Initiative and Referendum in Britain and Northern Ireland 2007," *Europa Magazine*, http://www.europa-magazin.ch/zone/.3bb51286/cmd.14/cert.99.EIjObJQkeN7.0.

18. Eric Weiner, "You Must Vote. It's the Law. Australia Requires Citizens to Vote. Should the U.S.?" *Slate*, October 29, 2004.

19. Tolbert, et al., op. cit., 23–41. See also this note for some of the points of view in the ongoing argument about direct democracy: "Some argue that direct democracy in liberal democratic governments around the world is making governments more participatory [Mendelson and Parker, 2001; Peters, 1996; Budge, 1996] while others suggest that ballot initiatives are 'derailing' or 'deluding' representative democracy [Broder, 2000; Ellis, 2002] tyrannizing minority groups [Schrag, 1998; Gamble, 1997; Bell, 1978] and weakening legislative institutions [Rosenthal, 1998]."

20. Jesse McKinley, "As Torch Reaches San Francisco, It Runs for Cover Before Its Run," *New York Times*, April 9, 2008. "Sarkozy Hints at Boycott of Olympics' Opening," Associated Press/*New York Times*, March 26, 2008.

21. On the unruly nature of colonial and revolutionary protest,

see Michael Beschloss, *Presidential Courage: Brave Leaders and How They Changed America, 1789–1989 (New* York: Simon & Schuster, 2007), 9, and Nash, op. cit., "Years of Insurgence," 44–88.

22. Kaminski, op. cit., 120, "We are not to expect to be translated from despotism to liberty in a feather bed."

23. Andrew Cornell, "Preempting Dissent," in Amitava Kumar and Michael Ryan, eds., *Politics and Culture,* http://aspen .conncoll.edu/politicsandculture/page.cfm?key=503.

24. Author interview, May 2008.

25. Author interview, November 2007.

26. http://www.NYC.gov.

27. William O. Douglas, *Points of Rebellion* (New York: Vintage Books, 1970), 11.

28. Author interview, May 2008. "The U.S. Army High School Program Guide: A Guide for Students, Parents and Educators."

29. On test prep, see, "March 2 Success: The Future Is Now!," www.macrh2success.com; U.S. Army, "Army Strong" at www .goarmy.com/recruiter; and the DVD *One on One: A Conversation with U.S. Soldiers and Their Families,* www.goarmy.com/for_ parents.

30. Mark Miller, *Fooled Again: The Real Case for Electoral Reform* (New York: Basic Books, 2005), xi-xviii, and Mark Miller, *Loser Take All: Election Fraud and the Subversion of Democracy, 2000–2008* (New York: IG Publishing, 2008). See also Damien Cave and Christine Sexton, "New Florida Rules Return More Than 115,000 Ex-Offenders to Voting Rolls," *New York Times,* June 18, 2008; Ian Urbina, "Decision Is Likely to Spur Voter ID Laws in More States," *New York Times,* April 29, 2008. See also William Poundstone, *Gaming the Vote: Why Elections Aren't Fair (And What We Can Do About It),* (New York: Hill and Wang, 2008), 3–22.

31. "Nica Elections: Interview with Jimmy Carter," National Public Radio, November 5, 2006, http://blythe-systems.com/ pipermail/nytr/Week-of-Mon-20061030/050459.html.

32. Author interview, American Democracy Institute, April 23, 2008.
33. Virginia Senate, http://www.sbe.virginia.gov.
34. Forms, http://www.sbe.virginia.gov.
35. You can get access to what Congress is doing day by day on its government site, but not in English, and not summarizing for ordinary Americans what the bills really mean—or even, if interpretation is a concern, "pro" and "con" or two-party summaries of what the bills actually mean. For example: Use the drop down menu to view Floor proceedings for the last 7 legislative days.

CURRENT HOUSE FLOOR PROCEEDINGS
LEGISLATIVE DAY OF JULY 9, 2008
110TH CONGRESS—SECOND SESSION
H.R. 6061:
to designate the facility of the United States Postal Service located at 219 East Main Street in West Frankfort, Illinois, as the "Kenneth James Gray Post Office Building"
6:48 P.M.—
DEBATE—The House proceeded with forty minutes of debate on H.R. 6061.
Considered under suspension of the rules.
Mr. Davis (IL) moved to suspend the rules and pass the bill.
H. Res. 1260:
supporting the goals and ideals of "National Internet Safety Month"
6:46 P.M.—
Motion to reconsider laid on the table Agreed to without objection.
On motion to suspend the rules and agree to the resolution Agreed to by voice vote.
6:34 P.M.—
DEBATE—The House proceeded with forty minutes of debate on H. Res. 1260.

Considered under suspension of the rules.
Mr. Hill moved to suspend the rules and agree to the resolution.
S. 2607:
to make a technical correction to section 3009 of the Deficit Reduction Act of 2005
6:33 P.M.—
Motion to reconsider laid on the table Agreed to without objection.
On motion to suspend the rules and pass the bill Agreed to by voice vote.
6:10 P.M.—
DEBATE—The House proceeded with forty minutes of debate on S. 2607.
Considered under suspension of the rules.
Mr. Hill moved to suspend the rules and pass the bill.
H.R. 6184:
to provide for a program for circulating quarter dollar coins that are emblematic of a national park or other national site in each State, the District of Columbia, and each territory of the United States, and for other purposes
6:07 P.M.—
Motion to reconsider laid on the table Agreed to without objection.
On motion to suspend the rules and pass the bill Agreed to by the Yeas and Nays: (2/3 required): 419-0 (Roll no. 479).
6:00 P.M.—
Considered as unfinished business.
H.R. 3329:
to provide housing assistance for very low-income veterans
Motion to reconsider laid on the table Agreed to without objection.
On motion to suspend the rules and pass the bill, as amended Agreed to by the Yeas and Nays: (2/3 required): 412-9 (Roll no. 478) . . .

36. Author interview, April 2008. In contrast to this is Representative Steve Kagen of Wisconsin, a doctor who voluntarily gave up his own health insurance until he could get his constituents affordable health insurance. He became a congressman because he could no longer stand to prescribe medication to his low-income patients who could not afford to get his prescriptions filled. Congresspeople, he says, have the power of life and death. "One of first things he did," says Ellis, who worked with him, "was say to his staff, 'I want every bill that comes before Congress to be explained: what do these bills mean to the people in my district.' Then he puts it on his website, he had a pocket card."

PRINCIPLE ONE: WE ARE REQUIRED TO SPEAK FREELY

1. Maxwell Taylor Kennedy, op. cit., 108.
2. Lord Charnwood, op. cit., 147.
3. Kaminski, op. cit., 345.
4. Maxwell Taylor Kennedy, op. cit., 18; Kaminski, op. cit., xxxi–xxxii.
5. Bill of Rights, www.law.cornell.edu/constitution/constitution .billofrights.html. See also www.firstamendmentcenter.org.
6. Sharansky and Dermer, op. cit., 10.
7. Author interview, June 2008.
8. Noam Chomsky and Edward S. Herman, *Manufacturing Consent: The Political Economy of the Mass Media* (New York: Random House, 2002), xi–xxx.
9. Kaminski, op. cit., p. 91.

PRINCIPLE TWO: WE HAVE A DUTY TO REBEL AGAINST INJUSTICE AND OPPRESSION

1. Maxwell Taylor Kennedy, op. cit., 4.
2. Author interview, November 2007. See also Jessalyn Radack, *The Canary in the Coal Mine: Blowing the Whistle in the Case of the "American Taliban" John Walker Lindh: A Memoir,* author

publication, ISBN #978–1–4276–0974–8; and Mayer, op. cit., 95–97.

3. Ibid., 281.

4. Connie Roberts, ed., *Wordsworth Dictionary of Quotations* (Hertferdshire, England: Wordsworth Editions Ltd., 1998), 182.

5. Nash, op. cit., 44–85.

6. Beschloss, op. cit., 6–9, 12.

7. Ibid., 18.

8. John D. Weaver, "Bonus March," *American Heritage Magazine,* June 1963, http://www.americanheritage.com/articles/magazine/ah/1963/4/1963_4_18.shtml. See also Paul Dickson and Thomas B. Allen, "Bonus March on Washington 1932," *Smithsonian,* February 2003, 84–94.

9. Reverend Martin Luther King Jr., "Letter from a Birmingham Jail," April 16, 1963, http://www.africa.upenn.edu/Articles_Gen/Letter_Birmingham.html:

> Nonviolent direct action seeks to create such a crisis and foster such a tension that a community which has constantly refused to negotiate is forced to confront the issue. It seeks so to dramatize the issue that it can no longer be ignored. My citing the creation of tension as part of the work of the nonviolent resister may sound rather shocking. But I must confess that I am not afraid of the word 'tension.' I have earnestly opposed violent tension, but there is a type of constructive, nonviolent tension which is necessary for growth.

10. "The Sound of Freedom," *Tailinn-Life,* http://www.tallinn-life.com/tallinn/estonian-singing-revolution.

11. "Suffragists Sing New March Song; Introduce It at Meeting to Get Pledges for the Big Parade on May 6," *New York Times,* May 1, 1911, http://query.nytimes.com/gst/abstract.html?res=9F0DE1DA1439E333A25752C0A9639C946096D6CF.

12. Abbie Hoffman, *Steal This Book* (New York: Thunder's Mouth Press, 2002), 146–55. See his recommendation that protesters wear motorcycle helmets or hard hats, gloves, boots or high sneakers, shoulder or leg pads, ski goggles, and carry

gas masks. The "demonstrations" chart he provides gives recommendations for dealing with such crowd control substances as tear gas, smoke pots, nausea gas, blister gas, or mace—effects of which are in stark contrast to the potentially lethal Tasering and other technologies of protest control in use today.

13. Al Baker, "Tasers Getting More Prominent Role in Crime Fighting in City," *New York Times,* June 15, 2008; "Police Sergeants to Carry Stun Guns," *New York Times,* June 8, 2008; Alec Wilkinson, "Annals of Technology, Non-Lethal Force," *New Yorker,* June 2, 2008, 26.13. For protest in Europe, see Jeffrey Stinson, "In France, Protest Is Almost a Ritual," *USA Today,* April 4, 2006, http://www.usatoday.com/news/world/2006–04–03-france-protest_x.htm. For more on crowd control, see Steven Greenhouse, "Demonstration Turns Violent at Trade Talks in Miami," *New York Times,* November 21, 2003. See also "USA: Amnesty International's Continuing Concerns about Taser Use," http://www.amnesty.org/en/library/asset/AMR51/151/2007/en/dom-AMR511512007en.html. One hundred fifty people had died by 2005. Amnesty International called for law enforcement agencies to suspend use of Tasers until there was further study, and "more than 7,000 law enforcement agencies in the U.S., out of a total of 18,000, now count Tasers as part of their arsenal." The number of Taser-related deaths are escalating every year. "Tasers, powerful electric weapons used by law enforcement agencies . . . conduct 50,000 volts of electricity into a suspect. . . . The electrical pulses induce skeletal muscle spasms immobilizing and incapacitating a suspect and causing them to fall to the ground."

14. "Student Tasered at Kerry Forum in Fla.," *USA Today,* Sept 18 2007, http://www.usatoday.com/news/nation/2007-09-18-student-arrest_n.htm.

15. Alec Wilkinson, "Annals of Technology: Non-Lethal Force," *New Yorker,* June 2, 2008.

16. Kirk Johnson, "Convention Preparations Prompt Suit by A.C.L.U.," *New York Times,* May 3, 2008. Andrea Costelo and

Matthew Strugar on "The Battle to Defend Dissent," Center for Constitutional Rights, June 17, 2008: "In November 2003, dozens of law enforcement agencies launched a deliberate and coordinated disruption of lawful protests in Miami, Florida, against the FTAA's 'free trade' policies. Hundreds of activists were politically profiled, unlawfully arrested, subjected to pepper spray, rubber bullets, and more as part of the 'Miami Model' of policing mass demonstrations. A historic settlement was reached in the Killmon case in April 2008, but the battle to defend dissent is not over. In November 2006, Congress and President Bush furthered the attack on political dissent by passing the Animal Enterprise Terrorism Act (AETA). The AETA criminalizes lawful, expressive conduct such as protests, boycotts, and demonstrations against animal and natural resource industries."

17. Author interview and statement, December 2007 and May 2008.

18. Kirk Johnson, "Convention Preparations Prompt Suit at ACLU," *New York Times*, May 3, 2008. Author interviews with Zach Heiden, Maine Civil Liberties Union, April and June 2008.

19. Ibid.

Principle Three: Ordinary People Are Supposed to Run Things

1. Gordon S. Wood, *The Radicalism of the American Revolution* (New York: Vintage Books, 1991), 3–8.

2. Ibid., 6–8.

3. Ibid., 180.

4. Ibid.

5. Ibid., 295.

6. Ibid., 185.

7. Ibid., 235. See also Nash, op. cit., throughout, but especially p. 18, "Too many working artificers, seafaring men, and low sorts of people," and page 20, "the newspaper insisted that 'All men are by nature on a level; born with an equal share

of freedom and endowed with capacities nearly alike.' " Also, pp. 96 and 101, quoting a broadside, "importing merchants 'will be dealt with by the Mechanics Committee.' To call artisans 'a Rabble,' continued A Lover of Liberty, and to 'assert that Mechanics are men of no consequences' was not to be tolerated."

8. Author interview, January 2008.

9. Wood, op. cit., 304.

10. http://www.townofmilton.org/public; and Joseph Zimmerman, *New England Town Meeting*, (Westport, Connecticut: Greenwood Publishing Group/Praeger Publishers, 1999), p. 22.

11. Maxwell Taylor Kennedy, op. cit., 14.

12. Author communication with Zach Heiden, June and July 2008.

13. Dane M. Waters, "A Brief History of the Initiative and Referendum Process in the United States," www.ianrinstitute.org. Statistical data and information from David Schmidt, *Citizen Lawmakers* (Temple University Press, 1989); Deborah K. McKnight, "Information Brief: 'Initiative and Referendum,' " February 1999, explains the process in other states and shows how it could be implemented in Minnesota. For information on the referendum system in other countries, see for Australia, Honorable Justice Michael Kirby, "The Australian Republican Referendum: Ten Lessons," http://www.lawfoundation.net.au/ljf/app/&id=DF4206863AE3C52DCA2571A30082B3D5.

14. For an overview of Switzerland's system of direct democracy, see http://direct-democracy.geschichte-schweiz.ch/. For UK reporting guidelines on British referenda, see http://www.bbc.co.uk/guidelines/editorialguidelines/edguide/politics/reportingukelec.shtml. For the EU in general, see http://www.democracy-international.org/41.html. For example, the EU constitution was submitted to citizens across Europe in a referendum.

15. Uta Harnischfeger, "Swiss to Decide on Secret Votes by Public on Citizenship Candidates," New Yorker, June 1, 2008,

and Mathieu Von Rohr, "Swiss Referendum: A Debacle for Xenophobes," http://www.spiegel.de/international/europe/0,1518,557089,00.html.

Principle Four: Americans Cherish the Rule of Law

1. Paine, *Common Sense*.
2. Maxwell Taylor Kennedy, op. cit., 105.
3. Nash, op. cit., 134. See also Cookie Roberts, *Founding Mothers: The Women Who Raised Our Nation* (New York: HarperCollins, 2004), 1–35.
4. Nash, op. cit., 417.
5. Ibid., 419.
6. Ibid., 320–39.
7. Ibid., 127.
8. Ibid., 407–10.
9. Ibid., 409.
10. Bill of Rights, http://www.law.cornell.edu/constitution/constitution.billofrights.html. See also www.firstamendmentcenter.org.
11. Ibid.
12. Summarized from author communication with Zach Heiden, June and July 2008.
13. Author interview, July 22, 2008.
14. Bill of Rights, http://www.law.cornell.edu/constitution/constitution.billofrights.html.
15. "Army's Documents Detail Secrecy in Tillman Case," Associated Press/*New York Times*, April 21, 2007, and Monica Davey and Eric Schmitt, "2 Years After Soldier's Death, Family's Battle Is With Army," *New York Times*, March 21, 2006.
16. Michael Moss, "Former U.S. Detainee in Iraq Recalls Torment," *New York Times*, December 18, 2006.
17. Alissa J. Rubin, "Iraqi Cabinet Votes to End Security Firms' Immunity," *New York Times*, October 31, 2007. Editorial, "What the FBI Agents Saw," *New York Times*, May 22, 2008.
18. Mayer, op. cit., 280, 311.
19. Mark Mazzetti and Neil A. Lewis, "Military Lawyers Caught

in Middle on Tribunals," *New York Times,* September 16, 2006. See also William Glaberson, "Lawyers for Guantánamo Inmates Accuse U.S. of Eavesdropping," *New York Times,* May '7, 2008.

20. Mayer, op. cit., 311.

21. Mark Mazzetti, " '03 U.S. Memo Approved Harsh Interrogations," *New York Times,* April 2, 2008.

22. Adam Liptak, "Power to Build Fence Is Above U.S. Law," *New York Times,* April 8, 2008. See also Ted Robbins, "Bush Signs Border Fence Act; Funds Not Found," NPR Radio, October 26, 2006.

23. John F. Kennedy, *Profiles in Courage,* 200.

24. Ibid.

25. Ibid.

26. Ibid., 199.

27. Ibid., 180–201.

28. Mayer, op. cit., 310. See also David Johnston, "Bush Intervened in Dispute Over N.S.A. Eavesdropping," *New York Times,* May 16, 2007, and Scott Horton, "A New Task Order from the Ministry of Love," *Harper's Magazine,* October 4, 2007.

29. Ross Tuttle, "Rigged Trials at Gitmo," *The Nation,* February 20, 2008, http://www.thenation.com/doc/20080303/tuttle.

30. D. D. McNicoll, "It's All in the Timing" *The Australian,* February 25, 2008, http://www.theaustralian.news.com.au/story/0,25197,23268312–25090,00.html.

31. Manjeet Kripalani, "E-Resistance Blooms in Pakistan," *BusinessWeek,* November 12, 2007, http://www.businessweek.com/globalbiz/content/nov2007/gb20071112_430063.htm.

PRINCIPLE FIVE: "AMERICA" ESTABLISHES NO GOD

1. "On the Right to Rebel," preached in 1776, Grant, op. cit., 110–45.

2. Steven Waldman, *Founding Faith: Providence, Politics, and the Birth of Religious Freedom in America* (New York: Random

House, 2008), xvi. See also Elwyn A. Smith, *The Religion of the Republic:* (Philadelphia: Fortress Press, 1971).

3. Walter Isaacson, *A Benjamin Franklin Reader* (New York: Simon & Schuster, 2003), 172–74.

4. Isaacson, op. cit., 173–74.

5. Kaminski, op cit., xiv, 352–55, and Merrill D. Peterson, *Thomas Jefferson and the New Nation: A Biography* (Oxford: Oxford University Press, 1970), 47.

6. Kaminski, op. cit., xviii.

7. Ibid., 48.

8. Wood, op. cit., 330.

9. Ibid., 331.

10. Ibid., 332.

11. Kaminski, op. cit., 352.

12. Perry Bacon Jr., "Foes Use Obama's Muslim Ties to Fuel Rumors About Him," *Washington Post,* November 29, 2007; "Poll: 1 in 10 Voters Think Obama Is Muslim; Flap Over Former Pastor Hasn't Changed View of Some," Associated Press, March 28, 2008; John M. Broder, "Democrats Wrangle Over Words and Beliefs," *New York Times,* April 14, 2008; "Transcript of Interview with Senator Clinton," *New York Times,* July 6, 2007, http://www.nytimes.com/2007/07/06/us/politics/07clinton-text.html; and Rebecca Sinderbrand, "Clinton, Obama Put Politics Aside to Discuss Faith," CNN, April 14, 2008. Cathleen Falsani, "Obama: I Have a Deep Faith. Barack Obama Credits His Multicultural Upbringing for His Theological Point of View," *Chicago Sun-Times,* April 5, 2004. See also Niebuhr, "The 2000 Campaign: The Religion Issue; Lieberman Is Asked to Stop Invoking Faith in Campaign," *New York Times,* August 29, 2000.

13. Neela Banerjee, "Soldier Sues Army, Saying His Atheism Led to Threats," *New York Times,* April 26, 2008.

14. Ibid.

15. Ibid.

16. Author interview, April 2008.

PRINCIPLE SIX: AMERICANS DELIBERATE WITH THEIR NEIGHBORS; WE DISAGREE WITHOUT VIOLENCE

1. Nash, op. cit., 95–96.
2. Ibid., 96.
3. Ibid., 95.
4. Bruce Ackerman and James S. Fishkin, *Deliberation Day* (New Haven: Yale University Press, 2004), 52–59.
5. Ibid., 6.
6. Ibid., 8.
7. Ibid., 8.
8. Ibid., 52–53.
9. Ibid., 54.
10. Ibid., 26.
11. Ibid., 54.

PRINCIPLE SEVEN: LIBERTY IS UNIVERSAL: "AMERICA" CANNOT MAINTAIN AN OPPRESSIVE EMPIRE

1. Paine, as quoted by Robert Kennedy, speech at Stellenbosch University, South Africa, June 7, 1966, http://www.rfksa.org/speeches/speech.php?id=2.
2. Maxwell Taylor Kennedy, op. cit., 17.
3. Ibid.
4. Kaminski, op. cit., p. 16.
5. Ibid.
6. Ibid., p. 18.
7. Popescu and Seymour-Jones, op. cit., 223–31.
8. Stephen Kinzer, *Overthrow: America's Century of Regime Change from Hawaii to Iraq* (New York: Henry Holt, 2007), 2.
9. Ibid., 2–3. See also Cullen Murphy, *The New Rome? The Fall of an Empire and the Fate of America,* (New York: Scribe Publications, 2008), 24–59. For an alternate view, see Michael Mandelbaum, *The Case for Goliath: How America Acts as the World's Government in the 21st Century* (New York: Public Affairs, 2005).
10. Kinzer, Ibid., p. 3.

11. Ibid., p. 43.

12. Ibid., p. 70.

13. Greg Gandin, *Empire's Workshop: Latin America, the United States, and the Rise of the New Imperialism* (New York: Henry Holt, 2007), 11–51.

14. Kinzer, op. cit., 118.

15. Ibid., 147.

16. Kaminski, op. cit., 34–35.

17. Author interview, January 2008.

18. Kinzer, op. cit., 85–86, 91, 96.

19. Sharansky and Dermer, op. cit., 143.

20. Ibid., 197–98.

21. Ibid., 143.

22. Ibid., 123–32.

23. Ibid., 60.

24. Maxwell Taylor Kennedy, op. cit., p. 152–53.

25. Popescu and Seymour-Jones, op. cit., xiv. The United States, as I write, is holding journalists in abusive conditions in prisons in Iraq and other U.S.-held prisons, http://www.cpj.org/news/2006/mideast/iraq16jan06na.html. See also http://www.legitgov.org/#breaking_news for reports of an AP photographer held.

26. Popescu and Seymour-Jones, op. cit., 30.

27. Ibid., 26.

28. Mayer, op. cit., 332. Air Force Colonel Morris Davis said that Jim Haynes, the general counsel for the Pentagon, told him "We can't have acquittals! We've got to have convictions!" See also Jeffrey Rosen, "Conscience of a Conservative," *New York Times,* September 9, 2007.

29. Popescu and Seymour-Jones, op. cit., 48–53.

30. Ibid., 68–75.

CONCLUSION: LEAD A NEW AMERICAN REVOLUTION

1. Grant, op. cit., 76–78.

2. Editorial, "Laura Berg's Letter," *New York Times,* April 27, 2008.

BIBLIOGRAPHY

Ackerman, Bruce, James S. Fishkin. *Deliberation Day*. New Haven: Yale University Press, 2004.

Bergman, Paul, Sara J. Berman-Barrett. *The Criminal Law Handbook: Know Your Rights, Survive the System*. Berkeley, California: Nolo Publishing, 2006.

Beschloss, Michael. *Presidential Courage: Brave Leaders and How They Changed America 1789–1989*. New York: Simon & Schuster, 2007.

Brookhiser, Richard. *Alexander Hamilton, American*. New York: Simon & Schuster, 1999.

Lord Charnwood. *Abraham Lincoln*. New York: Henry Holt and Company, 1917.

Clinton, Catherine. *Fanny Kemble's Civil Wars*. New York: Simon & Schuster, 2000.

Davis, Kenneth C. *Don't Know Much About the Civil War: Everything You Need to Know About America's Greatest Conflict but Never Learned*. New York: HarperCollins, 2004.

Douglas, William O. *Points of Rebellion*. New York: Vintage Books, 1970.

Ellis, Joseph J. *Founding Brothers: The Revolutionary Generation*. New York: Vintage Books, 2002.

Frothingham, Richard. *The Rise of the Republic of the United States*. Boston: Little, Brown and Company, 1881.

Grant, George. *The Patriot's Handbook: A Citizenship Primer for a New Generation of Americans*. Nashville, Tennessee: Cumberland House, 1996.

Giddings, Paula J. *A Sword Among Lions: Ida B. Wells and the Campaign Against Lynching*. New York: HarperCollins, 2008.

Hoffman, Abbie. *Steal This Book*. New York: Thunder's Mouth Press, 2002.

Isaacson, Walter. *A Benjamin Franklin Reader.* New York: Simon & Schuster, 2003.

Kaminski, John P. *The Quotable Jefferson.* Princeton: Princeton University Press, 2006.

Kennedy, John F. *Profiles in Courage.* New York: HarperCollins, 1955.

Kennedy, Maxwell Taylor. *Make Gentle the Life of This World: The Vision of Robert F. Kennedy.* New York: Broadway Books, 1998.

Kinzer, Stephen. *Overthrow: America's Century of Regime Change from Hawaii to Iraq.* New York: Henry Holt and Company, 2007.

Kurlansky, Mark. *1968: The Year That Rocked the World.* New York: Random House, 2004.

Levy, Leonard W. *Origins of the Bill of Rights.* New Haven: Yale University Press, 2001.

Maier, Pauline. *American Scripture: Making the Declaration of Independence.* New York: Vintage Books, 1998.

Mandelbaum, Michael. *Democracy's Good Name: The Rise and Risks of the World's Most Popular Form of Government.* New York: Public Affairs, 2007.

Mill, John Stuart. *On Liberty.* New York: W. W. Norton & Co., 1975.

Miller, Mark Crispin. *Fooled Again: The Real Case for Electoral Reform.* Cambridge, Massachusetts: Perseus Book Group, 2005.

Morris, Richard B. *Witnesses at the Creation: Hamilton, Madison, Jay, and the Constitution.* New York: Henry Holt and Company, 1985.

Murphy, Cullen. *The New Rome? The Fall of an Empire and the Fate of America.* Victoria, Australia: Scribe Publications, 2007.

Moveon.org. *50 Ways to Love Your Country: How To Find Your Political Voice and Become a Catalyst for Change.* San Francisco, California: Inner Ocean Publishing, Inc., 2004.

Nash, Gary B. *The Unknown American Revolution: The Unruly Birth of Democracy and the Struggle to Create America.* New York: Viking, 2005.

Nelson, Craig. *Thomas Paine: Enlightenment, Revolution and the Birth of Modern Nation.* New York: Viking, 2006.

Peterson, Merrill D. *Thomas Jefferson & The New Nation: A Biography.* New York: Oxford University Press, 1970.

Popescu, Lucy, Carole Seymour-Jones (ed.). *Writers Under Siege: Voices of Freedom From Around the World.* New York: New York University Press, 2007.

Sabato, Larry J. *A More Perfect Constitution.* New York: Walker & Company, 2007.

Sharansky, Natan, Ron Dermer. *The Case for Democracy: The Power of Freedom to Overcome Tyranny & Terror.* New York: Public Affairs, 2004.

Siegle, Joseph. *Effective Aid Strategies to Support Democracy in Africa.* "Africa Beyond Aid" Conference, Brenthurts Foundation, et al.

Tocqueville, Alexis de, Democracy in America. New York: Harper Perennial, 2006.

Thoreau, Henry David. *Walden, or Life in the Woods, and On the Duty of Civil Disobedience.* New York: Collier Books, 1962.

Waldman, Steven. *Founding Faith: Providence, Politics, and the Birth of Religious Freedom in America.* New York: Random House, 2008.

Wills, Garry. *Lincoln at Gettysburg: The Words That Remade America.* New York: Simon & Schuster, 1992.

Wood, Gordon S. *The Radicalism of the American Revolution.* New York: Vintage Books, 1991.

Zinn, Howard, Mike Konopacki, Paul Buhle. *A People's History of American Empire.* New York: Henry Holt and Company, 2008.

ACKNOWLEDGMENTS

This book would not have been possible without the help I received from many gifted patriots, all of whom took time from pressing concerns to contribute their expertise and guidance. I am grateful to them all for educating me: civil rights attorneys and activists Michael Ratner, Vince Warren, Annette Dickerson; Lauren Melodia and Jen Nessel of the Center for Constitutional Rights, and Heidi Boghosian; Marjorie Cohn of the National Lawyers Guild; grassroots leaders Raymond Powell and Trevor Oyate of the pro-Constitution Revolution March; journalist Josh Wolf; Vietnam veteran and pilot David Antoon; deliberative-democracy activist Mary Jacksteit and the staff of the Search for Common Ground Project for Life and Choice; attorneys Steven Bennett and Suzanne Telsey, who wrote and edited the User's Guide to the Constitution and Bill of Rights; fund-raiser Stephanie Berger; executive director of the Woodhull Institute for Ethical Leadership Wende Jager-Hyman and her colleague Elizabeth Curtis; NYU professor Mark Crispin Miller; ethical-investment specialist Diane Keefe; Lisa Witter of Fenton Communications; Curtis Ellis of The Campaign Network; Rep. Steve Kagen of Appleton, Wisconsin; Barry Lynn and Rob Boston of Americans United; Steve Brigham of AmericaSpeaks; my colleagues Steve Fox, David Fenton, William Haseltine, Bruce Charash, David Phillips, and Wes Boyd of The American Freedom Campaign; host of *Political Lunch* Will Coghlan; and Hardin Lang and Karina Gerlach at the United Nations. Zach Heiden of the Maine Civil Liberties Union provided ongoing legal readings of the manuscript and offered enlightening explanations of civil liberties issues. His dedication to and skill in the crucial task of making U.S. law, civil liberties debate, and the Constitution accessible to lay readers is inspiring. David Rosenthal, my publisher, and Amanda Murray, who has been my editor, incisively guided the conception of the idea for this book; my current editor, Dedi Felman, was both brilliant and tireless in moving it forward; Michele Bove and

Acknowledgments

Kate Ankofski were an invaluable help in the process, as were my dedicated research assistants, Rashmi Sharma and Mary Fratini. Jonathan Evans of my publishing house production department deserves great kudos for addressing multiple streams of information from many sources with tremendous grace under pressure. Erica Jong encouraged me to write about these issues and provided invaluable friendship in the process, as did Dr. Robin Stern, Susan Devenyi, Catharine Orenstein, and my extended family members, Tom Molner, Andrew Brimmer, Will Schwalbe, and David Chang.

Avram Ludwig was a source of encouragement, moral support, and careful readings, as well as a great informant about the Bonus March. My editors at the Huffington Post and at Firedog lake.com were generous with giving me room to develop these ideas, as were my editors at Project Syndicate. Carlton Sedgeley, Lucy LePage, and Helen Churko were early and steadfast advocates for this message. Laura Dawn got the message out through helping to present the ideas in lecture format. I am indebted to the Virginia Center for the Creative Arts, as well as to Doug Liman and Mrs. Ellen Liman, for making available to me tranquil places in which to work.

Hundreds of citizens I heard from in town hall–type settings shared ideas and information as a community and confirmed my certainty that, as the founders knew, the nation would be best off in their hands. I wish I could acknowledge each by name. I wish to express appreciation especially for the discussions we had in Rochester, Michigan; Spokane, Washington; San Diego, California; and Chicago, Illinois. My faith in the creativity and good sense of the American people was confirmed many times over.

Stephanie Venetsky, along with my wonderful parents, Leonard and Deborah Wolf, helped keep the children happy and engaged during the process, as did their dad, the world's best father, David Shipley.

Most of all I want to thank my beloved children, Rosa and Joseph Shipley, for whose sake, above all, I care about a legacy of freedom. For, as Joey rightly asked, "Isn't America supposed to be the freedom country?"

ABOUT THE AUTHOR

Naomi Wolf's first book, *The Beauty Myth,* was a landmark international bestseller. She is the author of six other books, most recently the *New York Times* bestseller *The End of America: Letter of Warning to a Young Patriot,* and her essays have appeared in *The New Republic, The Wall Street Journal, Glamour, Esquire, The Washington Post, The New York Times,* and on The Huffington Post. *The End of America* has been adapted as a feature-length documentary by award-winning filmmakers Annie Sundberg and Ricki Stern *(The Devil Came on Horseback).* Wolf is the cofounder of The Woodhull Institute for Ethical Leadership, an organization devoted to training young women for leadership roles, and the American Freedom Campaign, www.americanfreedomcampaign .org, a U.S. democracy movement. She lives with her family in New York City.